The Case of Odell Waller
and Virginia Justice

The Case
of Odell Waller
and Virginia Justice,
1940–1942

Richard B. Sherman

The University
of Tennessee Press

KNOXVILLE

Grateful acknowledgment is made to Frances Collin, literary agent,
for permission to quote the lines from Pauli Murray's poem
"Dark Testament," copyright © 1970 by Pauli Murray.

The paper in this book meets the minimum requirements
of the American National Standard for Permanence of Paper
for Printed Library Materials.
∞
The binding materials have been chosen
for strength and durability.

Library of Congress Cataloging in Publication Data

Sherman, Richard B., 1929–
    The case of Odell Waller and Virginia justice, 1940–1942 /
Richard B. Sherman. — 1st ed.
            p.   cm.
    Includes bibliographical references and index.
    ISBN 0-87049-732-4 (cloth : alk. paper)
    ISBN 0-87049-733-2 (pbk : alk. paper)
    1. Waller, Odell—Trials, litigation, etc. 2. Trials (Murder)—Virginia
—Pittsylvania County.   3. Discrimination in criminal justice administration
—Virginia.   4. Jury—United States.   5. Virginia—Race relations.
6. Blacks—Virginia—Social conditions.   I. Title.
KF224.W28S48   1992 345.73 '02523'09755581—dc20

Contents

Illustrations

Preface

Odell Waller is not a familiar name in American history. One is unlikely to find him mentioned even in books on black or southern history. Thus it came as a surprise to discover that for a relatively brief historical moment between 1940 and 1942 an obscure black sharecropper from Gretna in Pittsylvania County, Virginia, who was convicted of killing his white landlord, became the central figure in a widely discussed controversy that raised important questions about justice in the United States. His case became the concern of thousands of Americans across the country, and it had a lasting impact upon the lives of some of those who were most closely involved in the unsuccessful campaign to save his life. The end came in July 1942, just seven months after Pearl Harbor, and the memory of Odell Waller was soon overwhelmed by the pressing events of World War II. Most of the records of the case lay buried and forgotten in not readily accessible archives. Later, historians interested in southern racial and civil liberties issues were inevitably drawn to a far bigger story, the civil rights movement of the 1950s and 1960s. Thus the Waller case receded into the largely forgotten past.

Odell Waller's name first came to my attention a few years ago while I was reading a microfilm edition of some of the Harold Ickes papers. Buried there were some materials on the case that the Workers Defense League had sent to Ickes in the spring of 1942. As I began to check back into contemporary newspapers it soon became apparent that there was an important story that deserved to be told. Further research revealed the presence of a considerable collection of previously unused records. On the surface it was a simple story. A black sharecropper had shot and killed his landlord in a dispute over the distribution of the shares of the crop. There was no doubt that Waller had done the shooting. After a quick trial he was sentenced to death in the electric chair.

Throughout the South in the twentieth century there have been numerous examples of poor black defendants who were tried, convicted, and executed under circumstances that were little reported or noticed beyond their immediate area. Waller's fate might easily have been the same; indeed, to some extent it was fortuitous that his plight became a matter of national concern. Had he not fled to Ohio after the shooting, had the story of his capture not been noticed by a number of key organizations, had outside defense not been provided at his trial, the subsequent campaign to spare the life of Waller would probably not have taken place. But once that happened it became increasingly apparent that the story involved more than a simple, if fatal, shooting. It involved a long history of economic and political injustice and of grievances for which the established order provided no meaningful redress for the poor and powerless; it involved the fundamental issue of the right to be tried by an impartial jury of one's peers; it involved the disparate punishments meted out to whites and to blacks for apparently similar offenses. Thus the case said much about the relationship of economic status, political power, and race to the quality of justice in the United States at that time.

The Waller case had other interesting features. One was the degree to which Waller was supported by radical organizations, ones that were indeed alien forces in rural Pittsylvania County. At his trial Waller's defense was provided by an obscure group of Trotskyites known as the Revolutionary Workers League of the U.S. The subsequent campaign to save his life, however, was directed by the Workers Defense League, an organization founded by the Socialist party but, unlike the Revolutionary Workers League, one that was supported by many eminently respectable Americans. The disputes between these two groups is a continuing subplot of the story. Inevitably the Waller case invites comparison with the more celebrated Scottsboro case in which radicals, in that instance Communists, played the leading role in the defense efforts. There are indeed similarities, beginning with the race and economic status of the defendants, while the question of what constituted a fair trial was a central issue in both cases. But there are also significant differences. In the Scottsboro case the guilt of the defendants of the alleged crime of rape was a crucial question. In the Waller case there was no dispute over his having shot his landlord; rather his defense involved the more subtle issues of background, motivation, and extenuating circumstances that might explain the event. In the Scottsboro case the "radical outsiders" were members of the Communist party, but in the Waller case they were mainly Trotskyites or Socialists (or merely concerned liberals). The Communists did not play a central role in Waller's defense. Finally, the Scottsboro tragedy was much harder to forget precisely because the defendants remained alive. With the continual appeals and retrials their case dragged on throughout the 1930s, and the last of the defendants remained imprisoned until 1950. In contrast, the Waller case ended with the death of the defendant about two years after it began.

In the half a century since then the conditions that accounted for the tragedy of Odell Waller have changed considerably. Economic conditions in south-side Virginia have significantly improved; the poll tax is gone; the civil rights movement has greatly strengthened the political and legal status of blacks. Thus there is little likelihood that the events of 1940–1942 could be closely repeated. But at another level the tragedy of Odell Waller is still relevant. Great disparities in economic status remain, and in some respects the gap between the wealthy and the poor has gotten worse in recent years. Regrettably, it is still true that the quality of justice in America is very much related to one's economic position, and if racial discrimination is less overt when it comes to such matters as selection of a jury in a criminal case, race remains a factor in many aspects of the criminal justice system, especially when it comes to the question of the death penalty. The case of Odell Waller deserves to be remembered both as a measure of the progress that has been made since the early 1940s and as a reminder of how far we still have to travel to create a truly just society.

In the course of my research I benefited from the generous assistance provided by many individuals and institutions. This book would not have been possible without their help. In particular I wish to thank Minor T. Weisiger and Conley L. Edwards of the Virginia State Archives for locating the apparently lost files on the Waller case and for their assistance, along with that of their colleagues, with numerous other materials. Carol S. Linton of Swem Library at the College of William and Mary cheerfully responded to my frequent requests for interlibrary loans. Warner W. Pflug and Thomas Featherstone of the Archives of Labor and Urban Affairs in the Walter P. Reuther Library at Wayne State University provided expert assistance in using the Waller case materials in the Workers Defense League Collection and in locating relevant photographs. My thanks also go to Esme E. Bhan of the Moorland-Spingarn Research Center at Howard University, to Alexandra Chisholm of the Schlesinger Library on the History of Women at Radcliffe College, to Hilary Cummings of the University of Oregon Library, to Corey Seeman of the Chicago Historical Society, and to Daniel T. Williams of the Hollis Burke Frissell Library at Tuskegee University. In addition I am indebted to librarians in the Manuscript Division of the Library of Congress, in the Manuscript Department in the Alderman Library at the University of Virginia, in the Wilson Library of the University of North Carolina at Chapel Hill, and in Widener Library at Harvard University.

I would also like to thank Linda Welborn for assistance with my Freedom of Information Act request from the FBI and James O. Trotter for help in locating a photograph of Odell Waller. Similarly, I am grateful to L. Duncan Brogan of the Virginia Department of Corrections, who went out of his way to make negatives of Waller's prison picture for me, and to Charles P. Schober who produced the print. Others who kindly responded to my requests for help include Virginius Dabney, Esther Cooper Jackson, Oliver W. Hill, Preston Moses, and the late Caroline F. Ware.

My thanks is also due to the Committee on Faculty Research of the College of William and Mary for a grant awarded in the early stages of my research and to Donna Lyons for typing substantial portions of my manuscript.

As this book began to take shape I benefited from the comments of several individuals who read all or part of earlier versions of the manuscript or who helped me in other ways. In this regard Jon Bloom, executive director of the Workers Defense League, deserves a special word of thanks for his generous assistance. I would also like to express my appreciation to my son, Professor Alan T. Sherman, for his critical reading of sections of the manuscript, and to the late Samuel H. Friedman, former publicity director of the Workers Defense League. I am also grateful for the suggestions made by my readers at the University of Tennessee Press. In particular I would like to thank Professor Patricia Sullivan, who was helpful in a number of ways.

There are two people to whom I feel most indebted for their generous assistance with this work. One is my colleague, Cam Walker, who made many useful suggestions about the entire manuscript, and, thanks to her rich knowledge of black and southern history, was a continual source of help and encouragement throughout the entire project. The other is Morris Milgram. A central figure in the defense of Odell Waller, Mr. Milgram could bring a perspective on the case shared by no one else today. His critical reading of my work saved me from several errors, and his suggestions and encouragement proved to be invaluable. For this I am grateful.

Finally I wish to express my thanks to my wife, who not only read and commented on major portions of an early draft of this work but who also cheerfully put up with my seemingly endless commentary on the Waller case and encouraged me to continue.

As always, of course, I alone am responsible for any errors that may appear in this work.

1
A Farmer's Death

The cramped surroundings were painfully familiar. He had seen little else for well over a year and a half. It had been nearly two years since he had last walked through the dusty fields and wooded ravines of Gretna. Now there was so little time left to try once again to tell his story, to make sense of the events that had brought him to his cell on death row. The Richmond newspaper, which the guard had brought to him, lay there as a constant reminder: "Waller Faces Electric Chair as Governor Rejects Appeal." It was dated July 1, 1942. Less than twenty-four hours remained.[1]

Odell Waller returned to his pencil and paper. He wrote slowly and laboriously, but the results—ten large pages—were neat and mostly clear, despite the vagaries of his spelling. "First I will say dont work for a man two poor to pay you he will steel and take from you. . . . I was frightened. . . . I dont no [know] how many times I shot. . . . the good Book sais a lie is the worst thing a person can tell so I no [know] lies was told one [on] me. . . ."[2] Eventually he finished writing. His lawyer would see to it that others could read his statement. He desperately wanted the world to know that Odell Waller was not the ruthless killer portrayed by his prosecutors.

The chain of events that brought Odell Waller to his final moments in the state penitentiary in Richmond, Virginia, began a little over two years earlier in the spring of 1940. But these in turn were the product of a much longer history that created the social, economic, and political structure of the American South in general and of Pittsylvania County in particular. And there Waller's story began. Eventually, however, this obscure young black man had an impact on others far beyond Pittsylvania County, or even Virginia, as his troubles came to symbolize for many the deep-seated racial and economic injustice that still deformed much of American society.

Pittsylvania County is situated in the Piedmont region of south-central Virginia. Its southern boundary adjoins that of the state of North Carolina; its northern, some forty miles away at its greatest extent, is formed by the Staunton River. In 1940 it was Virginia's largest county, not only in area but in population, although it would soon be surpassed during the years of World War II by the rapidly growing suburban Washington, D.C., counties of Arlington and Fairfax. In the south, Pittsylvania surrounds the independent textile manufacturing city of Danville. Some fifteen miles north of Danville lies the county seat of Chatham, which in 1940 was a pleasant village of some eleven hundred people and home to Chatham Hall, an Episcopal school for girls, and Hargrave Military Academy, a preparatory school for boys. A red brick courthouse, which dates from 1853, is located in the center of the town. The surrounding streets have some fine tree-shaded homes. About ten miles north of Chatham is the smaller, less impressive village of Gretna in whose vicinity lived both Odell Waller and the white man whose death he caused, Oscar Davis.

Like most residents of Pittsylvania County, both Waller and Davis were dependent on the land and agriculture. Indeed, the county's greatest resource was its land. It was a resource that brought wealth to few, but it sustained life for the many. Part of the Piedmont plateau, Pittsylvania County tends to slope upward to the north and west forming rolling countryside that is dissected by numerous streams. In 1940 much of the land was fertile and under cultivation, although a considerable amount of woodland remained, particularly in the steeper areas adjacent to its streams and rivers. It was a land of long, hot summers and short, relatively mild winters. Its principal industry was agriculture—the census classified two-thirds of its people as farm population—and it produced nearly a fifth of the state's tobacco crop. Next in importance were corn and wheat. Pittsylvania County was not a region of large farms, with the average size in 1940 being only 80.4 acres. Even this was an increase over the 1930 average of 73.9 acres and reflected the impact of the Great Depression, during which the number of farms decreased from 7,563 in 1930 to 6,932 a decade later. In 1939 the average farm income per farm inhabitant in Pittsylvania County was only $165, compared to a national average of $256. Although it was better off than some parts of the rural South, it was not a land of rich men and women, and many of its inhabitants were intimately acquainted with unceasing toil and poverty.[3]

One of the most significant features of the farms of Pittsylvania County

Virginia, with Pittsylvania County highlighted.

was that a large proportion—58.2 percent in 1940—were run by tenants, not owners. The comparable figure for the state of Virginia in that year was 26.9 percent. Nearly all of the tenants in Pittsylvania County were either share tenants or the even more lowly sharecroppers. Share tenants owned most of their farm implements and paid their landlords a share of the crop in return for whatever supplies they got, but sharecroppers owned nothing and were totally dependent on their landlords. They were paid for their labor by shares of the crop they raised. Uncovered by any wages-and-hours legislation, or by Social Security, or by laws protecting the right to organize and bargain collectively, sharecroppers also had virtually no means of forcing unscrupulous landlords to live up to their contracts. In theory sharecroppers could sue for breach of contract; in practice, lacking any funds, they were nearly powerless to do so.[4] Moreover, these same conditions, combined with Virginia's poll tax, meant that sharecroppers were effectively barred from political activity, and thus they had no meaningful voice in state and local government. These problems cut across racial lines but were clearly worse for blacks. In 1940, 53 percent of Pittsylvania County's white farm operators were tenants; 26 percent were sharecroppers. But an astounding 74 percent of the black farmers were tenants, and 48 percent were sharecroppers.[5] Whether black farmers were owners or tenants, their economic status in Pittsylvania County compared unfavorably to that of their white counterparts. For example, the average value of the land and buildings of a white farmer was almost twice that of a black.[6] These disparities do not mean that life was easy for most white farmers in Pittsylvania County, only that it was likely to be considerably harder if one were black.

In 1940 there were 61,697 people living in Pittsylvania County. Of these, 42,708 were white, some 69 percent, while 18,989 were black. On the surface at least, the relations between the races were considered to be fairly good. It was not a region characterized by violent confrontation, and there were even some examples of interracial cooperation, such as the recent erection of a community center to provide a place of recreation for black children. But, as was so often the case, the facade of relative harmony covered over many problems and tensions. In most matters racial lines were sharply drawn, and in a fashion that relegated the black population to a clearly subordinate role. This was most obvious in politics and education as well as in economic status. In 1940, only about 200 blacks were registered to vote in Pittsylvania County out of a voting age population of over 8,000. At the same time there were about 6,000 registered whites out of a voting age population of about 23,000. A major reason for the low percentage of registered voters, one that affected whites as well as blacks, was the poll tax. To be eligible to register, one had to have paid an annual poll tax of $1.50, with a cumulative provision necessitating payment for the three years prior to an election.[7] For many, particularly the numerous share tenants and sharecroppers, the cumulative total of $4.50 was an insuperable obstacle to voting registration. The system ensured that the county, and much of the state, would be controlled by a limited, white elite.

Another serious problem in Pittsylvania County, and a source of considerable bitterness, was the disparity between the public education provided white and black children. During the 1939–40 school year the per capita cost of elementary education was $23.69 for each white pupil but only $10.86 for each black. For secondary education the figures were $42.06 for whites and $15.62 for blacks. The average annual salary of white male high school teachers was $1,278; of black males it was only $584. The county provided school libraries with 33,995 volumes for its 10,821 white pupils but only 4,182 volumes for its 4,753 black pupils.[8] A major grievance for black parents was the lack of adequate high school facilities. In 1940 there was only one high school, grades eight through eleven, open to blacks, and, as it was located in Gretna in the northern part of a large county, it was simply inaccessible to many black children. Moreover, it had been built to hold only 200 students. In 1939–40 only

244 students, out of a potential black high school population of 1,714, attended high school. During that same year 2,111 whites attended the ten high schools provided for them. In the summer of 1940 a number of black parents, teachers, and citizens submitted a petition to the county school board requesting the building of a new high school for blacks, and, until that was done, asking that the board make arrangements for the children involved to attend high school in Danville or some other place.[9] The issue was resolved, at least temporarily, after the National Association for the Advancement of Colored People (NAACP) threatened to go to court for a writ of mandamus to force the county to admit the black children to the nearest white high school unless a new black school were built. Thus, on September 6 the school superintendent agreed that the county would pay the fees for those children who attended the black high school in Danville.[10] But the inequities in the county's educational system remained a source of discontent among many blacks who were well aware that the practice of separate and unequal in Pittsylvania County had drastically limited the opportunities for their children. The school dispute appears to have been a somewhat unusual disturbance on the racial scene. Still, what some whites considered to be good relations between the races was in fact achieved at an enormous social cost that seemed to require the uncritical acceptance by blacks of innumerable inequities and injustices.

It was in such an environment that Odell Waller was raised, and such was the setting for the tragic conflict that arose between him and Oscar Davis. For most of their lives there was nothing unusual about either Waller or Davis, nothing that is, within the context of rural south-side Virginia. Had their paths not crossed, both men would probably have remained unknown to all but a few neighbors and family. Both came from families that labored in a never-ceasing struggle to keep what they had against the economic odds, especially during the depression years of the 1930s. They lived in a society that condemned many of its members to a life of economic marginality and that maintained racial barriers that for generations had impeded progress in the region. The fears and hostilities connected to questions of race affected both blacks and whites, but in unequal ways, especially in matters relating to law and the authority of the state. Few blacks had to be reminded that justice was not color-blind. Still, both Waller and Davis were shaped by the system in which they lived, and the result of such conditioning was directly related to the death of each.

In July of 1940 Oscar Weldon Davis was a forty-six year old tenant farmer who lived near the Chalk Level section of north-central Pittsylvania, about three and a half miles southeast of the village of Gretna. He and his wife Ethel rented a small house—"cabin" was the term used in some descriptions of the structure—at the end of a dirt lane that was surrounded by tilled fields. To the east the land sloped into woods that were bisected by Georges Creek. Immediately adjacent was a considerably larger frame house occupied by his brother Henry C. Davis.[11] The available records reveal little of Oscar Davis's background, but they give hints that he was a man of some pride who had had to deal with a number of adversities. Twice a widower, Davis married for the third time in the spring of 1939. As a result of his earlier marriages he had two grown sons, Frank and Edgar, and a daughter, Kathryn.[12] Many years before, in July 1917, he had attempted to purchase some eighty-one and a half acres of land situated about a mile and a half south of Chatham. The contract price for the land was the then considerable sum of $3,000, with $500 having to be paid in cash on January 1, 1918, and the remainder to be paid in ten annual installments of $250 plus interest each subsequent January 1 through 1928. But Davis was plagued by misfortunes. His first wife, Annie, died on January 10, 1919. Although he subsequently remarried, his dream of becoming an independent, landowning farmer was crushed by the harsh economic realities of his region. Unable to maintain his payments, he failed to gain title to his land, and, like so many others in Pittsylvania County, was forced into tenancy. Thus for many years he had lived and worked as a tenant farmer on lands owned by A. S. Shields.[13]

Among Davis's acquaintances in Pittsylvania County, his reputation and character were matters of some dispute. In July 1940 the *Danville Register* referred to him as a "well known farmer," but County Sheriff A. H. Overbey later asserted that "he was more or less what we call an obscure farmer. He wasn't a man of any prominence."[14] One former resident of the area noted that some whites thought that "Davis was imbued with the spirit of taking advantage of those who couldn't help themselves," although he believed that Davis "was a hard worker" and "a fairly respected man who bootlegged a little."[15] Dr. Ernest D. Overbey, a Chatham dentist and personal friend, praised Davis as "a fine Masonic brother . . . a good father to his children, a kind husband and a hard working man." He was "a most honest man with principals [*sic*] of Justice. He was as fair in his dealings with his fellow man as many man I know."[16] Although opinions were not unanimous, Davis's white neighbors generally seem to have regarded him as a decent, hardworking, God-fearing man.[17] Blacks in the area, however, often saw him in a different light. To many he was "a mean white man" who failed to keep his promises and who "liked to dawg the colored man."[18] Odell Waller later testified that "Mr. Davis was mighty crabby," but he added that Davis "didn't bother me at all but would jump on the boys [his sons] for the least thing. He carried a pistol and his oldest son had threatened to kill him."[19] Waller's assertion about both the pistol and Davis's relations with his sons would be challenged, and, given the circumstances, must be treated with caution. What seems clear is that Davis was a person of no unusual attainments, one who had experienced a number of personal and material losses, and who had to work hard to make ends meet. He undoubtedly vented his frustrations at times on those around him, and his treatment of the family of Odell Waller set in motion a series of events that ultimately led to disaster.

Odell Waller's background, like that of Oscar Davis, is shrouded in obscurity. At the time of his trial in September 1940 he stated that he was twenty-three years old and that he "was born in Pittsylvania about a half mile from Mr. Davis." But there was confusion about the exact date of his birth. In trial testimony he referred to his birthday as being on July 13, but in a written statement issued on January 2, 1941, he said that he was born on February 17, 1917. The date carved on his tombstone is March 6, 1917.[20] Odell's natural mother was Mrs. Dollie Jones. Shortly after his birth, however, his father died, and Dollie then permitted her older sister Annie and her husband Willis Waller to adopt Odell, who was given the family name of Waller. Dollie later married Carl G. Harris and moved to Logan, West Virginia. Thus Annie and Willis Waller raised Odell as their own (and only) child on their farm near Gretna about a mile from the Davis place.[21] Odell always referred to Annie as "mother." Annie was clearly proud of Odell. From Willis he "learned how to work" and at about the age of twelve began taking on odd jobs for other people near his home. After completing the third year of high school Odell left school at the age of sixteen to help his family work their farm. At that time Willis Waller owned about twenty-five acres, and Willis, in conjunc-

Former home of Annie, Willis, and Odell Waller near Gretna.
Photograph by Richard B. Sherman.

tion with another man, had acquired a wheat binder. Willis's cousin, Robert Waller, owned fifty-one acres nearby.[22] Among whites in the area, the members of the Waller family appear to have been relatively well regarded. In summarizing the opinions of a number of white neighbors, one former resident asserted that the Wallers "were far above the average" when it came to honesty, hard work, faithfulness, and dependability. Some whites said that they were "as honorable Negroes as you could want."[23] Ownership of their own land placed them in a different status from that of many blacks (and whites) in Pittsylvania County. Still, Annie and Willis led a life of hard and unceasing labor that allowed them little margin of safety, especially during the depression years of the 1930s. After the death of Willis in April 1938, Annie could no longer make payments on his debts. Six weeks later the mortgage was foreclosed, and Annie and Odell were reduced to the status of tenants. At first Odell had wanted to give up farming and leave the area, but it was the only work Annie knew, and for her sake he decided to stay and make do the best they could.[24]

Odell's reputation, like that of Oscar Davis, was subject to considerable differences of opinion. The same man who praised the Waller family noted that Odell "seemed to be a black sheep, a fair worker, but a bootlegger, high tempered and inclined to be treacherous when he was a little mad."[25] Others alleged that Odell had a "very bad reputation" and a "violent and turbulent nature" or that he was known as "a law violator" and as a "mean nigger."[26] Odell had, in fact, been convicted of a number of offenses. In August 1935 he was fined five dollars for an assault; in May 1936 he was convicted of reckless driving and of possessing six pints of illegal liquor; in November 1938 he was convicted of reckless driving; in June 1937 he was convicted of possessing two "turkey-killing" dogs; in January 1938 he was convicted of driving without a permit; in October 1938 he was convicted again of driving without a permit and of reckless driving. Another conviction, in November 1937 for carrying a concealed weapon (a razor), was more serious. For this he was fined twenty dollars and given a sixty-day jail sentence. But even here the circumstances, at least as Odell later explained them, appear to have been relatively innocent and may well have involved prejudicial behavior on the part of the arresting sheriff's deputy. Odell later acknowledged that he used to sell illegal whiskey as a means of paying for his car, but this was a practice far from uncommon in his area, and it certainly carried no great moral stigma in the minds of many of his neighbors in Pittsylvania County.[27] However unfortunate, Odell's prior offenses were not matters of great moral or legal consequence and may tell us as much about race relations in Pittsylvania County as they do about Waller's character. In startling contrast to these negative assessments, moreover, were the views of Percy Dalton, a white contractor for whom Odell had worked on a number of occasions. "Odell was a white man's negro," he said, "and would stand up for a white man against a negro. He was a quiet, steady worker and could be depended upon when he promised to work. He was honest. From time to time he borrowed small sums of money from me and he always paid me back. He was not a trouble maker. I could always count on him to be on the job and to put in a good day's work."[28] Whatever the truth may have been about Odell Waller's character, his reputation did not become a matter of particular interest until after the events of July 1940, and subsequent opinions were obviously colored by feeling about the death of Oscar Davis.

At the beginning of January 1939 Annie and Odell began working as sharecroppers for Oscar Davis, and they moved into a small house at his place. They were joined by Odell's wife Mollie, whom he had married a few days after moving to the Davis farm.[29] According to the sharecropping arrangement, Odell, Mollie, and Annie were to work corn, wheat, and tobacco. In return they were supposed to receive one-fourth of the corn and wheat crops and one-half of the tobacco crop.[30] At his trial Odell testified that during the first year (1939) "we got along all right, didn't have no trouble."[31] But in the middle of January 1940 the Agricultural Adjustment Administration notified Davis that his tobacco acreage allotment, which was 14.3 acres in 1939, was to be cut back to 6.3 acres in 1940. Although his wheat acreage remained about the same, 15.5 acres for 1940 compared to 15 acres in 1939, the severe cut in the tobacco allotment had a drastic impact on the Wallers. Presumably Davis kept the cash benefit paid by the AAA for the acreage reduction, but he would allow the Wallers to work only about four thousand hills of tobacco. The date when Davis notified the Wallers of the reduction was disputed, but it may not have been until April 1940. In any event, such a reduction in their cash crop put the Wallers in a desperate situation. Odell asked Davis to allow him to work more tobacco, but Davis refused and suggested that, if what he had allowed was not enough, Odell should look for work elsewhere.[32] In April 1940 Odell got just such an opportunity from Percy Dalton. Dalton had constructed electric lines for the Rural Electrification Administration and from time to time had hired Odell. In 1940 Dalton was given the job of building an electric line in Denton, Maryland, near Baltimore, and he hired seven local blacks, including Odell, as laborers.[33] Thus from mid April 1940 until his return in mid July, Waller left his home to work with Dalton in Maryland.

Meanwhile Annie and Mollie Waller remained in the house on the Davis farm and continued to help with the tobacco and wheat crops. Davis also allowed them to tend to a vegetable garden. Odell sent some of his earnings in Maryland back to Annie in order to pay Robert Waller to assist Davis in harvesting and threshing the wheat and thus be assured of saving their share of the wheat crop.[34] Earlier in the year Annie had also spent three weeks taking care of the ill Mrs. Davis, an arrangement for which she was supposed to have been paid $2.50 a week. But Davis failed to give Annie the $7.50 that was due her. In June, Annie asked him to give her half a sack of fertilizer out of what he owed to her, but his response, as recalled by Annie, was a flat "Hell, no." Finally, sometime in June, Annie refused Davis's request to go out to work some tobacco. "I told him, 'Mr. Davis, I don't know'—just that way. I said, 'Annie has been working and working and I don't see anything. It is all for Mr. Davis and nothing for Annie.'"[35] A few days later Davis sent a deputy sheriff to evict Annie and Mollie from their home. They found another, smaller house in the area which they rented from John Miller near the home of Robert Waller, and they coped by doing whatever work they could. Davis did allow them to continue tending their vegetable garden at his place, but this did not compensate for his actions. As Annie later testified, "he treated us like a dog; he certainly treated me wrong."[36]

During this same period another incident occurred that reflected on the strained relationship between the Wallers and Davis. The Wallers owned three dogs. One of them got loose and followed Annie and Mollie when they went to the Davis farm to attend to their garden. As they worked they paid no attention to the dog until suddenly it ran up to them "as bloody as he could be." Someone at the Davis farm, either Davis himself or his hired hand, a young, seventeen-year-old black named Henry Davis, or both, had mutilated the dog. What role this incident may have played in the subsequent chain of events is unclear. Odell did not mention it at his trial, perhaps fearing that it could be used against him to build a case of premeditation. But, as one of Odell's lawyers later observed, "it is certainly one of the things that shows somebody's contempt for the rights of Odell Waller and his mother."[37]

Although they had been evicted from their house on the Davis farm, the Wallers retained their rights to their agreed-upon shares of the crops, including one quarter of the wheat. So when it came time to cut the wheat, Annie provided Davis with the use of her binder (harvester-binder) as well as the labor of Robert Waller. The threshing of wheat in that area was traditionally done as a cooperative venture by the neighboring farmers who would move the threshing machine from one farm to another.[38] According to a statement by Robert Waller, they threshed the wheat from the Davis farm on July 11 and 12. As he worked Robert Waller separated the bags of wheat, three for Oscar Davis and one for Odell Waller. But when Davis saw what he was doing he ordered him to stop, and when they had finished Davis took all 208 bags of wheat to his own house.[39]

At Robert Waller's suggestion Annie wrote to Odell to tell him what had happened to their wheat. Subsequently, Percy Dalton stated that the black workers on the Maryland job told him that Waller had received a letter from home which said that Davis had refused to turn over the wheat and that Oscar Davis and Henry Davis "had cut off the privates of" his dog. Shortly thereafter, on Saturday, July 13, Odell decided to return home for the weekend. As he later explained, it was his birthday, and he was anxious to find out what had happened to his wheat.[40]

Until this point there was little disagreement about the main outline of the story. But it is a different matter when it comes to determining what happened on Sunday, July 14, and Monday, July 15. These disputed events will be examined later at some length. What was clear, however, was that Odell was back home on Sunday, July 14, and heard from Annie about the doings on the Davis farm. Odell attended church services in the morning and again in the evening. He also arranged to have Thomas Younger (who was the grandson of a sister of Willis Waller) take him in his truck over to Oscar Davis's farm early the next morning in order to get his wheat. Thus, at about 6:30 A.M. on Monday, July 15, Odell arrived at Davis's house. He was accompanied by Younger, Annie Waller, Archie Waller (the husband of Willis Waller's sister), and Buck Fitzgerald, a friend who drove Younger's truck. As soon as the truck stopped, Younger got off and left the scene. The other three remained on the truck while Odell went to talk to Oscar Davis, who was accompanied by Henry Davis. Odell carried a .32 caliber pistol in his pocket. He had also left a shotgun, under wraps, in the truck. Within a few minutes Odell fired several shots at Oscar Davis, then fled across the cornfield and into a neighboring woods.[41] The exact number and location of Davis's wounds subsequently became a matter of dispute. Dr. John C. Risher, the physician who attended to Davis at Lynchburg Memorial Hospital a few hours after the shooting, testified at Waller's trial that Davis "had four bullet wounds, one on the right side of his head, his scalp, another in his arm and two in the lower part of his back."[42] Examination showed life-threatening wounds. Later that day Risher conducted an apparently successful operation to repair the abdominal injuries, although a serious danger of infection remained. On Tuesday, Davis showed signs of improvement. But on Wednesday, July 17, at 2:00 P.M. he died. The immediate cause of death was a collapsed lung, which, Dr. Risher testified, was a consequence of the operation.[43]

Within an hour of the shooting Sheriff A. H. Overbey arrived at Oscar Davis's house where he questioned Henry Davis at length. Then Overbey began his search for Waller. After failing to find him at Annie Waller's house, he went back to Chatham, the county seat, and gathered a group of men at the courthouse. Eventually some forty armed men returned to

Former home of Oscar W. Davis near Gretna and scene of the shooting, with the enlarged house as it appeared in 1989. In 1940 Oscar Davis's house was separate from the larger building on the left. Photograph by Richard B. Sherman.

the Chalk Level area where for three days and nights they searched the swamps and woods within a radius of ten miles of the Davis farm. Overbey also offered a reward of twenty-five dollars (later raised to seventy-five) for information leading to the arrest of Waller.[44] In the meantime the terrified Waller was desperately trying to get away, hoping, as he later testified, "to keep 'em from stretching me up."[45] Eventually he made his way to Halifax in the adjoining county east of Pittsylvania. From there he traveled by bus first to New Jersey and then on to Columbus, Ohio, where his uncle, Sam Hairston, brother of Annie, lived. But his trail proved to be easy to follow. Overbey contacted the police in New Jersey, Ohio, and Michigan, places Waller was known to have had friends or relatives. On July 19 the state police in Woodstown, New Jersey, reported that Waller had left there on the seventeenth and that he might be found in Columbus. At Overbey's request the FBI joined the search on July 20. He also had a school photograph of Waller circulated widely. On Wednesday afternoon, July 24, less than forty-eight hours after arriving in Columbus, Waller was captured by local police and federal agents.[46]

Joseph Whitehead, Jr., the commonwealth's attorney for Pittsylvania

County, immediately requested Governor James H. Price to issue a requisition upon the governor of Ohio for the extradition of Waller.[47] On July 29 Price sent the request, and on August 2 Governor Bricker approved the extradition. As a result Sheriff Overbey and a deputy went to Columbus on August 3 to pick up Waller and return him to Virginia.[48] The extradition was delayed for several days, however, as a result of legal maneuvers in Columbus. After Waller's capture, newspaper accounts of his case attracted the attention of a number of outside groups, including the National Association for the Advancement of Colored People, the Revolutionary Workers League of the U.S., and the Workers Defense League, which sent attorneys to the Court of Common Pleas in Columbus to argue on his behalf, claiming that threatened mob violence in Pittsylvania County would prevent him from receiving a fair trial. The Ohio court rejected their contention, and after a few days Waller was handed over to the Virginia authorities.[49] It was the opening round of what became a long legal battle to secure justice for Odell Waller.

2
Trial in Chatham

On August 7, 1940, Waller was returned to Pittsylvania County and placed in the Chatham jail. After a preliminary hearing on September 13 before Trial Justice Hubert D. Bennett the case was sent to the grand jury. On September 16 the grand jury returned a two-part indictment which charged that Waller "unlawfully, feloniously, wilfully [*sic*] and of his malice aforethought did kill and murder" Oscar Davis.[1] The defense was given a mere three days to prepare for the trial, which was set for September 19, 1940.

During these preliminary legal proceedings Waller was represented by Thomas H. Stone of Richmond, a thirty-eight-year-old attorney who had been hired by an obscure Chicago-based radical organization, the Revolutionary Workers League of the U.S. In a meeting with reporters on August 13, Stone stated that other lawyers would be brought into the case. One name mentioned was that of Francis Heisler of Chicago, an attorney who had worked in labor cases and who was a member of the National Executive Board of the Workers Defense League, the organization that later played the principal role in the effort to save Waller from execution. As it turned out, however, Heisler was unable to be present at the trial. Instead, Stone got the assistance of J. Byron Hopkins, a black attorney from Richmond. Thus, from the time he was returned to Virginia through his trial for murder, Waller's principal defender was a lawyer brought in by the Revolutionary Workers League.[2]

Unknown to most Virginians, this organization seemed to be singularly out of place in rural Pittsylvania County. Indeed, throughout the long struggle to save Waller's life, reporters and others frequently misstated the name of the Revolutionary Workers League (RWL), at times confusing it with the Workers Defense League (WDL). The two were, however, very different organizations in their origins, ideology, and tactics, and their disagreements over how best to handle Odell Waller's defense soon developed into an acrimonious conflict. As both the RWL and the WDL played a prominent role in the Waller case, it is essential they be understood at the outset.

The origins of the RWL go back to the small band of Trotskyites who were expelled from the Communist party of the United States in 1928. In December 1934 a number of these Trotskyites merged with the American Workers party, a native radical group that had been organized in 1933. The guiding spirit behind that organization was A. J. Muste, a Dutch-born preacher and pacifist who had spent years promoting the cause of labor. The result of the merger was the formation of a new organization, the Workers party of the United States, in which the Trotskyites soon came to have the dominant role. The unity did not last long. In conformity with Trotsky's directives the leaders of the Workers party voted to enter the Socialist party in hopes of capturing the left wing of that group. But, led by Hugo Oehler and Tom Stamm, some of the Trotskyites opposed such a move and as a result were expelled from the Workers party in October 1935. The Oehlerites then formed a new organization, the Revolutionary Workers League of the U.S. [Marxist Internationalists]. In its newspaper, *The Fighting Worker*, which began publication on November 30, 1935, the new party identified itself as "Formerly the LEFT WING of the Workers party, U.S."[3] The professed purpose of the RWL was "the organization of a revolutionary Marxian, that is, a Communist party; the education and organization of the working class for the overthrow of capitalism, establishment of the dictatorship of the proletariat, and the establishment of a Communist society."[4]

The RWL began as a small group of some two hundred persons, and, in the words of Sidney Lens, one of its members, "it was all downhill, almost from the start."[5] It not only failed to win many new members, it was also hurt by numerous splits over minor issues. Nevertheless, the RWL participated in a few significant activities, most notably being efforts to organize auto workers in Detroit. With the coming of World War II in September 1939 the RWL, like a number of other radical groups, took the position that the conflict was an imperialist war for markets. This was not a popular position in America, particularly after the United States government stepped up aid to Great Britain and its own military preparedness. But by keeping a low profile the RWL leaders avoided the fate of some of the main group of Trotskyites who, in 1941, were tried and convicted for violation of the 1940 Alien Registration Act (the Smith

Act) and sentenced to twelve to sixteen months in prison. After September 1939 the principal activity of the RWL seems to have been the publication of *The Fighting Worker* until it got involved in the defense of Odell Waller during the summer of 1940.[6]

Compared to the RWL, the Workers Defense League was close to the American mainstream, although many Virginians viewed it suspiciously as an organization of radical outsiders. The WDL was founded on August 29, 1936, as a "militant, politically nonpartisan organization which would devote itself exclusively to the protection of labor's rights."[7] The idea for such an organization was prompted by a number of labor crises in the mid 1930s and was endorsed by Norman Thomas, the leader of the American Socialist party. To some extent the WDL was patterned after, and was a rival of, the International Labor Defense, a Communist-dominated organization that from late 1931 to 1935 led the legal fight in defense of the Scottsboro boys. Thus Thomas saw the WDL as being, among other things, a means of seeing that credit for supporting strikers or other workers in need of assistance would go to the Socialists instead of the Communists. On May 28, 1936, the National Executive Committee of the Socialist party voted to establish a Workers Defense League.[8] Implementation of that decision was due in large measure to the work of a remarkable young man named David L. Clendenin, who brought together a group of like-minded laborites at his home in New York on August 29, 1936. Clendenin became the organization's secretary-treasurer and from the start was its guiding figure. Son of a wealthy business executive, Clendenin was born in 1907 and educated at Phillips-Exeter Academy and Yale University, from which he graduated in 1928. Although he continued his studies at the University of Munich and at Yale for several more years, during the Great Depression he began to develop an acute social conscience. In 1934, while still a graduate student at Yale, he was arrested for picketing the Colt Arms Company plant in Hartford. From 1936 until his untimely death in an automobile accident on August 30, 1941, Clendenin worked ceaselessly for the underdog and in the process gained the deep respect of those who worked with him and shared his commitment to the fulfillment of the democratic promise.[9]

Although the WDL was a creation of the Socialist party, it pledged from the start that it would be an independent organization. Still, its leading figures were members of that party, and the two groups worked closely together to advance their mutual interests. Both were strongly

David L. Clendenin in 1941. Courtesy of the
Schlesinger Library, Radcliffe College.

committed to the defense of civil liberties, but the WDL focused exclusively on the rights of labor, and not, per se, on problems of racial
discrimination. The WDL used two principal tactics: legal services to defend workers' rights in the courts and publicity to mobilize public opinion in support of its objectives. Since 1937 it had been involved in many
cases in both the North and the South, many in defense of workers arrested for various strike-related activities. Along with numerous other
organizations and individuals representing a wide range of political
views, it participated in the convention held in Birmingham, Alabama,
in November 1938 that created the Southern Conference for Human
Welfare. In 1938 the WDL began to take a special interest in the plight
of sharecroppers. Working with the Southern Tenant Farmers' Union,
an organization also founded by members of the Socialist party and another participant at the Birmingham Conference, the WDL sponsored

an annual National Sharecroppers Week as a means of acquainting the public with the problems of sharecroppers and of raising money for the Union, for which it also provided legal defense.[10] Given these interests it was understandable that the WDL was drawn to the case of Odell Waller.

Members of the WDL first became aware of Waller following his capture in Columbus, Ohio, on July 24, 1940. On August 1 some members of the Chicago branch asked Francis Heisler to see what he could do to block Waller's extradition back to Virginia, but by that time the Ohio governor had already signed the papers. After Waller's return to Chatham, Heisler wrote to Clendenin about these events. He also noted that "some organization" had obtained the services of Thomas H. Stone as defense counsel for Waller. Although Clendenin was interested, he approached the case cautiously. At this early stage he not only lacked detailed information, he also feared that Waller was doomed unless it could be shown that he acted in self-defense.[11] After receiving Heisler's report, Clendenin wrote to Stone, who sent back a statement of the facts as he then understood them. Stone also applied for membership in the WDL. Acknowledging that he had been retained by the RWL, Stone noted that "in correspondence with them, they assure me that they would be glad to have the participation of any working class organization"[12] Clendenin was not favorably impressed by this indirect overture from the RWL. "If we decide to handle the case and give it widespread publicity," he replied to Stone, "it will be necessary for the Revolutionary Workers League to withdraw from active sponsorship; this political angle should not be allowed to prejudice Waller's chances and we would not want to risk the 'Red issue' being introduced on either side."[13] The RWL, however, had no intention of handing over Waller's defense to the WDL. Thus Clendenin's position had the effect of insuring that it would be Stone, backed by the RWL, who would be in charge of defending Waller at his forthcoming trial for murder.

Although Stone lived in Richmond, his presence in Pittsylvania County seemed to local whites almost as incongruous as that of the RWL. Born in Baltimore in 1902, Stone had studied for one year (1919–20) at the University of Virginia.[14] He had first attracted public attention at the end of 1932 as a result of his activities as one of the leaders of the Richmond Unemployed Council, one of a number of such groups organized across the United States by the Communist party in hopes of creating a mass organization of unemployed.[15] The Richmond Council was largely com-

posed of blacks. Stone's connections with the Communists and his activities in support of the council made him anathema to the good citizens of
Richmond, especially to Mayor J. Fulmer Bright who hounded Stone
and his little group at every opportunity. Between December 1932 and
December 1933, Stone was arrested several times on minor charges stem-
ming from his demonstrations and other actions on behalf of the council.[16] Stone's widely publicized conflicts with authorities in Richmond
turned out to be only a passing phase of his career. In October 1934 he
published a series of four articles in the *Richmond News Leader* in which
he described the fading of his dream in a communist, Soviet-style solu-
tion to the country's economic problems and his newfound acceptance
of the New Deal.[17] For a while he studied law at the University of Richmond, but without completing a law degree. On December 15, 1934, he
was admitted to the bar (the only requirement at that time being at least
two years of college education and passage of the bar examination), and
he began to practice law in Richmond. In the spring of 1935 he announced that he was planning to enter the city primary the next year as a
candidate for the mayor of Richmond. Thus Stone had apparently abandoned his radical ideology and his tactics of confrontation. But he could
not escape his background, including his reputation as a leader of the
Communists in Richmond in the early 1930s; nor did he give up his
interest in the cause of labor and the exploited. It was not surprising that
the RWL turned to him when it sought a Virginia attorney willing to
defend Odell Waller.[18]

To the discomfort of local authorities, the RWL lost no time in making its presence known in Virginia. On September 12, the evening before the preliminary hearing, the RWL's candidate for president, C. B.
Cowan, spoke at a meeting held at the Leigh Street Methodist Church in
Richmond.[19] The RWL certainly had nothing good to say about conditions in Pittsylvania County and claimed that a lynch-mob atmosphere
prevailed. Comparing the Waller case to that of the Scottsboro boys, *The
Fighting Worker* asserted that Waller "stands the danger of being framed
for a crime of self-defense for which he is not at all guilty; a case of the
usual robbery which the Southern landlord practices on his sharecroppers and tenants with impunity."[20]

Coming from radical outsiders, such attacks upon local conditions
certainly irritated Judge James Turner Clement, in whose court Waller
was soon to be tried. A native of Pittsylvania County, Clement was a mem-

ber of a large, well-known, and influential family. He had studied law at Washington and Lee University and had been admitted to the bar in 1894. A few years after that, he and his older brother, Nathaniel Elliott, opened a law office in Chatham. Nathaniel became a leader of the Democratic party in the area and was a member of the Virginia House of Delegates from 1916 to 1918 and the Virginia Senate from 1922 to 1927. James Clement served as the local commonwealth's attorney for a number of years and in 1922 was named circuit judge of Virginia's Seventh Judicial District. Sixty-six years old at the time of Waller's trial, Clement was an experienced judge with strong opinions on public questions and the way things should be run in his court.[21]

To have Waller's defense handled by a lawyer of Stone's background was undoubtedly troublesome to Judge Clement. But matters were made worse by what he interpreted to be the efforts of radicals to influence his court by a letter and some telegrams that were sent to him between the eighteenth and twenty-first of September. These, he complained in private to Sheriff Overbey, were sent by "Communists," and he professed to believe that the messages were "more or less threatening." Clement was also upset by the presence of several strangers at the opening session of the trial on September 19, one of whom was from Chicago and who represented, in his words, "some workers league." Like many others, Clement was unsure of the correct name and ideological identification of these radical outsiders, people who were in fact members of the RWL. But he did not welcome them. After the session on September 19, he instructed Sheriff Overbey to inform the FBI and to request that one or more agents be present at the trial, which had been postponed to September 26. As a result, an FBI agent came to Chatham on September 26, and without making his presence known to the public, observed the latter part of the proceedings on that day and the conclusion of the trial on September 27.[22]

At the opening session of Waller's trial on September 19, Stone and Hopkins moved for a continuance on the grounds that they needed more time to prepare the case. They pointed out that they had been informed of the trial date only two days before, on September 17, the same day they received the notice of the indictment. Clement immediately objected to their reasoning. "I am telling you this: A man charged with a criminal offense has no right to await the action of the Grand Jury. He should anticipate that he may be indicted." Nevertheless, Clement did agree to postpone the opening of the trial until Thursday, September 26.[23] Stone then filed two more motions. The first was "to quash the indictment on the ground the grand jury has been selected from a list exclusively of polltax payers." The second, if this first motion was not sustained, was "To quash the whole *venire facias*, on the same ground."[24] Stone took the position that "the payment of a poll tax is a prerequisite to voting and by implication also a prerequisite to jury service." Hence, in regard to the grand jury, Stone argued that Waller "has been unconstitutionally deprived of the protection of Section Eight of the Constitution of Virginia and the Fourteenth Amendment of the United States, and has been deprived of a trial by a jury of his peers." When pressed as to how it applied to Waller, Stone replied: "Persons who are unable to pay their poll tax are excluded and the accused is in the same general social and economic category." Unfortunately, Stone did not offer any evidence to sustain his contention that the juries had been selected from a list of poll tax payers. Nor did he offer any evidence as to whether Waller had paid his poll tax. His failure to present evidence of these matters turned out to be the most crucial mistake by the defense at the trial. Clement rejected Stone's argument forthwith, pointing out that he himself had selected the grand jury and he didn't know whether the members of it had paid their poll tax. Clement also overruled the motion to throw out the petit jury panel.[25]

In retrospect it seems possible that the final outcome of the Waller case might have been different had Stone and Hopkins been given more time to prepare and had they been assisted from the start by more experienced defense counsel, especially if this had resulted in the presentation of the vital evidence concerning the juries, Waller, and the poll tax. One person who might have helped was the WDL's Chicago attorney, Francis Heisler, but, unfortunately, he was unable to be at the opening session on September 19. For a while, however, it still seemed possible that he would be able to come to Chatham to serve as an associate counsel when the trial resumed on September 26. Heisler wrote to both Stone and Clendenin that he was anxious to help and would do all that was possible to be there. Although Stone said that he would welcome Heisler's help, Clendenin remained deeply concerned that the WDL at least be kept separate from the RWL. On September 24 he telegraphed to Heisler: "Imperative you get written authorization that WDL is in full charge of case before proceeding further. We will have to plan extensive campaign for funds to meet expenses and cannot do so with divided responsibility."[26] Heisler replied the next day that he had spoken with Mr. Okun of the RWL's executive board and that the RWL insisted on handling the case, although they would allow the WDL to support the Waller Defense Committee that they had set up.[27] Clendenin could not agree to such an arrangement. As he explained to Heisler, the members of the WDL's Administrative Committee believed that the "RWL figured they had got hold of another Scottsboro case and would use it as a political football." Thus on September 26 Clendenin explicitly instructed Heisler that the Chicago branch of the WDL was not to take any action in the Waller case unless it had the prior approval of the Administrative Committee, although he added that he had no objection if Heisler assisted at the trial as an attorney for the RWL. Heisler was willing to do this, but it was already too late. Prior commitments made it impossible for him to be in Chatham on the twenty-sixth, and Judge Clement was unwilling to postpone the trial any further, even by one day.[28] Waller's defense thus remained solely in the hands of Stone and Hopkins.

When the trial finally got underway on the morning of September 26, Stone's first step was to move that Judge Clement disqualify himself. Stone argued that Clement had disparaged one of the counsel for the defense (Mr. Hopkins) and had made remarks that indicated the "abrogation of the presumption of innocence" when, in the presence of the jury panel on September 19, he sharply questioned the reasons Stone and Hopkins had set forth for a continuance and asserted that a man charged with a criminal offense "should anticipate that he will be indicted."[29] It was a questionable tactic. As another of Waller's lawyers later observed, the motion rested on a flimsy basis, and it was certainly not calculated to endear the counsel with Judge Clement. "It was baiting the judge without any grounds."[30] Clement promptly rejected the motion as well as a second one requesting the dismissal of the entire jury panel that had been present on September 19.[31]

Stone next moved for a change in venue. This motion, he claimed, was based on new evidence that had come up since September 19. After Clement had the jurors removed from the courtroom, Stone placed one Edmund Campion on the stand to testify as to the prejudicial atmosphere in Pittsylvania County. Campion, a twenty-eight-year-old resident of Richmond, was a member of the RWL who had been sent as an investigator by the Waller Defense Committee. Newspaper accounts of his testimony claimed that he spoke "in broken English" when he described overhearing three conversations that allegedly indicated that public opinion in the area was highly hostile to Waller.[32] Campion testified that the owner of a garage in Gretna remarked to him on September 19 that the "damn niggah ought to be killed," and that, while eating lunch in Chatham on September 25, he overheard three men say that "Waller ought to be given the chair." Campion also testified that a gas station operator had complained that Waller was "being defended by a 'nigger' lawyer from Richmond and a communist lawyer from Chicago and deserved the chair," and "that the defense lawyers in the case ought to be lynched."[33] To counter Campion's testimony, Commonwealth's Attorney Joseph T. Whitehead called a number of citizens of Pittsylvania County, including Sheriff Overbey, who testified that they had not heard any remarks that would indicate that Waller could not get a fair trial in Chatham.[34] Overbey did state, however, that a few days after he had brought Waller back from Ohio some people told him "that crowds were coming here to get him out of jail to lynch him," and he added that on "the same day I heard a crowd of Negroes were coming to free him." But he also insisted that nothing like these threats had happened and that there had been no violence. In fact, he and some of the other witnesses testified that there seemed to be little interest in the case among the citizens of Pittsylvania County.[35] The latter may well have an exaggeration, but the fact remains that, if the defense could come up with no more evidence than that cited by Campion, then the case for a change of venue was not very compelling. Judge Clement was certainly unimpressed and rejected the motion as being "entirely without foundation."[36]

A much more serious issue concerned the composition of the jury. There were twenty-three veniremen from which the jury of twelve was to be selected. Stone began by moving to challenge "all of those on the panel employing sharecroppers" because the case involved "a killing of a landlord by a sharecropper and since it is our contention it arose out of economic circumstances." The implication, of course, was that it would be impossible for anyone employing sharecroppers to try the case fairly. Judge Clement showed little sympathy for this line of reasoning. "Mr. Stone," he retorted, "we try cases in court according to law and evidence and not because of some social standing that may exist. Motion overruled."[37] Nevertheless, Stone asked each prospective jury similar questions about his occupation and whether he had heard anything or read anything that had caused him to form an opinion in the case. Of the twenty-three men on the jury panel, twenty were farmers, nine of whom stated that they employed sharecroppers. One of the three others was in the outdoor advertising business; another was a carpenter and contractor; and the other was in the garage business.[38] All were white. Stone asked no questions about the payment of poll taxes. The jury that was finally picked was composed of eleven farmers, six of whom hired sharecroppers, and the carpenter-contractor.

In one respect the case against Odell Waller was very simple, for it rested on the uncontested fact that he had shot Oscar Davis. Beyond that, however, nothing was really clear-cut. The state's contention that this was a case of willful, premeditated murder was based primarily on the testimony of one of the two living eyewitnesses to the shooting, Henry Davis, and on the statements of two other witnesses who alleged that Waller had made threats against Davis the day before the shooting. The conclusions that the state drew from this evidence, moreover, were ones made with little sensitivity for the social and economic circumstances in which the events occurred. The prosecution, in other words, tended to regard the case as a cut-and-dried legal matter and showed little appreciation of the tragic circumstances that had blighted the lives of both Oscar Davis and Odell Waller and that made a mockery of many of the judicial and legal abstractions.

The first witness for the prosecution was Henry Davis, the seventeen-year-old black employee of Oscar Davis. In brief testimony he explained that he was walking beside Oscar Davis when Odell Waller got out of a truck and said that he had come after his wheat. According to Henry Davis, "Mr. Davis said, 'After we finish threshing if I can't get nobody else I will get Henry to bring it' and we walked on towards the house and then Odell shot him twice. I *turn* round like that and he shot at me" (emphasis in original transcript). After the shooting Henry Davis ran into the house and told Mrs. Davis. Then he "run down to the gear room and stopped and helped Mr. Davis back into the house." In response to questions from Whitehead, Henry Davis declared that Waller shot Oscar Davis four times. He also said that there had been "no cross words" before the shooting, that Oscar Davis was carrying no weapons, and that he was about twenty-five feet from him at the time of the shooting.[39] In his cross-examination Stone brought out that Henry Davis had talked about the case with Commonwealth's Attorney Whitehead three times. Stone also asserted that Henry Davis had told a somewhat different story at the preliminary hearing on September 13, and, under questioning, Henry Davis then acknowledged testifying at that time that Oscar Davis had said to Waller: "It looks like you are mad" (implying, but not specifically stating, that there had been some words between the two). Henry Davis also admitted saying that Oscar Davis had been good to him and that he had a definite sense of loyalty to his employer.[40]

Although the testimony of the next witness, Thomas Younger, was far from clear in some aspects, it was an important part of the prosecution's case. According to Younger, Waller spoke with him at church at about 11:00 A.M. on Sunday, July 14, at which time he asked Younger to take him to Oscar Davis's farm and then "said he was going to Mr. Davis' and get his wheat or kill Mr. Davis." Younger also stated that he saw Waller another time at church that day and that Waller "said he was gonna get his wheat or Mr. Davis one."[41] Nevertheless, when Stone asked Younger if he believed that Waller "was going to do something to Mr. Davis," he answered: "No, sir. I didn't think he was."[42]

The third of the state's witnesses was John Curtis Williams, a friend of Waller, who testified that he was at Waller's home around 4:00 P.M. on Sunday, July 14, and heard a conversation between Odell and his mother. According to Williams the conversation went as follows:

> Odell said, "Mr. Davis hasn't given me my wheat." Mr. Davis said as soon as they finished threshing he will bring it down himself if he can't get nobody else and Odell say, "I am going to get my wheat or Oscar Davis one."[43]

Under cross-examination Williams acknowledged, as had Younger, that he did not take the alleged threat to Oscar Davis seriously. All three of these state's witnesses, Henry Davis, Younger, and Williams, also acknowledged that they had discussed the case with Whitehead. But Stone did not press any of the three vigorously on cross-examination, despite the interesting questions their testimony raised. One was the nearly identical wording of the alleged threat as stated by Younger and Williams. Another question—one that cried out for further examination—concerned the curious fact that in recounting conversations that were supposed to have taken place on Sunday, July 14, Williams reported what Oscar Davis allegedly said to Waller on July 15 just before the shooting.

Moreover, Williams used words that were almost identical to those reported in the testimony by Henry Davis. There was certainly a suggestion here that the state's three key witnesses had been coached.[44]

The only medical testimony presented at the trial was from Dr. John C. Risher, the physician who attended to Oscar Davis at Memorial Hospital in Lynchburg. Curiously, neither the prosecution nor the defense subpoenaed the physician who examined Oscar Davis at his home after the shooting, a Dr. Anderson from Chatham. Nor did either side get the hospital record. It is at least conceivable that some of the discrepancies about the location of the wounds and in turn the facts of the shooting might have been resolved had Dr. Anderson and the hospital documents been subjected to careful scrutiny at the trial. Dr. Risher testified that Oscar Davis "had four bullet wounds, one on the right side of his head, his scalp, another in his arm and two in the lower part of his back."[45] He also asserted that Davis would have died had he not been operated upon, that the intestinal wounds were infected and could have led to his death, but that the actual cause of death was a collapsed left lung, which was a consequence of the operation.[46] Because of this fact, the defense would later attempt, with no success, to argue that Davis's death was not caused by the shooting. It was a wasted effort that did nothing to enhance the defense's position.

Three members of Oscar Davis's family testified for the prosecution: Mrs. Davis and Oscar's two sons, Frank and Edgar. Mrs. Davis stated that immediately after the shooting she had led her husband into the house and had helped him take off his pants. Her most important statement was that Oscar Davis was unarmed, that he had nothing in his pocket but a billfold, and that he did not own a pistol or have one at his house.[47] Both sons also testified that their father did not own a pistol.[48] The most significant aspect of their testimony, however, was their recounting of a statement made by their father to them in the hospital on Tuesday evening, July 16. Stone immediately challenged the admissibility of that evidence and insisted that the jury be removed from the room until a foundation had been laid that it could be properly considered a dying declaration. Stone contended that the medical testimony showed that at the time the statement was made, Tuesday evening, Davis's condition had apparently improved, and that reasonable grounds did not exist to believe that death was imminent. Whitehead, in turn, argued that the important point was simply that Oscar Davis thought he was going to die. Judge Clement ruled that the testimony was admissible.[49] According to Frank Davis the statement by his father was merely this:

> Frank, I am going to die. Odell shot me without any cause. He shot me four times, twice after I fell.[50]

Although Frank Davis testified that he had been with his father for about one hour, that simple statement was "about all he said."[51] Edgar Davis testified that he went into the hospital room "about the same time" as Frank, and that their father "said he was feeling mighty bad; said he wasn't going to live, that Odell shot him without any cause at all."[52] Frank and Edgar Davis could not testify directly about the facts of the shooting, but by introducing their father's alleged dying declaration they strengthened the prosecution's case that the shooting had been unprovoked and had not been an act of self-defense.

The testimony for the defense was even briefer than that of the prosecution. Stone called four witnesses: Archie Waller, Annie Waller, Mollie Waller, and Odell. Archie Waller, the brother-in-law of Annie's late husband Willis, was a man about sixty-four years old. He first testified briefly as to Odell's character and reputation, asserting that "he seemed to be all right to me" and to other people. He also stated that he did not hear Odell make any threats against Oscar Davis.[53] Archie Waller was on the truck that went to Oscar Davis's place on the morning of July 15, but he remained there while Odell went to speak to Davis. Nevertheless, he claimed to have heard Odell tell Davis that he had come for his wheat and that Davis replied: "I will finish threshing and you will get your wheat." He also asserted that he had his back to them and that after hearing that conversation "I looked around again and both had disappeared. In a second or two I heard a shot from a revolver."[54] Archie estimated that the truck was about eighty or ninety feet from Odell and Oscar Davis.[55] Archie Waller's testimony was of limited value to the defense. What he claimed to have overheard was a part of a conversation that suggested no threats by either party. But, according to his testimony, he had neither seen nor heard what happened in the few seconds immediately prior to the shooting. For those crucial moments the court had the contradictory testimony of only two living witnesses, Henry Davis and Odell Waller.

Annie Waller's testimony might have been of great significance. But the court would have had to allow a broad perspective and make the effort to understand the plight of black sharecroppers and particularly the enormous obstacles such people faced in attempting to resolve disputes with white landlords. Judge Clement was not inclined to allow such latitude. Some sixty-five years old and under great emotional stress, Annie clearly faced a difficult ordeal in taking the stand. After she began a rather labored attempt to explain her family's work as sharecroppers, Clement abruptly cut her off, criticized her remarks as "not relevant," and demanded, "What's the object of all this?" Stone attempted to explain that "everything leads up to an aggregate in that the defendant might have been justified in exercising self-defense." "The witness is old and uneducated," he continued. "I apologize for the rambling, but do respectfully insist that, in the main, the testimony is relevant."[56] Clement then relented and allowed Annie to continue, but only to a point. Thus he cut her off again when she attempted to explain that Oscar Davis had refused to pay the $7.50 he owed her for taking care of his wife.[57] As to the specific events on the morning of July 15, Annie could add little. She did insist that Odell seemed to be "in a good humor" when he left to go to Oscar Davis's place to get his wheat. She was on the truck when Odell got out to speak to Davis. "Then I heerd the firing of the gun—like to scared me to death. That's all I know about it."[58] Whitehead's brief cross-examination elicited no changes in this story.

The next witness was Odell's twenty-two-year-old wife Mollie. She testified that Odell had been in a good frame of mind on Sunday, July 14, and that he had never said that he was going to do anything against Oscar Davis. As for events on the morning of July 15, Mollie testified simply that "he told me he was going to get part of his wheat and told me to cook breakfast and have it ready when he got back."[59] Although neither Stone nor Whitehead made anything of this comment at the time, Mollie's remark was conceivably of significance in attempting to understand Odell's mood and intent as he left to go to the Davis farm. Had he been planning murder at that time, it would be hard to believe that he would calmly have asked his wife to have breakfast ready upon his return.

Finally, the defense put Odell Waller on the stand. The direct examination was conducted entirely by Hopkins, not Stone. Waller's testimony was useful at the outset in shedding light on the sharecropping arrangements with Oscar Davis, although some of the details were lacking in clarity, and on Davis's treatment of the Wallers. There were a few crucial points of dispute with the testimony of some of the prosecution witnesses. One was Waller's insistence that Oscar Davis carried a pistol, in flat contradiction to the testimony of Mrs. Davis and Frank and Edgar Davis. Another was his assertion that Oscar Davis had quarreled with his oldest son, Edgar, and that on one occasion Edgar had threatened to kill his father. (In his testimony Edgar Davis denied that there had been contention between himself and his father, although he said that he had quarreled with him in the presence of Odell Waller and others.)[60] In short, the Oscar Davis portrayed by Odell Waller was a more vexatious individual than the person described by his friends. A more important contradiction concerned the testimony of Thomas Younger and John Curtis Williams. Although Waller acknowledged seeing both on Sunday, July 14, he flatly denied telling them that he was going to harm or kill Oscar Davis.[61]

The biggest discrepancy was between Henry Davis's and Odell Waller's description of the confrontation between Waller and Oscar Davis and the actual shooting. Henry Davis testified that Oscar Davis told Waller that he would get his wheat after they finished threshing, that there were no cross words between the two, and that Waller just started shooting. Waller's version was entirely different. According to Waller:

> Mr. Davis said I won't get that damn wheat away from here. I said, "I got a truck." He said, "I told you you won't go carry it away from here." I told him I wouldn't of, and he used some dirty words, and from one word to another, and he usually carried a gun and run his hand in his pocket like he was trying to pull something. I had my gun and out with it. I opened my pistol and commenced to shoot at him— I don't know how many times. I didn't look at it. Mr. Davis hollered and fell. I went on down by the barn by the woods and stayed there until the evening.[62]

During his cross-examination, Whitehead tried to get Waller to say that he knew that Oscar Davis was carrying no weapon, but Waller stuck to his story. "The reason I shot was because he was going to do something to me."[63]

Waller also contradicted Henry Davis's claim that he had shot at him. In response to Hopkins's question, "Did you shoot at Henry Davis?" Waller answered: "No. I don't know where Henry Davis was; I didn't see Henry Davis. I didn't have no intention nor consider of doing anything to him."[64] Finally, Waller denied the charge, allegedly made by Oscar Davis in the dying declaration presented by Frank Davis, that he had shot Oscar Davis twice after Davis had fallen to the ground. (Significantly, the only other eyewitness, Henry Davis, did not make such a claim in his trial testimony.) In short, on several crucial points Waller contradicted the testimony of Henry Davis and Oscar Davis's dying declaration.

After Waller had finished testifying, the defense rested its case. The prosecution then put one final witness on the stand, Herbert Bailey, a special county officer, for the purpose of claiming that Waller's reputation in both the white and the black community was "bad" and that he was known as being "law violator" and a "mean nigger." When Stone pressed Bailey for specific illustrations that might provide a factual basis for such a reputation, Bailey had to admit that the only thing he had been able to catch Waller with was driving after his permit had been taken away and bootlegging. Bailey also claimed that Waller had once pulled a razor on him. Beyond this, the defense made no effort to explain Bailey's charges. At this point the brief trial came to an end. It had taken less than a day.[65]

Unfortunately, the evidence presented at the trial was scanty. In retrospect it was apparent that the defense could have done much more on several key points, beginning with the selection of the jury. Here specific data should have been presented regarding the actual payment or nonpayment of the poll tax by the prospective jurors and by Waller himself. The medical evidence was certainly inadequate. A more careful and detailed examination here might have shed light on the question of whether Waller had shot Davis after he had fallen down. In addition, the defense could have scrutinized far more carefully the crucial testimony of Henry Davis, Younger, and Williams for inconsistencies and evidence of possible coaching by the prosecution. Beyond that, there was certainly need for a fuller exploration into Waller's relationship to Oscar Davis and of his status as a black sharecropper in a white-dominated rural society, if there was to be any hope of understanding Waller's state of mind, and fears, at the moment of crisis. Instead, the short trial largely pitted Waller's admittedly self-interested interpretation of events against those of several prosecution witnesses. The defense wanted the jurors to see Waller as a frightened, exploited black man who had acted in what he truly believed was self-defense; the prosecution portrayed Waller as a vicious, habitual lawbreaker who deliberately planned and carried out a cold-blooded murder. Given the context, and in the absence of other testimony, the outcome of the trial at this point was quite predictable.

The court reconvened the next morning, Friday, September 27, before a large, but reportedly orderly, crowd of spectators. Judge Clement gave the jury more than twenty instructions, explaining in some detail the difference between murder in the first degree, murder in the second degree, and voluntary manslaughter. One of the instructions also stated that "any person has the right to peaceably demand his property and has the further right to arm himself if he reasonably believes that a proper and lawful demand for his property will be met with force dangerous to his life or calculated to do him great bodily harm."[66] Stone and Whitehead then spent about three hours in final arguments. The case went to the jury at 2:05 P.M. After a deliberation of only fifty-two minutes the jury returned a verdict of guilty of murder in the first degree and fixed punishment at death. Stone and Hopkins immediately moved to have the verdict set aside as contrary to law and evidence, but Clement promptly overruled their motion. The defense announced that they would draw up a bill of exceptions and apply to the Virginia Supreme Court of Appeals for a writ of error. Clement then sentenced Waller to die in the state's electric chair in Richmond on December 27, 1940.[67]

The verdict and sentence seemed to have the approval of many of the whites in the area. From the start the two local newspapers, the *Pittsylvania Tribune*, a weekly published in Chatham, and the *Danville Register*, a daily, had covered the case fairly extensively, but nothing in their accounts was calculated to elicit much sympathy for Waller. In an editorial entitled "Virginia Justice Sustained," the *Register* claimed that "the tradition of Virginia courts for meting out justice acquired added prestige" as a result of the trial's outcome, and it praised the court for exercising "extreme caution" in assuring "the Negro defendant every right and privilege" in what it believed was a "fair and impartial trial."[68] From such a perspective, which was undoubtedly shared by many other whites in Pittsylvania County, the matter was considered closed. It was also little known beyond the immediate area. Without the continued support of the Revolutionary Workers League and the subsequent entry into the case by the Workers Defense League, Waller would probably have gone to his death at the end of 1940 unknown to most of the world.[69]

3
"Save Odell Waller!":
The Campaign Begins

The determination of the Revolutionary Workers League to mount a campaign on behalf of Waller insured that his plight was not going to be easily forgotten. But the transformation of the case from one of merely local interest to one of national significance, in which Odell Waller became a symbol of racial and economic injustice in the United States, did not get underway until the Workers Defense League finally decided to come to his defense in early November 1940. By mid December, Waller's defenders had achieved their first objective, a reprieve of his scheduled December 27 execution in order to allow an appeal to the Supreme Court of Appeals of Virginia. The efforts were considerably complicated, however, by the conflict between the relatively moderate tactics of the WDL and the radical goals of the RWL.

From the moment the RWL first became involved, its ideology and tactics invited controversy. Immediately after the trial the *Pittsylvania Tribune* published a story asserting that attempts had been made to intimidate the court through "ugly worded telegrams" sent to Judge Clement. According to the *Tribune*, one of these telegrams used "insulting words" and accused the court of bias. This had been signed by "L. Drone, secretary of the District Project Worker's Union." In addition the "Workers Union" had sent a special delivery letter which, the *Tribune* alleged, had "threatened the court." Claiming that these were threatening communications, Clement had sought the assistance of the FBI. More than a year later he reiterated this charge and suggested that they had come "from the crowd these lawyers [Waller's counsel] apparently represented."[1] But Clement seems to have taken a different position publicly from what he had expressed privately to an FBI agent immediately after the trial. According to the report of the agent who was present at the trial, Clement told him on September 27 that "there was no threat and he had no fear" in regard to the letter and the telegrams he had received. Subsequently, the agent in charge of the Richmond office of the FBI reported that those communications did "not appear to constitute a violation of the law." Although Clement may have hoped to discredit the RWL and Waller's lawyers by releasing information about the letter and the telegrams, the charge that the senders had attempted to intimidate the court cannot be sustained. What these messages did was simply to "protest the speeding of the case without adequate time to prepare the defense." They contained no threats.[2]

The controversy had, however, attracted attention to the Waller case and to the possibly disturbing role played by the RWL. For example, Norfolk's black newspaper, the *Journal and Guide*, published an editorial on October 12, 1940, entitled the "Kiss of Death," in which it attacked what it erroneously called the "American Revolutionary League" for defending Waller. It was "extreme recklessness," the editorial charged, to risk whatever chance Waller might have had by bringing such an organization into a southern court. It "prejudiced the case and identified the defense with the usual headquarters of the workers' revolution—Soviet Russia."[3] The *Journal and Guide* exaggerated the damage the RWL may have done. It had, after all, provided counsel for Waller when others were unable or unwilling to do so. And it did not take the presence of outside radicals to explain that a conservative white judge and landowning white jurors had little sympathy for a black sharecropper accused of murdering his white landlord. But there can be no doubt that the RWL was not welcomed by most residents of Pittsylvania County and that its tactics complicated the efforts of the WDL and others who wished to come to the defense of Odell Waller.

While Thomas H. Stone and Byron J. Hopkins set to work preparing Waller's appeal, what publicity the case got at this early stage was largely the work of the Richmond Waller Defense Committee (RWDC). Created by the RWL in August, this organization had three professed objectives: "One, to defend Waller in court. Two, to begin building Waller Defense Committee [*sic*] throughout the nation for the purpose of giving the widest publicity to the Waller case. Three, to interest all other labor and sympathetic organizations in the case and get their cooperation."[4] The first chairman of the Richmond Waller Defense Committee was Edmund Campion, the man who testified at the beginning of

Waller's trial as to the allegedly prejudicial atmosphere in Pittsylvania County. From the start the position of the RWL was "that the only place in which the ruling class will allow the Negro equal rights is in the electric chair." It sought funds to assist in the appeal. "Here is a real working class issue, which needs the support of every working class organization in the country."[5] By the latter part of October the RWL claimed to have Waller Defense Committees set up in Chicago, Philadelphia, and New York in addition to the one in Richmond, although it complained that the committees were "still woefully weak." The New York committee had to be reorganized, it noted, "because of the sudden withdrawal of both factions of the Trotskyites." Although the RWL referred to the interests of all labor groups, it vigorously complained that the larger labor and Negro organizations had not entered the case. It particularly singled out the WDL in this regard for allegedly taking the position that it would become involved only if other organizations, including the RWL, withdrew.[6]

Before the trial, David L. Clendenin had made it clear to Thomas H. Stone and Francis Heisler that the WDL would take over Waller's defense only if the RWL withdrew and left the WDL in full charge.[7] On September 25, Hugo Oehler, the national secretary of the RWL, replied that they would have no objection to having the WDL conduct the defense, provided "it is agreed between us that the case shall be handled on a class struggle basis, with the legal defense an auxiliary to attempted mass action of trade unions, Negro organizations, political organizations, etc.," and that the mass actions were to be "a concomitant of the legal defense" organized as a "united front" by a Waller Defense Committee."[8] In Clendenin's opinion Oehler's propositions simply showed that he "had no conception of the purposes and functioning of the Workers Defense League. . . . The RWL is a minute splinter group with a few hardy souls like Robbins and Campion to carry on the Oehler wing and it seems to us rather Icarian for them to attempt to build a national defense movement around the unfortunate Waller."[9] Stone disagreed. Although he professed to have nothing to do with such organizational matters, he thought that the WDL should agree to take up Waller's defense on the terms proposed by Oehler. It was wrong, he suggested, for the WDL to take the position that it should "have the whole case or leave Waller to his fate. Frankly, this looks to me like the WDL is playing around with the 'unfortunate Waller.'"[10]

Although Stone had recently joined the WDL, he obviously was not attuned to the principles of that organization. On October 7, Clendenin replied in detail to Oehler, after a discussion of his proposals by the WDL's Administrative Committee. The WDL, he pointed out, was a nonpartisan organization that was on the job all the time in defense of labor victims. It did not proceed sporadically by ad hoc defense committees. It thus regretted the formation of dual organizations, such as the Waller Defense Committees. If the WDL were to handle Waller's defense, then, Clendenin suggested, the RWLers would do well to join the WDL, "thus demonstrating their belief in the solidarity of labor." If the WDL were in charge, it "would take very little effort to enlist the support of the N.A.A.C.P. and many trade unions. Your action in sanctioning Waller Defense Committees however leaves us no alternative but to keep our hands off unless we can reach some further understanding."[11]

This did not end the exchange between Clendenin and Oehler, but they could reach no agreement. The WDL insisted upon independence and autonomy if it were to take charge of Waller's defense. The RWL insisted on the formation of Waller Defense Committees and maintaining its political position. Oehler did state, however, that the RWL was willing to "subordinate and merge our local groups into a broad Defense committee, under the WDL."[12] He obviously tried to present this position, then and later, as evidence of the willingness of his organization to be reasonable and cooperative. But such a step would still have involved the WDL with the dual organizational structure that it rejected in principle and would have inevitably associated the WDL with some of the ideological or political positions of the RWL. It was apparent, a month after Waller's trial, that if the WDL were to enter the case in a meaningful way, it would have to act completely separately from the RWL and its Waller Defense Committees.

Although Stone did not share Clendenin's views about the role of the RWL, which, after all, had retained him as counsel for Waller, he still hoped that Francis Heisler could be brought in to help with the appeals process. Heisler continued to indicate his willingness to assist, but as the Midwest attorney for the WDL, he insisted on following the position of that organization. It was, he reminded Stone, a "non-partisan labor defense organization," and he opposed the creation of new organizations for every new case.[13] Meanwhile, the Administrative Committee of the WDL sent Clendenin to Richmond on October 14 to talk to Stone in hopes of persuading him to turn over the case to Heisler and the WDL. Clendenin did not succeed, although he did find that Stone was "upset over the whole business."[14]

By that time Clendenin was leaning towards the position that the WDL should "take over the case bodily and organize . . . [its] own defense." He noted with interest that the RWL had had no success in organizing a Waller Defense Committee in New York City, and that members of the Socialist party, the Socialist Workers party, the Workers party, and the IWW had come out in favor of the WDL handling the case.[15] A decision was finally reached at a meeting called by the WDL in New York City on November 2. Present were Clendenin; Morris Milgram, the WDL's assistant national secretary; other WDL officials; Thurgood Marshall, the national counsel of the NAACP; and Stone. Stone gave a detailed presentation of the background of the case, the trial, and the basis of his appeal. Asked about the chances of success in the appeal, Stone replied that "we are reasonably sure of getting a writ of error from the Virginia Supreme Court." Clendenin reported that the principal role of the WDL at that stage would be to finance the appeals. He estimated that a minimum of two thousand dollars would be needed to take the case to the Supreme Court of the United States. To raise the money the WDL would have to mount a publicity campaign. In the end all present agreed to a statement that "the Workers Defense League shall handle the case, its directions and fund raising, with Mr. Stone handling the legal phase of the case."[16] After some two and a half months of hesitation, the WDL had finally made a definite commitment to aid Odell Waller. As it turned out, it was to become a considerably lengthier and costlier process than anyone anticipated at the time.

On November 2, 1940, the WDL issued a "Statement of Facts on the Case of Odell Waller" which was signed by both Stone and Clendenin. It contained a couple of comments that some critics of the defense efforts would find objectionable. One was that during his confrontation with Waller, just before the shooting, Oscar Davis "ran his hand in his front pocket where he usually carried a pistol." The other was "that Davis did not die from the wounds, but from collapse of the left lung." The statement concluded with an appeal for funds, to be sent to WDL headquarters in New York City, with $350 needed by November 19 "to cover the cost of the record in the appeal to the Supreme Court of Appeals of Virginia."[17] To support the fund drive the WDL also sent out two special news releases on November 7 to the Negro press to be used as the basis of editorials and feature stories. They noted that the NAACP was cooperating with the WDL on the Waller case, and Clendenin called for the support "of all those who are opposed to the poll tax and other instances of racial and social discrimination in the South." Clendenin also sought financial aid from the Sharecroppers Defense Fund of the Southern Tenant Farmers' Union.[18]

The most significant early move by the WDL was to send Pauli Murray, a young black woman then working for the WDL, to Richmond, Virginia. Her principal objectives were to begin raising funds for Waller's defense and to organize a committee to carry on her work. For Murray involvement in the case proved to be a turning point in what was to become a distinguished career. Born in Baltimore in 1910, Murray had been raised by her maternal aunt, a teacher, in Durham, North Carolina, after the death of her mother in 1914. Upon her graduation from high school, the young Pauli was determined to attend a nonsegregated college, and through hard work and the help of family in New York City, she managed to graduate from Hunter College in Brooklyn in January 1933. For several years afterward, times were difficult, although she found work for a while with the National Urban League selling subscriptions to its journal, *Opportunity*, and, from 1936 to 1939, with the Workers' Education Project of the WPA as a teacher of remedial reading. In the spring of 1940 Murray and a friend were arrested and jailed in Petersburg, Virginia, for violating the state law requiring segregated seating on buses. With the help of an NAACP lawyer they appealed their conviction, but, predictably, they lost after a trial in Hustings Court. Rather than pay the fine they decided to return to jail, but after a few days they were released when David L. Clendenin and Morris Milgram of the WDL sent money to pay the fines. During the summer of 1940 the WDL in New York offered Murray a job on its Administrative Committee, a position she readily accepted out of gratitude for the assistance it had extended to her during her troubles in Petersburg.[19]

Accompanied by a white friend, Gene Phillips, Murray arrived in Richmond in the evening of November 7. It proved to be no easy outing. On November 8 they conferred at length with Stone, who filled them in on the details of the case. Although he welcomed their assistance in raising funds, he provided no logistical support for Murray and Phillips, who, short of cash, faced daunting problems in simply finding a place to sleep. Stone put them in contact with Hilliard Bernstein, the local secretary of

MRS. ANNIE WALLER
PM Photo

YOU *can save a Life!*

ODELL WALLER

Sentenced To Die December 27th

TWO DAYS AFTER CHRISTMAS!

ODELL WALLER
Journal & Guide

Negro Sharecropper and Family,

including aged MOTHER—ROBBED, CHEATED, AND EVICTED BY WHITE LANDLORD!!!

ODELL WALLER, born in Gretna, Virginia, 23 years of age, who worked long days for the miserable one-fourth of the crop that meant food and shelter for himself, his wife and his old mother, now faces death on December 27th in a Virginia electric chair for the self-defense shooting of his landlord, Oscar Davis.

Picture this sharecropper cheated by his landlord as people of his race have been cheated and beaten for generations of Southern history. Picture for yourself a desperate boy, home from Baltimore where he had gone for work, finding his family evicted and its share of the bread crop withheld. Remember that a contract between landlord and tenant means nothing; if it is violated, the tenant has no redress and no money to secure legal aid. A sharecropper or a Negro has few rights in the American South.

Picture for yourself Waller—asking for his share of the wheat crop and Davis, brief and profane, refusing; his aging mother, waiting in the truck for the bread crop she had toiled to raise; Davis cutting short his talk with a gesture toward his "gun" pocket. Then Waller, fearful, shooting for his life. The Virginia law allows a man to carry a gun if he feels his life is in danger.

Hunted by armed lynch mobs and dogs, Waller was caught and tried by an all-white jury made up of ten landlords, a carpenter and a business man.

Sharecroppers, who are the majority of county residents, were excluded from the jury because they were unable to pay the $1.50 Virginia poll tax. The tax adds up for years, and poor people can never catch up on payments. In that way, six million white people and four million Negroes in 8 States are prevented from voting and from serving on juries. Is this democracy?

THE WORKERS DEFENSE LEAGUE is fighting the death sentence, with the cooperation of the NATIONAL ASSOCIATION FOR THE ADVANCEMENT OF COLORED PEOPLE and the BROTHERHOOD OF SLEEPING CAR PORTERS. The crime for which Odell Waller stands condemned is the outgrowth of unbearable conditions facing Negro and white sharecroppers and migrant workers in the South. He symbolizes the tragic lives of so many of the disinherited and dispossessed citizens of our country, both white and colored, whose condition has long been the shame of the greatest democracy on earth. The defense of Waller is one way of bringing to the attention of the American people a condition which must be wiped out.

To appeal his case to the United States Supreme Court, FUNDS are needed.

SNATCH ODELL WALLER FROM THE JAWS OF DEATH! RUSH CONTRIBUTIONS!

TEAR OFF AND MAIL

| National Headquarters
WORKERS DEFENSE LEAGUE
112 East 19th St., New York City
— or —
NATIONAL ASSOCIATION FOR THE ADVANCEMENT OF COLORED PEOPLE
69 Fifth Avenue, New York City

Issued jointly by Workers Defense League and the N. A. A. C. P. | Here is my contribution to help save the life of sharecropper Odell Waller. $................
Name................................
Address................................
City................................
Organization................................
(Please list on reverse side friends who may be interested) |

Workers Defense League flier, November 1940.

the Socialist party, who put them up for the night. Bernstein was pessimistic about Waller's chances. He frankly stated that Stone's association with the case was the biggest problem in getting the support of liberals and labor, who were alienated by his past connections to the Communist party and his continued association with the RWL. His assessment proved all too accurate. Murray found that the labor unions and liberals on her list were unwilling to contribute as long as Stone was associated with the case. Nor did she have any luck with the local NAACP and Negro groups. Some potential contributors turned her down because they confused the WDL with the RWL. After several days of effort Murray and Phillips returned to New York with only $36.50 in cash and $25.00 in pledges. They were clearly very discouraged. "Frankly, if a man's life were not at stake, we would recommend that the WDL withdraw from the case because of these complications," they wrote in their report of their visit.[20]

Murray and Phillips were less than enthusiastic about Stone's role in the case. One of their recommendations was that Stone accept another lawyer, Howard Davis of Richmond, as an associate counsel. Davis was quite willing and stated that he would "serve as a counterbalance to Mr. Stone, who is an excellent lawyer but has a tendency toward radicalism." They also recommended "that the exercise of restraint in dealing with public relations . . . be considered as a paramount responsibility, so that public sentiment may not be alienated from the merits of the case."[21] This was an obvious reference to the work of the RWL and its Waller Defense Committees, with which Stone sympathized, but which Murray believed had hurt Waller's case. Over the next few months Murray's negative opinion of Stone grew, and she ultimately concluded that his continued association with the RWL made "the work of the WDL incalculably more difficult."[22]

During their visit to Richmond, Murray and Phillips got the chance to discuss the case with Virginius Dabney, the influential editor of the *Richmond Times-Dispatch*. If he were to be persuaded to support Waller's appeal, it could have a considerable impact within Virginia. At that time however, Dabney regarded it as a simple case of murder, and he was unwilling to do anything without further study. Although his initial response was not very encouraging, eventually Dabney would come to play an important part in raising questions about the nature of Virginia justice in the Waller case.[23]

In the meantime, Odell Waller had to endure a lonely and stressful

Pauli Murray in 1941. Courtesy of the Schlesinger Library,
Radcliffe College.

period during the weeks immediately after his trial and sentencing. With
only limited contacts to the outside world, he was largely cut off from the
arguments that were raised over the handling of his case and the issues
he was coming to symbolize. On October 9, 1940, he was transferred
from the Chatham jail to a death row cell in the basement of building A
in the state penitentiary in Richmond. There he was allowed to see only
his immediate relatives, his spiritual adviser, and Stone. Pauli Murray
attempted, without success, to visit him during her visit to Richmond, so
on November 15 she wrote Odell a letter introducing herself and explaining her efforts with the WDL. "We want you to feel encouraged and

to know that you have thousands of friends all over the country. . . . Try to keep well and strong because you have a tough job ahead of you. Many people are praying for you." Murray enclosed two dollars "for your needs."[24] On that same day he had sent a letter to Annie Waller in which he noted that "I have wrote three letters to Stone haven't heard nothing get in touch with him and find out what sort of steps to take." Murray's letter was thus particularly welcome to Odell, who replied that he "was more than glad to hear from you and I know I have some friends same time I think every one have gone against me."[25] Over the next several weeks Murray kept up a steady correspondence with Odell in an effort to inform him of the work being done on his behalf and to keep his spirits up. In the long run this exchange, which brought home the human dimensions of the tragedy unfolding before her, probably had a greater impact on Murray than on Waller.

Although Murray was discouraged by the meager results of her trip to Richmond, the WDL leaders in New York were not dismayed. Upon her return they immediately asked her to work full time on the case as a special field secretary raising funds and seeking public support. By mid November the WDL had a substantial campaign of press releases, telephone solicitations, and mailings, and other activities well under way.[26] One of their first fliers, a collage of stories about Waller clipped from black newspapers, proclaimed that "$2000 *Can* Stop Judge Lynch . . . !"

> Waller is a typical victim of the planter justice which has ground down the poor people, white and colored, of the Southern states for generations. He was tried in a court presided over by a judge who made no attempt to conceal his anti-Negro bias and condemned by a jury consisting of a businessman, a carpenter, and *ten landlords.* Sharecroppers had no place on the jury list which was made up of those who paid the $1.50 Virginia state poll tax.[27]

The efforts of Murray and others in the WDL soon began to have some effect. Eleanor Roosevelt, for example, first showed interest in the case as a result of a letter Murray sent to her on November 20. Mrs. Roosevelt in turn forwarded that letter to Governor James H. Price of Virginia with the request that he "look into the case and see that the young man has a fair trial." Price responded that he would see to it that Waller had "every opportunity to present his case" and that "additional time will be granted" to allow his attorneys "opportunity to present the matter to the Supreme Court of Appeals."[28]

Other organizations also joined the list of Waller's defenders. One of considerable importance was the NAACP. Although this oldest of civil rights organizations had been interested in the case from the start, until mid November its assistance at the national level had been limited to the informal backing of the WDL's efforts by its counsel, Thurgood Marshall. But on Saturday, November 16, 1940, the national office of the NAACP formally announced that it would work with the WDL on Waller's behalf, and thereafter it regularly assisted the WDL in its fund-raising and publicity campaigns. The local NAACP chapters in Danville and Richmond had also expressed a concern about the case, but they too had provided no immediate help. After Stone addressed the State Conference of Virginia Branches of the NAACP at its meeting in Richmond on November 20, however, that group took up a collection for the defense fund.[29] The Brotherhood of Sleeping Car Porters, led by veteran black activist and labor leader A. Philip Randolph, who was also a member of the National Committee of the WDL, was another significant addition to the list of organizations that enlisted in the emerging campaign to save Odell Waller. In this case the union's executive board reached its decision on November 27 after listening to a plea from Annie Waller, who was then in New York on the first of several publicity and fund-raising tours. At the same time Murray announced the formation of a Harlem Committee, composed of representatives of several organizations, to aid in Waller's defense.[30]

The most important addition, however, was to the legal staff. In mid November the eminent attorney John F. Finerty, who was a member of the WDL's National Executive Board, agreed to enter the case. He was joined by WDL counsel Morris Shapiro, who was also a member of the National Executive Board.[31] Thus, from that moment on, first-rate legal talent became available to support the appeals process. Finerty in particular came to play a crucial role. Born in 1885, Finerty had a distinguished record as both a corporation lawyer and a civil libertarian. His father, John Frederick Finerty, who had been born in Ireland and emigrated to the United States in 1864, had been a reporter for a number of Chicago newspapers and had served one term in Congress (1883–85) as an Independent Democrat from Illinois. The younger Finerty studied law at Northwestern University and worked for a number of years as counsel for several major railroads. A champion of Irish independence, he served as counsel for Sinn Fein leader Eamon de Valera from 1922 to 1927 in litigation involving Irish Republican bonds. Finerty was also active in the American Civil Liberties Union and had volunteered his services in a number of cases involving underdogs or defendants who were unpopular with the ruling establishment. The most notable of these included Sacco and Vanzetti, for whom he drafted and argued their last writ of habeas corpus shortly before their execution in 1927, and Tom Mooney, whose case he argued before both the United States Supreme Court and the Supreme Court of California.[32] According to the WDL announcement, Finerty agreed to work as associate counsel in the Waller case, concentrating on the constitutional aspects while Stone would continue to handle the local and evidentiary side.[33]

On November 24, Murray wrote to Waller to explain how fortunate they were to have Finerty, "one of the best lawyers in the country," working on his case. "He will not charge you anything," she wrote, "but he wants you to write him."[34] Waller obliged. On November 27 he sent a moving short note to Finerty:

> I have been informed Thrue miss pauli Murry that the Negro organaizahan has employed you to help defend me.
> I hope you will put your hole heart in the movement.
> I am trusting the lord will give you the power to help me in my distress.
> I appreciate every step you good people do towards helping me I am a poor laboring boy All I want is one more chance at life.[35]

One of the WDL's most effective early publicity and fund-raising moves was to bring Annie Waller to New York to have her tell Odell's story to interested church, labor, and other groups, especially blacks. Arriving in New York on November 23, this small, stooped, but dignified woman had a telling effect on her audiences. Her presence attracted the attention of the press and led to increased publicity for the case.[36] As Murray later wrote, she "gave our efforts an immediacy and authenticity no other person could have supplied."[37] During her visit in New York,

Prison photograph of Odell Waller. Courtesy of
Department of Corrections, Commonwealth of Virginia.

which lasted to December 22, Mrs. Waller stayed with Pauli Murray, who
found her to be "one of the most courageous little souls I have ever
met." For Annie, the experience was difficult but exciting, as she found
herself "going from church to church and organization to organization."
But her hosts also found time to take her to a Broadway show, a China-
town restaurant, and other, for her, exotic places. As she wrote back to
Robert Waller, "I am among good people—some of the best white and
colored people I have ever known."[38]

Fortunately, the various fund-raising efforts brought some results. A
report of December 11, 1940, showed that $1,459.51 had been received
and $1,228.90 disbursed, leaving a balance of $230.61 in the Waller fund.

Annie Waller, November 1940. The WDL used this photograph extensively in its fliers. Courtesy of the Archives of Labor and Urban Affairs, Wayne State University.

Thus the WDL was able to cover the expenses incurred by Stone in preparing the appeal to the Supreme Court of Appeals of Virginia as well as to mount a publicity campaign.[39] Another result of the WDL efforts was seen in the increasing number of stories about Waller that began to appear in nationally circulated journals. The December 1940 issue of *The Catholic Worker*, for example, carried a sympathetic account that ended with an appeal for funds to be sent to the Waller Defense Fund that the WDL had set up in New York.[40] A rather different approach was taken by Jonathan Daniels, the writer and influential editor of the Raleigh *News and Observer*, in an article in *The Nation*. While not unsympathetic to Waller's plight, Daniels saw in the case "the violence of deep Southern poverty, white and black." He correctly pointed out that "Oscar Davis was a symbol too. He was no rich landlord. He was a white tenant. And the anger, the rapaciousness, the fear, the murder between white men and Negroes in the South need symbolizing as the conflict of men over the sharing of too little for all."[41] Daniel's observations were pertinent. The case of Odell Waller was important because it was far more than an isolated event. It could be regarded as the end result of the deeply rooted southern poverty that had long warped the lives of both whites and blacks and, in turn, the social, political, and legal structure of the society. These larger dimensions of the case were slowly beginning to emerge.

During these busy days Annie Waller and Pauli Murray did their best to keep Odell informed. "Just to let you know I haven't forgotten you, nor has your Mother," Murray wrote to him on December 7. "We've both been very busy speaking at two or three meetings each day in your behalf." Murray noted that she, Finerty, and Stone had now "read the Court Record very carefully. Your own testimony is straightforward and clear. The testimony of Henry Davis is utterly rediculous [*sic*]. I think your own testimony is your very best defense."[42] At the request of his mother Annie, Odell wrote a letter to Clendenin on December 14 in order to thank him and the others for all the work they were doing in his behalf.

> Words wont express how I doo appreciate what have been done on my case so far. . . . I do hope by the help of the Good lord you can save my life I feel like if I ever have another opertunity I will make good of it so you doo all you can for me please the good master may able me to help some one else[43]

At the time he wrote there were just thirteen days left before his scheduled execution.

Throughout November the RWL and the Waller Defense Committees struggled to come to terms with the entry of the WDL into the case.
The messages they sent out were not always clear. On November 9, Thomas Stamm of the RWL wrote to Clendenin that the RWL had agreed to
place his "time and services" at the disposal of the WDL for the defense
of Waller, asking only that the WDL pay Stamm's expenses.[44] Given the
previously stated position, the offer was of little interest to the WDL. On
November 23 a RWL publication, *Revolt*, complained that the WDL was
ignoring the Waller Defense Committees and that the divisions were
hurting Waller's defense.[45] A little over a week later, however, the Richmond Waller Defense Committee issued a statement welcoming the entry of the WDL, the NAACP, and other groups into the campaign to
defend Waller. "We are glad to report," said Edmund Campion, "that
after long and dangerous delay, the Workers Defense League and the
National Association for the Advancement of Colored People have come
into the fight to free Waller." But Campion insisted that cooperation
with the WDL did not mean that his organization was transferring
Waller's power of attorney, which was held by Stone for himself and the
RWDC, to anyone else, nor did "it relieve the Richmond Defense Committee of its duty and right of priority in the defense of Mr. Waller." Still,
Campion warned "against anarchy in the defense of Odell Waller" and
stated that the Richmond Committee would "continue to work for the
co-ordination of all the effort to free Mr. Waller."[46]

In fact, however, the relationship between the RWDC and the WDL
remained contentious, with the WDL doing its best to disassociate itself
from Campion's organization and others in the RWL. The WDL did, of
course, work with Stone, who continued to play a somewhat ambiguous
and increasingly controversial role in the defense efforts. Originally retained by the RWL, he remained sympathetic to the activities and positions of the RWL and its Waller Defense Committees. At the same time,
he had been, since August, a member of the WDL and had been a party
to the decision of the WDL on November 2 to come to Waller's defense.
Moreover, Stone remained the attorney of record in the case, approved
by Odell Waller, so for the time being the WDL had no option but to
work with him, and it continued to use its funds to pay for his expenses
in preparing the appeal. Stone professed to be "delighted" that Finerty

had agreed to serve as an associate counsel in the case.[47] On November 25, Frank McCallister, the Southern Secretary of the WDL, had a long talk with Stone in Richmond and came away "feeling that he knows his way around."[48] At the end of the month, Stone traveled to New York where on Sunday, December 1, he conferred with Finerty, Shapiro, Milgram, and Murray and presented them with a copy of the trial record. As Murray summarized it, they were all "convinced that Odell Waller acted through fear and not malicious premeditation." But Murray continued to have severe doubts about Stone. "You and I know," she wrote to McCallister, "that Stone can always retreat behind the set barriers of race when he wants to evade any pressing question I may ask. I'm quite worried about Stone."[49] In time Finerty would come to have similar reservations.

One point of contention at that time concerned Stone's disdain for Virginius Dabney. Murray and others in the WDL still hoped that Dabney could be persuaded to support their cause. When Murray first discussed the case with him in early November he gave them no encouragement, for he was unconvinced that Waller had shot in self-defense. Dabney was troubled by the evidence suggesting that Waller had shot Davis in the back and that Davis had been unarmed. On November 27, Murray wrote to Dabney explaining her view in these matters after talking with Stone and Annie Waller. Murray was convinced that Waller believed that Davis was reaching for something in his hip pocket. "If you could hear her story as a mother I think you would realize that her son is not a criminal but a frightened and desperate boy." Murray also pointed out that the medical testimony held that Davis had died of a collapsed lung, not the gunshot wounds, and urged him to call Stone to clear up any questions in his mind. "As I said to you when I was in your office, it will be the liberal people of Virginia who will create the sympathy necessary to give Odell Waller a chance for another trial. We want you with us on this issue."[50]

Dabney remained unconvinced. "I cannot see that the evidence in the Waller case justifies the effort you are making," he replied. "It seems to me that you have chosen an unfortunate set of circumstances on which to base a fight in the courts. I do not feel able to cooperate in your efforts."[51] It was a discouraging response. "If we are not able to win over such people as Dabney," warned McCallister, "our cause, so far as the public is concerned, is already washed up."[52] At the request of the WDL,

Finerty then wrote to Dabney, enclosing a transcript of the trial testimony of Henry Davis and Odell Waller. Finerty argued that Henry Davis's "testimony was obviously coached by the State to the point of absurdity," and that not even he claimed that Waller first fired when Oscar Davis's back was to him. To Finerty the fair inference was that the shock of the first two shots, which hit Davis in the head and arm, caused him to turn "so that the last two shots hit him in the back." He also suggested that it was not entirely clear that Oscar Davis was not armed. "Waller's testimony impresses me as frank and truthful," but that of "Henry Davis is wholly incredible." Finerty stated, however, that his connection to the case would "be confined to the Constitutional question arising from the apparent barring of non-payers of poll tax from both grand and petit juries."[53]

Finerty was no more successful with Dabney than Murray had been. "It seems to me to be a poor case on which to base a fight on the poll tax requirement for jury service," Dabney replied. "I fully agree that it is unjust to make the poll tax a prerequisite for jury service and the franchise, but there is no doubt in my mind that Waller is guilty of manslaughter or something worse, probably the latter." So Dabney concluded that the case did not deserve the publicity it was getting.[54] But his disapproval of the poll tax at least gave a hint that Dabney's mind was not closed. As Murray wrote, after reading an article Dabney had just published on "Civil Liberties in the South" as well as his correspondence with Finerty, "It grieves me deeply that while you agree with us in principle on all the issues we raise in this case, you still regard it as merely a murder case."[55]

On December 21, 1940, Dabney published his first editorial relating to the Waller case. In a piece entitled "Poll Taxes and Juries" he argued that "if Virginia juries are being chosen exclusively from lists of persons eligible to vote, and hence from persons who must have paid their poll taxes, we have one more argument against that unjustifiable levy." He suggested, however, that the Waller case was not the best one to make such a fight, and he repeated the charge that Waller had "shot Davis in the back as he was walking away." Dabney also said that he had not seen any evidence that the poll tax was in fact a prerequisite for service on the jury which tried Waller, although he acknowledged that the same results could have been obtained by picking the jury from a list of qualified voters. There should have been sharecroppers on the jury, he stated, although he would "feel better about it, if the issue was being drawn in the interests of a defendant who seemed less guilty than Odell Waller, and if the Workers' Defense League's inflammatory literature gave more evidence of a desire to state the issues fairly."[56]

Three days later, Dabney published a second editorial on the Waller case, which, he noted, was "being made a focal point for efforts of out-of-state organizations to attack the poll tax and sharecropping systems prevailing in Virginia and other Southern States." According to Dabney, there was "no law making payment of poll taxes a prerequisite for service on a petit jury in Virginia," but he acknowledged that such payment was apparently required for service on a grand jury, as the law required that such a juror be a citizen who was "entitled to vote and hold office." Dabney reported that officials from Pittsylvania County had stated that the list from which petit jurors were drawn was "not compiled exclusively from the list of voters, but also from persons known to the commissioners whose names do not appear thereon." A similar system was used in Richmond. In Henrico County, however, petit jurors were selected from the voting list. Such practices, he insisted, should be discontinued. He ended his editorial by criticizing the pro-Waller literature for failing to point out that Oscar Davis had been shot twice in the back and that he had been unarmed.[57] In short, Dabney's discomfiture over the manner of selecting some juries in Virginia did not mean that he had yet changed his mind about the case of Odell Waller.

Murray did not give up. Visiting Richmond on December 24 she again discussed the case with Dabney and, despite his editorials, she found some reason for optimism. Dabney was concerned about what he considered to be the "inflammatory" nature of the early WDL literature on the case. She explained that the WDL had accepted the facts as given to them by Stone but that since then they had had their own investigator in the field and had become more self-critical. Murray noted that Dabney had been much impressed by Jonathan Daniel's article in *The Nation* and that "he admitted to me that he had changed his estimate of the Waller case." Murray understood Dabney to believe at that time that "the death penalty was probably too severe, and that he was willing to see to it that Waller had another trial."[58]

In Stone's opinion all such efforts to influence Dabney were worse than a waste of time. It was a mistake, he argued in a statement addressed to the WDL's National Administrative Committee, "to base the public defense of Mr. Waller upon pseudo-liberals, such as Virginius Dabney and others of like sort." He also criticized Murray for not cooperating "in the formation of a Workers Defense League branch in the city of Richmond," which he considered essential if the public defense of Waller was to be correctly handled, instead of leaving it, as Stone suggested Murray wished to do, "in the hands of an avowed and dangerous enemy like Dabney."[59] Stone's vehemence in regard to Dabney, along with his sympathies for the tactics of the RWL and the Waller Defense Committees, thus continued to complicate the efforts of the WDL.

When Murray told Dabney that the WDL had sent its own investigator to check on facts in the case, her reference was to Murray Kempton, a young free-lance writer who had written a piece on Annie Waller at the time of her visit to New York. During the first week of December, the WDL sent Kempton to Pittsylvania County to gather data for an article on the Waller case. Kempton's initial report back to Pauli Murray was highly critical of Stone for failing to tell the WDL "that Davis was shot 4 times, twice in the back," that there was testimony that Waller had "twice sworn to get Davis," and that Waller had a pistol and shotgun with him when he went to Davis's house. While in Richmond, Kempton had talked to Dabney, who proved to be "a stone wall" and to Byron Hopkins, who "was considerably impressed by the fairness of the court and distressed at Stone's tactics." In Kempton's opinion, Hopkins and his partner seemed "like typical Booker T. Negroes," but "they sound sincere in their conviction that Odell's act was premeditated." Thus Kempton's initial reactions were not encouraging. "Frankly I can't see the case in either black or white, so far as the actual facts of the killing are concerned."[60]

A few days later, Kempton sent Murray a much longer handwritten report that explored the physical setting and the economic and social conditions in Pittsylvania County as well as the background to the dispute between the Waller and Oscar Davis. In this account the tone was much more sympathetic to Waller. He noted that white people in the area spoke well of the Waller family, including Odell, and that they "never heard anything against him before" the shooting. There was disagreement about Oscar Davis, mainly between the opinions of whites and blacks. "The Negroes who knew him and worked his crop speak of Oscar Davis with something very close to hatred." In summarizing the dispute between Oscar Davis and the Wallers, Kempton left little doubt that the Wallers had been treated badly.[61] Kempton followed up this account with a two-page typed report, dated December 9, 1940, that sum-marized the major points in his longer story. "Up to the killing," he concluded, "everything is on Waller's side." But he had doubts about the rest. Although Kempton noted that "in general the town [Chatham] is torpidly anti-Negro," he did not find that the atmosphere had been such as to preclude Waller's chances for a fair trial. According to Martin A. Martin, a thirty-year-old black attorney and president of the Danville branch of the NAACP, "whatever prejudice existed was against Stone." The biggest problem for Kempton was Henry Davis's testimony. Unless it could be broken, he wrote, "I think we're sunk and I'm pretty con-vinced of Odell's guilt myself."[62]

Although this was certainly not what Murray had hoped to hear, she was not dismayed. Unlike Kempton, she had been influenced by an ex-change of letters with Waller, and she continued to believe that he had shot out of fear for his life, not malice. Her close contacts with Annie Waller only reinforced this conclusion. At the same time Kempton's re-ports could not help but reinforce her negative opinions of Stone. De-spite some obvious differences in their views of Waller's culpability, Kempton and Murray pooled their efforts and produced an effective sixteen-page pamphlet, "All For Mr. Davis": The Story of Sharecropper Odell Waller, which was published by the WDL in 1941. This included a short preface written by Frank P. Graham, president of the University of North Carolina, in which he argued that it was a desperate time for freedom and democracy in the world and that Americans had to be sensitive to conditions that tested freedom at home. "This packed pamphlet, with its information, analysis, and democratic sympathy, is in the front line struggle for democracy in America."[63] This was a theme that would come to play an ever larger role as the case dragged on.

By mid December 1940 it was apparent that the defense of Odell Waller had become considerably more complicated than most members of the WDL could have imagined when they agreed to take on the case. Nevertheless, by that time they had achieved their first object—a post-ponement of Waller's execution, which had been scheduled for Decem-ber 27. In preparing his appeal Stone had filed a bill of exceptions with Judge Clement, along with a request for a transcript of the trial record, on November 23. A week later Stone formally requested Governor Price to grant Waller a reprieve until March in order to allow him time to appeal for a writ of error to the Supreme Court of Appeals of Virginia.[64]

Price responded on December 20 by granting Waller a reprieve until March 14, 1941.[65] It was the first of ultimately five reprieves that Waller would receive, and the first tangible results of the defense efforts. Pauli Murray immediately wrote to Governor Price on behalf of the WDL and its supporters to express their "deep gratitude for your kindness in giving this young man additional time in which to have his case reviewed by the higher courts."[66]

Shortly afterwards the WDL put out a flier with the title "Thank You, America!" in which it described how the efforts of the WDL, through its attorneys, John F. Finerty and Thomas H. Stone, with the cooperation of a number of organizations (the NAACP, the Southern Tenant Farmers' Union, and "other local labor and church organizations") had succeeded in obtaining the stay of execution. The Richmond Waller Defense Committee was not mentioned. At the top of the flier the WDL reprinted the touching short note written by Odell Waller on December 14 to David L. Clendenin in which he expressed his thanks for the efforts on his behalf.[67]

On December 20 the Richmond Waller Defense Committee issued its own press release, signed by Edmund Campion, announcing the reprieve. It stated that "its work and that of its supporting groups throughout the country—including the legal defense supplied by the Workers Defense League and the National Association for the Advancement of Colored People—has at last won the first battle in the fight to vindicate and free Odell Waller."[68] The statement implied that the reprieve was a product of the cooperative efforts of the RWDC and the WDL. The reality, however, was considerably different. From the start the WDL had attempted to distance itself from the RWL and the Waller Defense Committees, although its efforts were complicated by the ambiguous role played by Stone. During the next few months the differences between the WDL and the radicals widened into what at times was a bitter controversy.

4

Defending Waller:
Controversy and Commitment

With the reprieve until March 14, 1941, the immediate pressure on Waller and his defenders was somewhat lessened. But the relief was only temporary. "Odell's life is not saved by any means," Pauli Murray explained to Annie Waller. "One false step and this case is lost."[1] Much work remained to be done. This included the collection of data, particularly on the poll tax and the selection of jurors in Pittsylvania County, and the preparation of briefs to be presented to the Supreme Court of Appeals.

During this period the efforts of the WDL continued to be complicated by the tensions between it and the radicals, particularly the Richmond Waller Defense Committee. No one felt these strains more keenly than Murray. Since mid November she had been deeply affected by her exchange of letters with Odell Waller and her contacts with Annie Waller. These certainly reinforced her belief that Odell was a victim who had shot Oscar Davis out of fear for his own life, and they kept reminding her of the human dimensions of the Waller story. "It is lomsam and blue here now I am the only condemned man here now one boy got his sentence comuned to life," Waller wrote to Murray on December 5.[2] Murray did what she could to keep his spirits up by sending him letters and reading materials. She also asked him to write down his own story of the shooting, "just as everything happened."[3]

Another family contact for Murray was with Odell's natural mother, Mrs. Dollie Harris, of Logan, West Virginia. In November she wrote to Mrs. Harris to explain what the WDL was attempting to do for her son. Subsequently Murray also asked her to try to get some contributions for his defense from friends, her church, or other organizations to which she might belong. Although Mrs. Harris tried, she had no luck raising money.[4] In mid December, Murray learned that the RWDC was trying to get Mrs. Harris to go to Cleveland and Chicago to speak at meetings the Waller Defense Committees were arranging. Murray was strongly opposed to the idea. "It is very important that the Waller family take no action until they confer with the Workers Defense League," she wrote to Annie Waller. "Outside organizations not connected with the Workers Defense League may hurt this cause more than help it. . . . If other organizations enter the field and confuse things by suggesting tours for Mrs. Harris, the public will become confused and will ignore the whole case."[5]

Mrs. Harris did not accept the RWDC's invitation. Nevertheless, the situation prompted Murray to write a long, agonizing letter to Waller, on December 28, which she sent by special delivery, explaining the differences between the RWL and the WDL and warning him of the dangers of the RWL. The latter, she noted, "is not a defense agency; it is a political group, very small and with but a few members in the country. It has as its philosophy a belief in communism, but it is not part of the official Communist Party in this country." Their motives are very different from those of the WDL. "It has been our experience that such a group is more interested in making publicity out of the case than it is in saving the life of the person involved." Thus, Murray explained to Waller, two organizations claim to be defending you. "You must make the choice as whether you want to be represented by the Workers Defense League and its cooperating groups, or whether you want to be represented by the Richmond Waller Defense Committee or any other organization which may seek to aid you. I CANNOT MAKE THAT CHOICE FOR YOU OR INFLUENCE YOUR DECISION." She concluded by asking Waller to write to her immediately about his decision and, if he wanted to be represented by the WDL, to write also to Finerty.[6]

For Murray, as for Waller, this was a crucial moment. She obviously wanted the WDL to continue to work for Waller, but she believed deeply that he had to sever contacts with the RWL. "I hope that my judgment is correct in writing this letter" to Waller, she explained to Clendenin and Milgram later the same day. "Since I have tried every means to see Odell without success, there was only one recourse—to shoot the works." If this doesn't work, she continued, "I'm ready to recommend that the Workers Defense League withdraw from the case and make a public statement as to its reasons."[7] Murray also wrote to Finerty, enclosing a copy of her letter to Waller. She saw three difficulties that they had to face:

1) How to get prompt action from Attorney Stone in cooperating with you on the legal aspects of the case. . . . 2) How to deal with the complicated nature of the shooting in our relations with the press and other interested organizations, so as to keep our own integrity and at the same time to build sympathetic opinion for Odell's cause; 3) How to steer clear of the Revolutionary Workers League and other political front organizations.

She recommended that the WDL be prepared to withdraw from the case if Waller did not grant Finerty "complete power of attorney." She also recommended, among other things, that if they discovered that Stone deliberately failed to cooperate and continued to have relations with the RWDC without telling the WDL, then Finerty should consider whether it would be advantageous to have Stone continue as an associate counsel in the case.[8]

As Murray explained in her letter to Clendenin and Milgram, she had not been allowed to visit Waller. Nevertheless, she found that "Captain Brent of the Virginia State Penitentiary is an enlightened prison official." Furthermore, she believed that "we've made a good impression on the prison officials, and that helps in a crisis."[9] Two days later, on December 30, Brent relaxed the rules and allowed Murray, who was accompanied by Annie Waller, to have a long talk with Waller in his death cell. She was deeply impressed. Waller freely admitted his responsibility in the shooting, but he steadfastly denied that he intended to kill Davis. "I'm as sorry as I can be it all happened," he told Murray. "I wasn't trying to kill Mr. Davis. I was aiming to keep him from killing me." Murray came away "more convinced than ever that he was not guilty of premeditated murder. . . . Manslaughter, yes, but not intentional murder." Murray never saw Waller again, but, as she wrote many years later, "the image of that ominous door at the end of the narrow corridor was never erased from my memory. No argument in favor of capital punishment has overcome the shattering impact of that single visit to the death house."[10]

Murray also convinced Waller that her position on the role of the WDL was correct, and she came way with a letter that he wrote to Finerty along the lines she had asked. In it he said that

I want you to take my case in your hands and doo what you can I want you to Represent me as my Attorney in all matters Regarding my case. I will except what ever decisions you make until Further notice. I un-

derstand you Represent the Workers Defense League, the sole Orgina-
tion I give power to handle my case If you have the time you will come
and talk with me about the case[11]

After leaving the prison, Murray and Annie Waller conferred at some
length with Stone. Murray told him that they believed that the RWDC
would do more harm than good and that they did not wish to associate
with it in any way. She did not tell Stone about Waller's letter to Finerty,
feeling that it would be best if Finerty and Stone worked out the problem by themselves, although she wrote to Waller that "if possible, we do
want to keep Mr. Stone in on the case."[12] Stone responded with a statement on December 30 that he sent to the National Administrative Committee of the WDL. In it he reiterated his opinion that the WDL "has the
right of consultation" in the case as well as the right "to differentiate
itself in any manner that it sees fit from any other organization supporting a new trial for Mr. Waller." He promised to "extend assistance to any
organization whatever that seeks the release or acquittal or a new trial

The return address Odell Waller wrote on his letters to Annie Waller and Pauli
Murray was 500 Spring Street, the main entrance to the Virginia State Penitentiary in Richmond. Photograph by Richard B. Sherman.

for Mr. Waller." Stone took the position that his differences with Murray were due to her efforts seek the support of "pseudo-liberals such as Mr. Virginius Dabney." Unlike Murray, he welcomed the assistance of any group. "The defense of Mr. Waller cannot be the monopoly of any organization" although "the actual steps in the presentation to the Court or Courts of Mr. Waller's appeal should only be under the supervision and control of the Workers Defense League." Stone ended by again urging the "immediate formation of a local branch of the WDL in Richmond."[13]

Stone followed this up on December 31 with a proposal sent in separate statements to both the Waller Defense Committee in Richmond and the WDL. In these he suggested that each organization (the WDL and the RWDC) "select a representative or representatives to some sort of a contact committee" which would coordinate their efforts.[14] Stone also wrote to Waller and discussed the "difference of opinion" between him and Murray "concerning certain phases of the case." Stone enclosed a proposed letter from Waller to Stone, which he asked Waller to rewrite in his own handwriting. This stated that he favored having any organization help him that wanted to and that "its looks to me like your idea of having all these organizations work together is best." Instead of rewriting the letter drafted by Stone, however, Waller sent it to Murray. At the bottom he commented that "Mr John F Finetery I believe would be the best lawyers Mr Stone & Hopin let me down in the begining seem like Mr Stone is getting things baled up this is searus time not for foolishness."[15] Caught in the middle of the dispute, Waller decided to place his faith in Pauli Murray and the WDL.

Consistent with its previously stated position, the WDL did not look sympathetically upon Stone's suggestion that it coordinate its public activities with the RWDC through a contact committee, and it simply left unanswered letters proposing the same sent to it by the RWDC on January 6 and January 31, 1941.[16] Thus the WDL continued to do its best to keep its distance from the RWDC and others associated with the RWL. But it was not easily done, for the RWDC attempted to create the impression that it was in charge of the defense efforts by using a letterhead that listed, under "Legal Staff," Thomas A. Stone as senior counsel, and John Finerty of New York, Byran [*sic*] Hopkins of Richmond, Martin A. Martin of Danville, and Richard Tomkins of Washington, D.C., as associate counsel. After seeing one of these letterheads, Murray wrote to Hopkins to express her surprise, since he had not indicated any interest in continuing the case. He replied that he had not authorized the RWDC to use his name and complained that Stone owed him $35.16 for expenses in the case. Hopkins played no further role in Waller's defense.[17]

In addition to the listings on the RWDC letterhead, an article in the January 1, 1941, edition of the RWL's newspaper *The Fighting Worker* also implied that Finerty had been added to the RWDC staff.[18] After Finerty discovered what was happening, he repeatedly requested the RWDC to remove his name from their documents.[19] It was to no avail. Despite his protests, his name still appeared on a letter he received from the RWDC on January 31. Thoroughly disgusted, Finerty made no more attempts to communicate with that organization. Instead he decided to publicize the dispute in a letter to the editor that was published in the *Richmond Times-Dispatch* on February 28. In it he explained that "there was no other course open to me than publicly to repudiate any connection with that committee." He asserted that he had entered the case "wholly at the request of the Workers Defense League. . . . I never had, nor will I have, the slightest association with a committee so irresponsible as the Richmond Waller Defense Committee."[20] Writing to Dabney a few days later, Finerty expressed the hope that his letter would "serve to put a quietus on the Waller Defense Committee, or at least on their irresponsible activities and communications."[21]

It was appropriate that Finerty would decide to go public in his dispute with the RWDC through the pages of the *Richmond Times-Dispatch*, for during this same period the WDL renewed its efforts to win the support of that newspaper's influential editor. On January 13, 1941, the *Times-Dispatch* published a long letter by Clendenin. In it he attempted to clarify the WDL's position on the Waller case and to deal with some of the issues Dabney had raised in his December editorials. First, Clendenin pointed out that the WDL did not contend that Negroes as such had been excluded from Waller's jury. Rather, he argued, it was a situation in which the poll tax denied sharecroppers and "Negroes on low incomes the right to serve on juries. . . . With the exception of our first leaflet on the case, which was based on alleged facts given us by the local Richmond attorney for Odell Waller, our whole emphasis on this case has ben an economic one, complicated by the racial patterns of the South." And, he added, if Waller had been white and Davis black, "the verdict certainly would not have been first degree murder involving the death sentence." Second, Clendenin objected to the labeling of the WDL and the NAACP as out-of-state organizations, and he pointed out that the WDL sought the cooperation of local groups. He described the WDL as "a national non-Communistic, nonpartisan, labor organization," which, among its other activities, served as the official agency of the Southern Tenant Farmers' Union. But, he noted, because the WDL recognized that it created problems to have a New York–based organization lead activities in the South, in November 1940 it had established a Southern Workers Defense League, which was led by Frank McCallister of St. Petersburg, Florida, the southern secretary of the WDL.[22]

By this time Dabney had begun to modify his opinion on the Waller case. Although he still insisted that the WDL "got off on the wrong foot when it made such incorrect statements in the Waller case in its early stages," he now told Clendenin that "I hope Waller gets a new trial, even though I am not by any means as convinced as you are that he shot in 'self-defense.'"[23] Two weeks later Dabney wrote a letter to *The Nation* in which he further clarified his position. In response to the comment by Jonathan Daniels (in his December 21 article) that Dabney regarded the Waller case "as merely a murder," Dabney now declared that "I changed my opinion of the case's significance about a week after I discussed it briefly with him [Daniels] over long-distance telephone, and when I was better informed as to the circumstances." He concluded that "I am not prepared to say definitely that injustice was done, but I confess that I am not sure either way." At the same time, Dabney continued to criticize the literature being put out on the case for failing "to inform the public that Waller shot Davis twice in the back, when Davis, according to uncontradicted witnesses, was unarmed."[24]

In response Finerty tried once again to convince Dabney, and others, that there was an alternative explanation of the shooting. "The only testimony that Waller first fired at Oscar Davis when Davis' back was turned," he argued, "is the testimony of the only eye witness, an eighteen year old colored boy, Henry Davis, then employed by Oscar Davis and still employed by his family, who prior to the trial, refused to talk to the defense at all. His entire testimony is incredible and gives every appearance of being coached." Similarly, Finerty held that the testimony that Davis was unarmed was "open to the utmost suspicion," coming from the same Henry Davis and from Oscar Davis's wife and two sons. In any event, the issue was "whether Waller had reasonable grounds for believing him to be armed." Finerty concluded that he did. Finerty also commented on the poll tax issue. Although Pittsylvania County officials might state that payment of the poll tax was not used as a qualification for being selected to the petit jury list, in fact "an investigation shows that every member of that jury had paid his poll tax." Had the racial situation been reversed, "the same poll tax jury which sentenced Waller . . . would, on the same evidence, have either found a white land owner not guilty on the grounds he shot in self-defense, or would, at most, have found him guilty of manslaughter."[25]

A few days later Dabney tried once again to explain his evolving thinking about the Waller case. In an editorial published on February 16, 1941, he noted the conflicting interpretations by Pittsylvania County authorities and Finerty over how the petit jury had actually been selected. He now acknowledged that "the question arises whether the commissioners did not consciously, or unconsciously, lean toward the choice of the relatively well-to-do in this case involving economic and social conflict." But Dabney remained unconvinced by Finerty's interpretation of how Oscar Davis came to be shot in the back. He also insisted that "nobody has produced any evidence that Davis was armed." Dabney recognized that many people believed that a new trial was necessary in order to vindicate Virginia justice. The fact that Waller "was represented by something called the American Revolutionary Workers Defense League of Chicago . . . was almost enough to ruin his chances of getting an objective hearing. This group of ultraradical professional agitators is no longer handling the Waller defense, and the current approach is much more conservative. Another trial would be conducted in a different atmosphere."[26] Although Dabney did not explicitly call for a new trial at this time, he was moving closer to that position.

There was little in Dabney's latest editorial to please Waller's initial defenders, however. If Dabney really wanted to be fair, wrote Stone's wife, why didn't he call the attorneys who defended Waller as well as the commonwealth's attorney in Pittsylvania County?[27] Thomas H. Stone shot back with a long, emotional letter attacking Dabney's "untruths, half-truths, and damaging insinuations." He disagreed with Finerty, Murray, and others who believed in Dabney's liberalism. "I consider you a pseudo-liberal whose sole aim is to get a new trial for Odell Waller so that he may be electrocuted 'properly.'" Stone also complained that Dabney ignored his and Hopkins's continuing role in the case, as if to imply that Waller had been abandoned by those who had represented him at his trial. Like Finerty, Stone insisted that it was reasonable for Waller to believe that Oscar Davis had been armed. Stone was even more bitter over what he called Dabney's "campaign to burn Odell Waller" which, he said, was "based upon alleged shots in the back." But, insisted Stone, "There has been absolutely no testimony as to Oscar Davis being shot in the back." Stone also asserted that no such organization as that named by Dabney in his editorial represented Waller at his trial, but he did not go on to clarify the matter by stating the correct name of the group that had hired him. Finally he accused Dabney of only belatedly taking up interest in the case when it served "the political interests of yourself and your group," as in an attack on the poll tax, but not because he was "concerned with the guilt or innocence of a human being."[28]

Stone was not the only interested party angered by Dabney's editorial. Commonwealth's Attorney Joseph Whitehead, Jr., also took him to task on the question of the poll tax and the jury. Again Whitehead insisted that the jury commissioners did not consider whether prospective jurors had or had not paid their poll tax when they drew up the jury list and that there was no law in Virginia making poll tax payment a prerequisite to jury service. Whitehead concluded that Waller "had a fair trial at the hands of a jury, free from excitement or feeling and should pay the penalty of his crime."[29]

Dabney was understandably annoyed by Stone's vituperative letter. In another editorial he pointed out that the *Times-Dispatch* had "vigorously defended" Stone in 1932 and 1933, despite his being "a radical agitator with Richmond Communists," because it had felt that his constitutional rights were being denied. The earlier editorial did not mention Stone by name, said Dabney, because it was discussing Finerty's position. As for whether Davis had been shot in the back, Dabney held that Finerty himself had acknowledged that medical testimony showed that Davis had two wounds in the back. Dabney did admit to a "slight error" in his statement of the name of the organization that retained Stone, but otherwise he asserted he had no interest "in bandying words" with Stone over his other accusations.[30]

About a week later the *Times-Dispatch* published a letter by C. B. Cowan, then chairman of the RWDC, and Pauline Subienne, the secretary-treasurer, which called "attention to certain false, inaccurate and misleading statements" that appeared in Dabney's February 16 editorial. Most of their letter was concerned with clarifying the name and position of the RWL and the role of the RWDC in the Waller case. They insisted that, if there were to be a new trial, "there will be no leaning to conservatism or compromise." That was guaranteed by having Stone as senior counsel on the case. Finerty, they stated, "is one of the associate counsel for Waller and holds such a position by virtue of requests and agreement of Thomas H. Stone."[31]

Before publishing the letter by Cowan and Subienne, Dabney showed it to Finerty. As a result Finerty wrote the letter, which was published in the same edition of the *Times-Dispatch*, that brought out in the open his dispute with the RWDC. Finerty was particularly upset by Stone's letter to Dabney, as were others in the WDL, who feared it would hurt Waller's case. As Murray saw it, there was little they could do to "control the actions of Stone as an attorney for Waller" when he disagreed with WDL policy. For the time being, they needed him. The power-of-attorney Waller had granted to Finerty was "inadequate" because Waller had to be represented by a member of the Virginia bar, and Finerty was not one. Still, Murray hoped that there would be the possibility of "separating Stone from the case." She concluded that he was "too evasive to be depended upon" and that his "reputation in Richmond" was a definite "liability in efforts to establish proper public and press relations on the case."[32] Stone had certainly not changed his attitude toward the RWDC. Writing to C. B. Cowan on March 4, 1941, he stated that he was "entirely of a different opinion from Mr. Finerty in regard to the Waller Defense Committee. . . . I am for the highest possible degree of unity."[33]

Despite their disagreements, Stone and Finerty cooperated in preparing Waller's appeal. Stone, assisted by Howard H. Davis of Richmond, drew up the petition for a writ of error, which he discussed with Finerty, and filed on January 23, 1941.[34] Meanwhile, Finerty began to work on the constitutional questions concerning jury selection. To assist him in this the WDL engaged the services of Martin A. Martin of Danville, who began checking the jury lists to ascertain who were landowners, who were tenants, and who, if any, were sharecroppers. He was also to see if all twelve of Waller's jurors had paid their poll taxes and to check into the testimony of Henry Davis.[35] On the afternoon of February 24, Stone presented his oral argument on the petition for a writ of error before the Supreme Court of Appeals of Virginia. Waller's reprieve was due to expire on March 14, only two and a half weeks later. Having received no word of the court's decision by March 4, Stone wrote to Governor Price requesting that he extend the reprieve for three more months. Even if the Virginia court refused to grant the writ, he argued, there were features in the case "that would inevitably lead to a petition for a writ of habeas corpus to the Federal Courts."[36] On that same day, however, the court granted a writ of error and supersedeas.[37] Thus Waller's execution was put off once again until the court had time to hear and consider the arguments on the appeal and to come to a decision.

The constitutional ramifications of the relationship of the poll tax to the selection of jurors were important features of the defense's legal strategy. Similarly, the WDL's publicity in the Waller case continually played upon the injustices in Virginia's continued imposition of the poll tax. "Waller was convicted by a jury of poll-tax payers," proclaimed a statement issued on February 4, 1941, but in Pittsylvania County "out of a population of 61,000 (of which 36,000 were whites and 25,000 Negroes), only 6,000 white citizens and 200 Negro citizens are qualified to vote—less than 10 per cent. Is it any wonder that Odell Waller was not tried by a jury of his peers . . . ?"[38]

Insofar as the Waller case involved the poll tax, it came at a particularly propitious moment, for it coincided with a strong movement within Virginia and the nation to abolish the tax. Virginia was then one of only eight states that still required the payment of a poll tax as a qualification for voting. Three other former poll tax states, North Carolina, Louisiana, and Florida, had repealed their taxes between 1920 and 1937. The most important organization then fighting the poll tax was the Southern Conference for Human Welfare, which had persuaded Congressman Lee E. Geyer, a Democrat from California, to introduce a bill abolishing the poll tax in federal elections in September 1939. Nothing came of this first attempt, but support grew in 1940, and on January 3, 1941, Geyer reintroduced the bill. On March 31, 1941, Senator Claude Pepper of Florida introduced a similar measure in the Senate.[39] Data produced by poll tax opponents showed conclusively that a far smaller proportion of the population participated in the electoral process in the poll tax states than in others. As the WDL observed, it was "a definite obstruction to the functioning of democracy."[40] In Virginia only 20 percent of the potential voters cast ballots in the 1940 election. In the eight poll tax states a mere 7.21 percent of the total population (11.82 percent in Virginia) voted in the congressional elections, compared to 41.79 percent in thirty-nine non–poll tax states.[41] A large proportion of blacks clearly found it difficult to pay their poll tax. According to data collected by the Virginia Voters League, for example, of voting age blacks in 1942 the average percentage of those paying in Virginia cities was only 7.1 and in Virginia counties 8.3. The figure for Pittsylvania County was a mere 2.3 percent.[42]

On February 1, 1941, a group of poll tax opponents met in Richmond for the purpose of creating a Southern Electoral Reform League. Speakers included Eleanor Roosevelt and LeRoy Hodges, the Virginia state comptroller. Frank McCallister of the WDL served as secretary at that meeting and was later elected a member of the governing body of the new league. At a subsequent meeting in Washington, D.C., permanent officers were elected and an agenda was set. David George of Hanover County, Virginia, was named the director of the league, with headquarters in Richmond.[43] George was the former organizer of the Socialist party in Virginia and, in McCallister's words, he was "very close to us." McCallister urged the WDL to give the Southern Electoral Reform League all the help that it could, but he advised Clendenin that there was "no place they can fit in the Waller case," largely due to the lack of interest among its members in it.[44]

Opposition to the poll tax was one definite point of agreement between the WDL and Virginius Dabney. Every newspaper in the state, he claimed, backed its repeal, but he warned that, unless Virginia and the other poll tax states acted on their own, they might find that Congress would outlaw the tax or that the Supreme Court would hold it unconstitutional. Clearly he favored state action over these other possibilities.[45] Unlike the WDL and Dabney, the RWL, in an article in *The Fighting Worker*, bitterly denounced the anti–poll tax efforts. In its view, the Southern Electoral Reform League, Dabney, McCallister, the WDL, and others were really engaged in a disguised attempt to perpetrate Jim Crow under the banner of eliminating the poll tax, for which they would substitute stricter literacy tests designed to keep blacks from voting. The RWL claimed that a sellout of Waller was a necessary step to achieve that goal.[46] It was little wonder that the WDL saw no point in attempting to cooperate with doctrinaire radicals who were capable of such strident and emotional rhetoric.

For a while it appeared that the poll tax opponents in Virginia might be successful. On March 26, 1941, the Virginia Advisory Legislative Council, acting on Governor Price's suggestion, appointed a "Subcommittee for a Study of Constitutional Provisions Concerning Voting in Virginia," which was headed by Professor Robert K. Gooch of the University of Virginia. The subcommittee held hearings in Richmond and Roanoke in July and August and collected much data. It reported on November 7, 1941, with the recommendation that the poll tax be eliminated as a prerequisite for voting. But the full council voted to take no action on the subcommittee report, and the movement for repeal in Virginia ground to a halt. Similarly, efforts in Congress to pass anti–poll tax legislation were thwarted a year later in November 1942 as the result of filibustering by southern senators. Ultimately it would take many more years before the battle against the poll tax was won.[47]

The WDL's interest in the anti–poll tax movement was but part of a busy agenda in 1941. Much of the WDL's attention was focused on its publicity and fund-raising campaign for the defense of Odell Waller. The success of Annie Waller's visit to New York in late November and early December 1940 prompted the league to plan a much more extended tour throughout the Midwest. Eager to do whatever she could to help her son, Mrs. Waller agreed. Traveling alone, she left Washington on January 5 and proceeded to Chicago, where she was joined by Murray, who had come in separately from New York. For Murray the tour came "as a refreshing and reassuring experience." Riding the streamlined Zephyr train from Chicago to St. Paul and Minneapolis, the two black women were treated with "all the courtesy which any American citizen expects as a matter of course." The contrast with the "Southern Railroad, with its stuffy, dirty Jim Crow cars" deeply impressed Murray. "I felt like a free human being for the first time in my life."[48] Speaking under the auspices of local branches of the NAACP and the WDL, with the assistance of local churches, the YWCA, student groups, and others, Mrs. Waller and Murray made some twenty-two appearances between January 7 and January 27 in Minneapolis, Chicago, and Detroit before a total of 6,985 people. Everywhere they found a keen interest in the plight of Odell Waller and sharecroppers generally from audiences that included students at the University of Minnesota, teachers, trade unionists, social workers, and others. Despite Murray's original misgivings that the tour might not be a financial success, they raised some $458.00 (not including promises of future payments) while spending $172.64. Murray reported that the "publicity, reception and personal contacts on tour were *excellent!*"[49]

At the conclusion of this midwestern tour, Mrs. Waller and Murray

traveled to Boston before returning to New York, where Mrs. Waller remained until February 19. In New York the WDL put a special emphasis
on enlisting the support of black churches and organizations. This phase
of their efforts concluded with a mass meeting on the evening of February 18 held at the Abyssinian Baptist Church in Harlem. Murray again
introduced Mrs. Waller. Other speakers included the Reverend Adam
Clayton Powell, pastor of the church, and representatives of the Brotherhood of Sleeping Car Porters, the Urban League, the NAACP, the Fellowship of Reconciliation, and others, as well as Clendenin for the WDL.
A WDL flier advertising the meeting stressed that, although lawyers were
donating their services, "FUNDS ARE NEEDED DESPERATELY AND
IMMEDIATELY for other necessary legal expenses if the appeal is to be
fought and a life saved." It also explained that the WDL took up the fight
"because it believes the Waller case and the verdict are the outgrowth of
unbearable conditions facing white and Negro sharecroppers and migrant workers everywhere, but especially in the South. The WDL wants
to focus public attention on the tragic lives of the disinherited and dispossessed citizens of the greatest, the richest democracy on earth: Our
America."[50]

Mrs. Waller returned to Gretna on February 19 for a much-needed
rest. Her return to Virginia also gave her a chance to stop in Richmond
and see Odell, whom she found to be well. Murray was kept busy completing a pamphlet on the case which the WDL was anxious to have for
distribution to interested parties.[51] In addition to her correspondence
with Annie and Odell, Murray also exchanged letters with Dollie Harris,
who continued to follow the case as closely as she could. "I am very proud
to know that my son Odell Waller has had success in getting or having a
new trial in the Supreme Court of Virginia through the wonderful work
of your-self and the W.D.L. and sister Annie," she wrote to Murray.[52]

At the end of March, Murray was upset by a report from the Chicago
branch of the WDL that Odell's wife Mollie was going to Chicago to
appear at some gatherings sponsored by the RWDC. Murray immediately wrote to Annie Waller asking her to try to find Mollie and talk her
out of such a trip. "If Mollie goes to Chicago, it will ruin our tour and
make people think that Odell's case is just a racket."[53] She also telephoned Stone, who said that he was not going to Chicago, but he acknowledged that the RWDC was planning to have Mollie speak there
from April 5 to April 9. Murray asked Waller to write to Mollie and ex-

plain that his case would be hurt if she were to go on such a tour and to write to Clendenin to express appreciation for what the WDL had done for him.[54] The issue with Mollie and the RWDC was soon resolved. In a letter dated April 4, Waller informed Clendenin that Mollie had written to him that she was planning to go to work in Washington on March 30. Subsequently the Chicago office of the WDL reported that Mollie had not been in Chicago. The incident had simply reinforced Murray's deep mistrust of the RWDC.[55]

As Murray had requested, Waller wrote to Clendenin to express appreciation for what the WDL had done for him. In his letter he stated that the WDL was the only organization that he had authorized to handle his case and to distribute funds raised in his defense.[56] The latter comment was prompted by Murray's concern that the RWDC, and others associated with it, would solicit funds that would never be used in the defense of Waller and thus alienate potential contributors.[57] At that time the WDL needed all the contributions it could get, for the Waller case had become the most important, and by far the most financially draining, of that organization's projects. Between January 1 and April 30, 1941, the WDL spent $3,137.69 on the case. No other expenditure came close to that amount, with the next highest, that for the Southern Tenant Farmers' Union, being $431.53 for the same period. From the beginning of the Waller project in November 1940 through April 30, 1941, the WDL had taken in a total of $4,751.17, but its total expenditures and obligations incurred stood at $5,381.23.[58] As Clendenin observed in a report on May 9, although the WDL had made the Waller case known nationally, they faced a number of problems. Among these were the need to see if more evidence could be obtained to help Waller and improve his legal defense, the need to find a means of arousing greater public support, and the need to raise more money.[59]

Although there was always more that could be done, the growing public awareness of Waller's case was evident. One interesting example was the publication by the WDL on April 14, 1941, of a letter signed by six prominent Americans: Alfred Bingham, editor of *Common Sense* magazine; George S. Counts, president of the American Federation of Teachers; John Dewey, the philosopher and educator; Paul Kellogg, editor of *The Survey* magazine; the Reverend A. J. Muste, head of the Fellowship of Reconciliation; and A. Philip Randolph, president of the Brotherhood of Sleeping Car Porters. "In 1856," the letter began, "Dred Scott became a symbol for the abolition of slavery. Today another unknown Negro, Odell Waller, like that runaway slave, has in our time become the rallying point for those who would abolish the poll tax and the injustices of the sharecropper system. . . . There is still a chance to save Odell Waller, and in saving him, to enlist wider action on this grave problem." The letter appealed for donations to support legal research, the printing of briefs needed in the appeals process, travel and publicity.[60]

Another indication of increased public awareness of the Waller case was found in the letters that some concerned citizens began to send to the Virginia governor on Waller's behalf. One such correspondent was William Allen White, the celebrated newspaper editor from Emporia, Kansas. "I have been reading about the case of Odell Waller," he wrote to Governor Price in April 1941. "It seems to me that here is a place where exceptional care should be exercised to see that this man has a fair trial. I am writing to express my belief and hope—with other American citizens who hope to see better race relations promoted—you will do what you can to safeguard this man's rights whatever they are."[61] Although letters of this sort had only begun to trickle into the governor's office during the spring of 1941, as the campaign on Waller's behalf gained momentum, they would eventually reach flood proportions.

Increasing the public's awareness of Waller's plight and raising money were, of course, inherently interconnected. The success of Annie Waller's tour in January prompted the WDL to ask her to return to New York in mid April for a six-week period to speak in nearby localities. The proposal was soon upgraded to a nationwide tour. As before, Murray was to accompany Mrs. Waller.[62] Murray Kempton, a field secretary of the WDL, was to make the advance arrangements. For the tour and for general fund-raising purposes the WDL prepared a special folder which it mailed to twenty-two thousand persons. This included pictures of Odell Waller, Annie Waller, some black laborers in the fields, and Pauli Murray, along with the tour's itinerary. Under the picture of Odell were the words, in bold letters: "This man MUST DIE! Unless . . . you help him . . . FAST!"

> It's not just one man and his family—though they're important too. It's the whole setup: the terrible problem of white and colored sharecroppers, of tenant farmers and landlords. President Roosevelt called this "America's number one economic problem." . . . Odell Waller is on trial—but so is American Democracy![63]

HEAR
Pauli Murray!

poet, lecturer and travelling companion
of "Mother" Anne Waller

ON

1. Odell Waller Is Innocent!

Graphic description of a case that has
shocked America. Odell Waller is in Virginia today under sentence of death.

2. How the Poll Tax Affects You!

Did you know that every voter in California is a victim of the poll tax?

ABOUT PAULI MURRY...

She is a well known writer and liberal leader. Her appearance on the Negro Newspaper of the Air (KFVD, 2:15) last Sunday was a sensation!

Thursday, May 22, 1941, 8 p. m.
First A. M. E. Church

Corner Vernon and Kensington　　　　**Pasadena**
Rev. Dames, Pastor

ADMISSION FREE

California Eagle Press

Notice of a Pauli Murray talk in Pasadena, California, May 22, 1941.

In arranging local speaking engagements, the WDL had the cooperation of the NAACP and the Brotherhood of Sleeping Car Porters. Annie
Waller arrived in New York on April 18 and spent the next ten days in
the New York area. Then Murray and Mrs. Waller traveled to Boston,
Pittsburgh, Cleveland, Detroit, Chicago, Milwaukee, and Denver before
proceeding to the West Coast. After speaking in Seattle, Portland, San
Francisco, and Los Angeles, they made additional stops in Oklahoma
City, Kansas City, St. Louis, Louisville, Indianapolis, Cincinnati, Dayton,
and Columbus before returning to New York in early June.[64] It was an
exhausting trip for both women. "This tour has worn me out so thoroughly, that I'm not capable of making judgments about the whole
mess," Murray wrote to Milgram from Kansas City.[65] Short on funds, they
had to eat simply and sit up in day coaches during long, overnight train
rides. Some of their talks were before large audiences, but more often
they spoke to small groups in little halls or rooms in church basements.
At times the advance planning was poor, but they considered the visit to
Cleveland to be the only "flop" during the early part of the tour. Murray
regarded the week in Los Angeles (May 15 to May 22) as "one of the ups
and downs" of their tour. They collected $200 in six meetings, but, she
believed, they would have done better had the accusation of communism not been raised against the WDL, had there not been organizational problems with the NAACP, and had there not been so many other
events going on at the same time. Still, Murray at least concluded that
they had made some useful contacts.[66]

Despite some problems, they undoubtedly had an impact on their
audiences. Mrs. Waller movingly told her story in a simple, straightforward manner that clearly revealed her personal anguish. Murray would
follow this with a factual account of the problems of sharecroppers and
the poll tax system.[67] Upon her return to New York, Murray concluded
that, on balance, the tour had been "moderately successful." The total
expenses of the Murray-Waller tour were $363, but they raised $755.[68]
This was a useful, but not spectacular, addition to the Waller defense
funds. Ultimately the WDL would need many times that amount. Fund
raising would have to be a continuing activity if they were to keep up the
struggle to save Waller's life. Still, the tour had undoubtedly increased
public awareness of the case, and thus it laid the groundwork for some
future contributions.

Annie Waller returned to Gretna on Friday, June 13. A few days later

Murray left New York for a long vacation. In return for giving a few lectures on sharecropping to the Young People's Socialist League Summer Institute at a camp in the Catskill Mountains of New York, she was allowed to spend the summer in one of the simple cabins rent-free. She devoted her time to writing, although she did not publish any of the results of her summer's efforts. For Murray the work in charge of the Waller case for the WDL had been both physically and emotionally draining. On March 15, Frank McCallister had assumed the direction of the case, although she remained deeply involved in it until the end of her tour with Mrs. Waller. In September she entered Howard University Law School, and thereafter the defense of Odell Waller necessarily took up less of her time than it had during the previous year. But it continued to have a significant impact on her life.[69]

By the summer of 1941, the Waller defense efforts entered a new phase. Temporarily, the WDL's activities, at least its public campaigns, became far less obvious. So did its battles with the RWDC. Although the WDL remained just as firmly opposed to the ideas and tactics of the RWL and the RWDC, by that time the role of the radical organizations in Waller's defense had been so reduced as to have become substantially irrelevant. This, of course, was not true for Stone, who remained essential to the defense as it prepared to argue its case before the Supreme Court of Appeals of Virginia. Important as the WDL's efforts had been in awakening many Americans to the plight of Odell Waller and to the underlying problems he had come to symbolize, these alone could not save his life. His fate rested primarily in the hands of his lawyers and their ability to convince Virginia's highest court—or failing that, the federal courts—that he had been denied a fair trial. In the months ahead, the quality of Waller's legal defense became the critical issue.

5

"The Judgment . . .
Will Be Affirmed"

When the Supreme Court of Appeals of Virginia agreed to consider Waller's appeal on March 4, 1941, the defense assumed that its review of the case would take place before the end of the spring term. The court eventually set May 31 as the date for the filing of the defense's brief responding to the state's arguments against the appeal and June 2 as the date for the oral presentations. This put considerable pressure on Stone and Finerty, for they had much work to do to complete their brief. Their problems were compounded by Finerty's extremely heavy schedule of cases and by his becoming seriously ill in the spring. Consequently Stone, citing Finerty's illness, applied for and, "after quite a lot of argument," obtained a postponement until September.[1] Thus, after a very busy spring, the summer of 1941 became a period of relative quiet in the campaign to save the life of Odell Waller. From then through the fall of 1941 his defenders focused their attention almost entirely on the legal and constitutional issues on which so much depended.

In preparation for their oral presentation before Virginia's highest court, Stone, Finerty, Milgram, and another lawyer, Ernest Fleischman, conferred in Finerty's office in New York on the evening of Sunday, August 17. They were particularly concerned about the damaging nature of the testimony of two of the prosecution witnesses at Waller's trial and agreed that it would be desirable if they could get them to change their stories. One of these witnesses was Henry Davis, whom they believed had been "bribed or terrorized into falsely testifying." The other was Mrs. Oscar Davis, who they believed had lied when she stated that her husband had carried only a wallet, not a gun, in his pocket. They hoped that they could get a clergyman or some friend to persuade them "to testify to the truth," but their course of action was limited. As for the session before the court, which was scheduled to be held in Staunton on September 8, they agreed that every effort should be made to have the leading members of the WDL, as well as prominent intellectuals and trade unionists, be present. If possible they hoped to get Mrs. Roosevelt to attend. As Milgram saw it, "the more important the court thinks the case is the better its decision will be. The more influential our delegates are, the more effective."[2]

Although he was then a young man only twenty-five years old, Milgram had become acting secretary of the WDL in the summer of 1941 after Clendenin stepped down. Born in New York City in May 1916, he had studied at City College and the University of Newark, from which he was graduated in 1939. He brought idealism and enthusiasm to his work with the WDL and shared, with Pauli Murray, a deep commitment to the defense of Waller. After Clendenin's death in an automobile accident on August 30, 1941, Milgram became the national secretary.[3] In Pauli Murray's absence, it was Milgram who tried to keep Waller informed of developments. "Everything is going along very well in our plans for the oral argument of your appeal," he wrote on August 22. "I am confident that victory will be ours because I am certain that you are innocent."[4] Milgram also kept in touch with Dollie Harris, who planned to be present at the oral argument.[5] Unfortunately, neither Thurgood Marshall nor Walter White of the NAACP was able to get to Staunton. Nor could Mrs. Roosevelt. It is doubtful, however, that the Virginia court would have been seriously influenced by their presence, or that of others, no matter how distinguished, when it heard the oral arguments by Stone and Finerty in the session held on September 8.[6]

The legal basis for Waller's appeal was laid out in the petition for a writ of error which Stone had drawn up, with the assistance of Howard H. Davis, and submitted to the Supreme Court of Appeals in January 1941. In it they included every conceivable error that they could allege had occurred at Waller's trial. They listed ten specific points:

(1) The denial by the court of a motion to quash the indictment on the ground that it had been returned by a grand jury from which non–poll tax payers had been excluded.

(2) The denial by the court of a motion to quash the entire *venire facias* (jury panel) on the ground that there had been a systematic

exclusion of non–poll tax payers which had thus deprived Waller
of a trial by a jury of his peers.

(3) The refusal of Judge Clement to disqualify himself because of
prejudicial remarks made on September 19 to the court reporter
and counsel.

(4) The denial by the court of a motion to discharge the entire jury
panel because it was present when the prejudicial remarks were
made.

(5) The denial of a motion for a change in venue.

(6) The overruling of a challenge for cause against one of the jurors
who employed sharecroppers and against all others who did the
same.

(7) The overruling of a challenge for cause against another juror,
G. W. Farson, who employed sharecroppers and who indicated
doubts that he could be unprejudiced in viewing a conflict
between a sharecropper and a landlord.

(8) The admission of the alleged dying declaration of Oscar Davis.

(9) The refusal of the court to eliminate all the instructions to the
jury on homicide.

(10) The refusal of the court to set aside the verdict as contrary to law
and evidence.[7]

The state had answered these allegations in a "Brief on Behalf of the
Commonwealth" prepared by Attorney General Abram P. Staples and
Assistant Attorney General Joseph L. Kelly, Jr. The defense had responded in turn with a fourteen-page reply brief, which it submitted in
June. In preparing this brief, as well as his oral arguments, Stone was
assisted by Finerty and Shapiro as well as Davis.[8] Both Stone and Finerty
spoke at the September 8 session before the Supreme Court of Appeals.
The defense's hopes lay primarily in the argument over the relationship
of the poll tax to the composition of the grand and petit juries, and, to a
lesser degree, the occupational status and economic bias of many of the
jurors. The other alleged errors offered far less possibility of success, and
the argument for those can be summarized briefly.

The third and fourth errors cited in the petition related to the allegedly prejudicial remarks of Judge Clement on September 19, 1940, to
the court reporter and counsel. At this time Hopkins and Stone had
been arguing for a continuance on the grounds that they had not had

enough time to prepare their case. The judge then displayed, according to the petition, "not only a spirit of irritation but also an absolutist spirit not compatible with judicial temperament," when he rebuked the stenographer for asking people to speak louder.[9] This, admitted Stone, would not have been a reversible error by itself, had the judge not then stated in the presence of the jury panel that "a man charged with a criminal offense had no right to await the action of the Grand Jury. He should anticipate that he may be indicted."[10] Such a remark, argued Stone, "startlingly negatived [sic] one of the foremost principles of our criminal jurisprudence, the doctrine of the presumption of innocence."[11] In their brief, Staples and Kelly quickly dismissed this whole argument with the comment "that it seems to us obvious that the court's remarks related to the probability that the prisoner would be formally accused in due course of the offense for which he was being held—not to the question of whether he had committed it. They simply had nothing to do with the presumption of innocence."[12] To this the defense replied that the real vice here was that the offending remarks were made in the presence of potential jurors. "The criterion of error in such cases is not what a lawyer would think of them, but what the average juror would think, and in a case involving the life and death of a person, certainly no chances can be taken. The right to an absolutely fair trial for an accused is more important than the convenience of either the Court or a specific jury panel."[13]

The basis for the fifth error, the court's refusal to grant a change in venue, appeared rather tenuous to many observers. The argument here rested upon the assertion that the atmosphere in Pittsylvania County was so hostile that Waller was precluded from receiving a fair trial.[14] The evidence for this claim was the testimony of Edmund Campion, which had not been directly controverted, about overhearing three conversations hostile to Waller, and that of Sheriff Overbey, who had said he had heard some threats of a lynching about the time he returned Waller from Ohio. But the latter remarks were several weeks before the trial, and Overbey himself had testified that, not only had nothing happened, but that most of the people in the area showed little interest in the trial. Moreover, Campion had proved to be far from an impressive witness. As Staples and Kelly argued, Stone had not been able to produce evidence that there was "a general prejudice prevailing in the community at any time, or that an atmosphere of violence surrounded the trial."[15]

The seventh alleged error pertained to the response made by a prospective juror, Mr. G. W. Farson, to a question from Stone. Farson was a farmer who also employed some sharecroppers. Would that fact, Stone had asked, "have any effect in prejudicing you one way or the other" if testimony were to show that there had been a conflict between a share-cropper and a landlord? Farson replied: "I don't think I would have any trouble." Stone asked again: "Could you possibly state whether it would or not?" and Farson replied: "I don't think it would."[16] Stone had challenged this juror but had been immediately overruled by Clement. In his petition Stone insisted that his question had been one that could have been answered by a simple yes or no, and thus doubt about Farson's ability to be fair had been demonstrated. Staples and Kelly replied by simply quoting the exchange that had taken place between Stone and Farson and then remarking that "we cannot believe that the Court will consider seriously any contention that this juror's statement, taken as a whole, rendered him subject to a challenge for cause."[17] The defense's short response simply asserted "that a fair interpretation of the juror's answer is that he had a mental reservation or doubt in his own mind. It is so elementary that such a person should not be allowed on a jury panel that we do not deem it necessary to discuss this further."[18] Although Clement had overruled Stone's challenge to Farson, subsequently Farson was not selected as a member of the petit jury, so his possible doubt could not have been a factor in the jury's decision.

The admissibility of Oscar Davis's alleged dying declaration, the eighth error, was a more serious matter. Because the state's only witness to the shooting was Henry Davis, whose possibly coached testimony was suspect on many grounds, the inclusion of this dying declaration was, in Stone's view, "an absolute necessity" to the state's case. Stone's argument rested heavily on Dr. Risher's having testified that at the time Davis made his alleged remarks to his sons he had taken a turn for the better and was not *in extremis*, so the statement lacked the prerequisites for admissibility as a dying declaration.[19] Despite the potential importance of this issue, Staples and Kelly did not devote much space to a response and merely claimed that prevailing judicial interpretation in Virginia held that such statements are admissible if the deceased believed at the time that he was dying.[20]

The ninth alleged error, the failure of the judge to remove instructions to the jury on homicide, was based on the contention that the state "had not proved, as a matter of law, beyond reasonable doubt, that the deceased suffered death as a proximate or even indirect result of the wounds resulting from the shooting." At the trial Dr. Risher had, of course, testified that death was due to a sudden collapse of the left lung, and that this had been a consequence of the operation, which in turn had been necessitated by the shooting. But, Stone argued, the state had not shown at the trial that there had been a connection between the shooting and the pulmonary collapse. "This cannot be left to speculation or contingency. Certainly if doubt existed in the mind of the Commonwealth's medical expert doubt must exist as a matter of law, and, therefore, no instruction based on homicide could stand."[21] Staples and Kelly responded by citing the same case noted by Stone, *Livingston* v. *Commonwealth* (55 Va. 592). Here, they insisted, the court had upheld the principle that a person who caused a wound that was not itself fatal could be held criminally responsible for the death of that person should the victim later die as a result of conditions that were caused by the wound. They contemptuously dismissed Stone's argument here as "plainly groundless."[22] The defense's reply on this issue was again very short and merely argued that in the *Livingston* case the court had referred to the subsequent death of a person from a wound that originally had not been fatal. In the case of Oscar Davis, however, "there is no testimony that the wound turned to anything. The wound had cleared up. It was not the cause of the pulmonary collapse."[23] It is very doubtful that Finerty and Shapiro, at least, had their heart in this argument. From the start many observers had viewed Stone's contention that Davis had not died from the gunshot wounds as the rankest quibbling, although it was a point often made in the literature put out by Waller's radical defenders and a few others. But it was not an argument that Finerty wanted to embrace, and he later publicly dismissed it as an "absurd theory."[24]

It was obvious that several of the errors cited in the defense's petition were of dubious merit and were unlikely to impress the court. The issues raised over the composition of the jury, however, were quite different, for these went to the heart of the social, economic, and racial problems that underlay the whole tragic affair. The sixth error noted in Stone's petition was the overruling of his challenge for cause against one of the jurors who employed sharecroppers and against all the others who did the same. Nine members of the jury panel and six members of the petit jury employed sharecroppers.[25] Stone acknowledged that he was making "a new point, a point of first instance not only in Virginia but also, so far as counsel have been able to discover, in general." His contention was "that in a case involving the shooting of a landlord by a sharecropper, in which such shooting arose entirely out of economic circumstances, that it is impossible as a matter of law for an employer of sharecropper [*sic*] to act as an impartial juror." Stone sought support for his position in the 1939 case of *Pierre* v. *Louisiana* in which the United States Supreme Court had overturned the murder conviction of a Negro because of the systematic exclusion of Negroes from the grand jury because of race.[26] Stone argued, therefore, "that the exclusion of certain definite groups, classes or races is a denial of justice," and, reasoning by analogy, held that this should also be true for economic class.[27] Such an interpretation was especially relevant in the Waller case, he insisted, because the state's theory, "if it had any theory at all," was that Waller shot Davis "as a result of being exasperated by economic conflict," while the defense's theory was that it was a matter of self-defense in a situation that "again arose out of economic conflict. Now, to say that a fair trial could be given your petitioner by a jury whose whole social training, economic environment, and subconscious feeling inspired by pecuniary motives, is asking these gentlemen to be not men but super-men." The jury that was selected "was not, as contemplated by the law a cross-section of the community, but strictly a class jury." Stone did not claim that there had been any systematic exclusion of Negroes, but he pointed out, correctly, that there were no Negroes on the jury panel, so that Waller was "tried by a jury not only of landlords but of white landlords."[28]

Staples and Kelly showed little sympathy for Stone's appeal to such economic, social, and human realities. "The law is settled beyond all question," they asserted, "that a defendant is never entitled to a jury which is in any case 'mixed' for the trial of his own, particular case." Counsel was asking the court to create a new ground for challenging jurors, and "if such a sweeping rule is to be established it clearly must be done by the legislature."[29] To this the defense replied that the state's argument was "radically in error on its law" and cited the 1940 case of *Smith* v. *Texas* in which Justice Black held that a jury had to "be a body truly representative of the community."[30] Thus, the defense attacked the commonwealth for maintaining "two monstrous legal theses. First, that it constitutes a fair trial to exclude from the jury the whole section of the community to which the accused belongs and then to place upon the jury an overwhelming majority of the group to which the deceased belonged."[31] As Stone acknowledged, the defense was raising a new point in holding that exclusion of an economic class had denied Waller a representative jury. Regardless of the legal merits of this argument, it at least had the virtue of being concerned with the underlying problems of race and class and the obstacles to understanding these created in American society.

By far the most important challenge raised by the defense concerned the alleged exclusion of non–poll tax payers from the grand and petit juries. This was the basis for the first two assignments in error in Stone's petition, and it seemed to be the most promising ground for obtaining a reversal of conviction or a new trial. Stone's position was that the indictment against Waller "should have been quashed in that it was returned by a grand jury from which non–poll taxpayers had been excluded. Your petitioner himself was of this class and made offer of proof of same." In addition, he argued that non–poll tax payers were excluded from the petit jury panel and hence from the jury that tried Waller.[32] At the beginning of the trial, on September 19, 1940, Stone's first motion (after that for a continuance) had been to quash the indictment and the whole jury panel on the basis of this alleged exclusion.[33] But he had not, at that time, presented specific evidence about the selection of the juries or about Waller's nonpayment of the poll tax. In his petition Stone cited the recent cases of *Smith* v. *Texas* and *Pierre* v. *Louisiana* to establish the point that a jury had to be truly representative of the community in order to have equal protection of the laws, and that particular groups, classes, or races who are otherwise qualified may not be excluded as such from jury service. Therefore, he claimed, the only question was "whether non–poll taxpayers are excluded from juries and grand juries in Virginia."[34]

On this point Virginia law was not explicit. Stone's contention was as follows: Section 4853 of the Virginia Code held that "each grand juror shall be a citizen of this State, 21 years of age, and shall have been a resident of this State two years, and of the county or corporation in which the court is to be held one year, *and in other respects a qualified juror . . .* " (emphasis added). For petit jurors Section 5984 held that "all male citizens over twenty-one years of age who shall have been residents of this State one year, and of the county, city or town in which they reside six months next preceding their being summoned to serve as such, *and competent in other respects*, except as hereinafter provided, shall remain and be liable to serve as jurors" (emphasis added). (The exceptions were: "First, idiots and lunatics; second, persons convicted of bribery, perjury, embezzlement of public funds, treason, felony, or petit larceny.") Stone then looked at the qualifications for voters under Section 18 of the Virginia Constitution and concluded "that, with the exception of the possible question of women on the jury, not involved in this case, that the requirements for voting and the requirements for jury service are almost identically the same."[35] In an 1873 case (*Craft* v. *The Commonwealth*) the Virginia Supreme Court of Appeals had held that in order to be a qualified juror a person had to have the constitutional qualifications for being a voter. This was a reasonable interpretation of the 1873 Virginia Code which had provided that "all male citizens twenty-one years of age, and not over sixty, who are entitled to vote and hold office, under the Constitution and laws of this state, shall be liable to serve as jurors." As Stone acknowledged, the specific requirement of being a voter was later dropped from the code, and by 1902–4 "the statute was changed to approximately its present form of section 5984 of the present Code." But, Stone also argued that the Virginia Constitutional Convention of 1902, which adopted the poll tax, was called "for the specific purpose of disfranchising as far as possible the Negroes," and the same individuals who sat in that convention sat in the 1902–4 General Assembly. Stone reasoned that the phrase "competent in other respects" had to be construed to mean "that jurors must possess constitutional qualifications for voting."[36]

That being the case, Stone concluded "that both the grand jury in the instant case and the petit jury panel were selected solely from poll tax-payers. Therefore, *there was no necessity to offer proof that either the grand or petit juries were so construed*" (emphasis added).[37] If a jury had to be representative of the community and could not exclude any group or class, then both the grand jury that had indicted Waller and the petit jury that had tried his case could not have met that constitutional requirement, because Virginia law, as Stone interpreted it, excluded non–poll tax payers. Unfortunately for Waller, there were significant legal deficiencies in Stone's argument, even though he was manifestly correct in asserting that both the grand and petit juries were not representative of the community and that classes of people had been excluded. Inevitably, Staples and Kelly pounced on these deficiencies. "It is a sufficient answer," they argued, "to point out that the accused has not shown that he is a mem-

ber of the class alleged to be discriminated against, having neither introduced nor offered evidence as to nonpayment of his own poll taxes."[38]
Of course Waller had not paid his poll tax, and no one could have had
any serious doubt about that fact. But Stone's incredible failure to offer
evidence of this at the trial gave the prosecution an effective, if technical, rebuttal to his argument. Of equal importance was Stone's failure at
the trial to show that non–poll tax payers had in fact been discriminated
against in the selection of the grand and petit juries. Instead, Stone contended that the statutes "should be construed as requiring the discrimination of which they complain."[39] But these laws could be interpreted
quite differently. Thus Staples and Kelly argued that in an 1861 case
(*Booth & al.* v. *The Commonwealth*) the Virginia Supreme Court of Appeals had held that the phrase "in other respects qualified jurors" referred "to the broad, general grounds of disqualification existing at common law," such as being "an alien or villein," having been outlawed for a
crime or convicted of treason, a felony, or perjury. "We can conceive of
no reason for holding that the same phrase in the statute has a different
meaning now."[40] Moreover, they also insisted that the history of Section
5984 of the Virginia Code showed that the legislature had *not* intended
"to impose the same requirements for jury service as for voting." Thus
the statute enacted in 1902, a few days after the Constitutional Convention adopted the first poll tax, not only dropped the words "entitled to
vote and hold office" but prescribed residence requirements for jurors
that were "less strict than those prescribed for electors under the new
Constitution."[41]

The defense lawyers did what they could to rebut this argument. First,
they insisted that Stone *did* offer evidence at the trial that Waller had not
paid his poll taxes. When Stone originally introduced his motion to
quash the indictment on the grounds that the grand jury had been selected exclusively from poll tax payers and to quash the whole *venire
facias* on the same ground, his argument was based on his construction
of the laws that held that payment of the poll tax was a prerequisite for
jury service. Judge Clement asked: "Mr. Stone, what is the basis of your
motion in this case? What has the qualification or otherwise to do with
this defendant?" Stone replied: "Persons who are unable to pay their
poll tax are excluded and the accused is in the same general social and
economic category."[42] But Stone went no further and introduced no specific data as to whether Waller had or had not paid his poll tax. Never-

theless, the defense lawyers now asserted that this exchange had constituted an "offer of evidence."

Most of the defense's reply was an attempt to support Stone's position
that non–poll tax payers were barred as a matter of law from jury service.
They contended that the *Booth* case was irrelevant, as it pertained to the
Code of 1849, not the one in effect after 1902, but even if it were to be
used, the fact that the court had included the word "villeins" would be
enough to hold that non–poll tax payers and sharecroppers would be
excluded from jury service.[43] Moreover, they pointed out that the
registration requirement for voting was only a *statutory* requirement at
the time of the *Craft* case, but it had been elevated to a *constitutional*
provision by the Constitution of 1902, which also made payment of the
poll tax a prerequisite for registration. Referring to the remarks made by
Delegate Carter Glass at that 1902 convention, remarks that had been
quoted in the "Petition For Writ of Error," they again contended that it
had been the intention of the Constitutional Convention of 1902 to
disenfranchise Negroes, using the poll tax as a means to that end. That
being true, "it would certainly appear that an intention to deprive non–
poll taxpayers of the vote for reasons enunciated by Delegate Glass,
would also apply, and with still greater force, to excluding them from
juries."[44] Finally, they insisted that the words "and competent in other
respects" in Section 5984 could *not* refer to the exceptions listed thereafter, for that would be tautological. Therefore, they must refer to
something else. Once again they concluded that the General Assembly
of 1902 meant to "impose the same restrictions on jury service as they
did on voters."[45]

Stone's final assignment of error, the refusal of the court to set aside
the verdict as contrary to law and evidence, was, of course, made in part
for the record as a means of bringing all his arguments together. But he
also insisted that more was at stake here. The state's only eyewitness was
Henry Davis, and his testimony about the unprovoked nature of the
shooting was without substantiation "unless it be by the alleged dying
declaration of the decedent." In Stone's view, both Henry Davis's testimony and Oscar Davis's dying declaration were "incredible." "This again
leads to the inescapable conclusion that it was the composition of the
jury which prevented your petitioner from having a fair trial in any practical sense of the word."[46] The commonwealth saw the evidence differently. Staples and Kelly pointed out that the prosecution had produced

two witnesses who testified that, on the day prior to the shooting, Waller had said he was going to get either his wheat or Davis, that there were two witnesses (Davis's sons) to his dying declaration, that they and others had testified that Davis did not own or carry a weapon, and that the state had produced evidence that Waller had a "bad reputation for keeping the peace."[47] They concluded that "it is indeed difficult to believe that any sane man should designedly kill another in cold blood, but the Court can hardly be asked to hold that inhuman crimes are never committed."[48] To this the defense replied that the testimony of Henry Davis "is absolutely incredible and gives every appearance of being coached. . . . It is distinctly the contention of the plaintiff in error that to believe the story of Henry Davis is to believe that Odell Waller was absolutely insane," a point the defense had never maintained.[49]

After presenting their oral arguments on September 8 there was little more that Waller's lawyers could do until the Supreme Court of Appeals reached its decision. What hope for success they had at this level rested primarily on their arguments concerning the composition of the jury. But they could win only if the court was willing to venture beyond prevailing constitutional interpretations and hold that Waller had been denied a fair trial because he was a member of an economic class that had been systematically excluded from his jury, or if the court was willing to accept the contention that Virginia law did in fact exclude non–poll tax payers from juries, assuming in the latter case that the court did not then fall back on the technicality that at the trial Stone had failed to prove that non–poll tax payers had been excluded. There was abundant evidence that the trial court—judge, prosecution, and jury—had been insensitive to the social, economic, and racial dimensions of the controversy between Oscar Davis and Odell Waller. Hence it was understandable that the defense lawyers believed that a truly representative jury might have rendered a different verdict. But the chances were probably never very good that the justices on the Supreme Court of Appeals of Virginia would show a sensitivity that had been lacking in the trial court. The many debatable points in the defense's argument were likely to give the conservative justices a means of avoiding an imaginative and meaningful consideration of social, economic, and racial realities that underlay the case of Odell Waller.[50]

Five weeks later, on October 13, 1941, Chief Justice Preston W. Campbell delivered the opinion of the court. In terse, at times harsh, language it rejected every point raised by the defense and affirmed the judgment of the trial court. On the crucial question of the alleged exclusion of non–poll tax payers from the juries, the court held that the "accused did not offer any proof whatever to sustain the two motions." As for Waller himself, "There is not a scintilla of evidence in the record to show that accused had, or had not paid a poll tax; hence he is in no position to complain of such discrimination, had it existed."[51] The court also accepted the reasoning in the Commonwealth's Brief and dismissed as "untenable" the defense's contention that the laws must be interpreted to mean that the qualification for jurors are the same as those for voters.[52] All the other alleged errors were quickly dismissed. As for the refusal of Judge Clement to disqualify himself, the court held that no conclusion can be properly drawn that the judge's conduct denied the accused a fair trial according to law.[53] Similarly, it rejected the contention that the trial court erred in refusing a change of venue with the comment that "the record utterly fails to even indicate that the accused was tried in a hostile atmosphere."[54] The court was equally unmoved by Stone's argument about the inherent bias of those jurors who employed sharecroppers. "Counsel do not even remotely suggest that the challenged jurors were not men of worth and fully competent to try the issue between the Commonwealth and the accused. . . . In our opinion, no discrimination has been made against the accused and the assignment is without merit."[55] There was also no error in the rejection of the challenge to G. W. Farson.[56] Nor was there any error in the acceptance of Oscar Davis's dying declaration, because it was "beyond dispute that [he] . . . was fully conscious of his impending death."[57] Nor was there any error in the trial court overruling the motion to strike out instructions on homicide, for that argument rested on the contention that death was not due to the bullet wounds. The evidence conclusively showed "that the ultimate cause of death was the result of the wounds inflicted by the accused."[58] The court devoted more time to the contention that the trial court had erred in not setting aside the verdict on the ground that it was contrary to the law and evidence. But, after quoting part of the testimony of John Curtis Williams, Thomas Younger, and Henry Davis, as well as Odell Waller, it concluded that the evidence did indeed sustain a verdict of murder in the first degree.

It is hard to conceive of a case where the elements of premeditation and malice stand out more prominently than they do in the case at bar. In our opinion, the accused has had a fair and impartial trial, by an impartial jury; he has been convicted upon evidence adduced by members of his own race, which upon its face bears the impress of truth. There is no error in the judgment of trial court and it will be affirmed.[59]

However disappointing this decision was to Waller's defenders, it could not have been wholly unexpected. Still, Stone was angry. "In my mind it represents a complete evasion of practically all the legal issues, and not even a very clever evasion," he wrote to Finerty. Stone recommended that they present a petition for a writ of habeas corpus to the Supreme Court "at the earliest possible moment." He also prepared a letter to send to the governor requesting a stay of execution.[60] Milgram agreed with Stone. "We certainly will fight the case right up to the Supreme Court. The evasion of the legal issues by Virginia's highest justice deserves the vigorous action you suggest." Milgram also noted that the WDL had exhausted its funds on the case, and that they were "busy getting new support."[61]

The court's decision provided Virginius Dabney with another opportunity to comment on the Waller case on the editorial pages of the *Times-Dispatch*. He too regretted that the court had not ordered a new trial. "Another trial . . . in a calmer atmosphere and without radical propaganda in the courtroom, would have gone far to allay existing dissatisfaction over the death sentence," he wrote. But it was "not surprising that the verdict of the lower court was affirmed," given the lack of proof presented by the defense on the poll tax issue. "The Waller case never impressed us as an ideal one with which to test the constitutionality of making poll-tax payments a prerequisite to jury service, for the reason that Waller's guilt seemed so probable."[62]

Once again Dabney provoked a controversy. In a letter to the editor, Stone's wife, Dorothy C. Stone, demanded to know "where was the radical propaganda that he so often mentions?" She was present at both the trial and the oral argument before the Supreme Court of Appeals, so she felt better qualified than Dabney to express an opinion. If one is to be labeled a "radical" just for trying to help the underprivileged, she wrote, "then I think it would be well for all of us to strive to get into that category." She also asked "how could Odell Waller have a fair trial at all unless the jury were completely composed of Negro share croppers and nonpoll tax payers? And the fact that Waller did not prove as fact that he was a nonpoll tax payer, and thereby has 'no right to complain' seems just too technical."[63] Dabney responded in an editor's note in which he defended his use of the term "radical" by pointing out that the Revolutionary Workers League had employed Waller's counsel and that Edmund Campion, an official of the RWL, had testified at the trial. He ignored her other points, however.[64] Dabney's dislike of the RWL was obvious and predictable, but his response was slightly disingenuous. His editorial had complained of radical propaganda *in the courtroom*. Whatever the other activities of the RWL, the record of the trial simply does not sustain this allegation.

In an October 20 editorial entitled "Waller and the Facts," Dabney tried once again to sort out the disputed issues. Decrying the "misrepresentations" of the case that Waller's defenders continued to make, he cited a bulletin put out by the NAACP which said that "in Virginia no one can serve on the jury who is not able to pay the State's $1.50 cumulative poll tax." But, Dabney noted, the Supreme Court of Appeals has held that no evidence was presented in the Waller case about the exclusion of non–poll tax payers from the jury, and "the *Times-Dispatch* has been unable to discover evidence of widespread exclusion." Furthermore, he continued, it is a misrepresentation to assert that Waller shot in self-defense, when "uncontradicted witnesses" testified that Davis was unarmed and that Waller shot him twice in the back.[65] Earlier in the year Dabney had begun to express reservations about the trial, but the positions he took in these two editorials in October 1941, with their strong denunciations of Waller and their absence of even a hint that there were deeper social and legal issues at stake, showed that the hopes of Pauli Murray and others that he would become an ally had not been realized.

Dabney's editorials infuriated Stone. At first he planned not to reply, but after talking with Waller in his prison cell he changed his mind. According to Stone, Waller asked: "Mr. Stone, why does that man print all that junk about me in the Times Dispatch? Why can't he fight fair? You were down there and you know what he is saying is not the truth."[66] In a long, emotional letter, which Dabney declined to print in the *Times-Dispatch*, Stone denounced some of Dabney's "untruths." Among other things he emphatically denied that there had been radical propaganda in the courtroom at Waller's trial, and, as Dabney had a copy of the record, Stone accused him of making "a contemptible effort to try to convince your readers that Waller had been sacrificed for political reasons by some radical group." Stone was equally incensed by Dabney's dismissal of the claim that Waller had shot in self-defense. Dabney failed to note, said Stone, that the state's case on this issue rested on the testimony of the sole prosecution eyewitness, Henry Davis, a person who had refused to talk to the defense counsel and whose testimony was full of glaring discrepancies. Stone concluded by asking why Dabney had so misrepresented the issues. "The answer," said Stone, "is plain." Waller symbolized the plight of sharecroppers, black and white, against the exploitation by landlords.

> And knowing this, you properly take your stand with the exploiters. That is right. That is where you belong. . . . But in the sharpest social struggle, Mr. Editor, you have shown that it is necessary for your class to resort to the most vicious and most contemptible methods. I cannot imagine anything more despicable than for an editor of a widely circulated paper to resort to what you have done against an imprisoned sharecropper. I had thought that the actions of Hitler and others in the present imperialist carnage had reached the lowest depths of cultural depravity. I regret that you have convinced me to the contrary.[67]

Afterwards, Stone wrote to Waller to let him know that he had kept his promise and had responded to the attacks of the *Times-Dispatch.* "I hope, when you are released, that you will give the benefit of your experience to others similarly circumstanced, the victims of the 'liberal free press.'"[68]

John F. Finerty also responded to Dabney's editorials, but his approach was quite different from Stone's. In a letter published in the *Times-Dispatch* on October 31, he used carefully measured language to show that the poll tax issue had by no means been resolved as a result of the decision by the Supreme Court of Appeals in the Waller case. That court had decided that non–poll tax payers were not barred as a matter of law from jury service. But it "did not and could not pass on the factual question as to whether or not nonpayers of poll taxes were actually barred from such grand and petit juries. That question was not before them." In what in effect was a public rebuke of Stone, Finerty explained that the defense had not presented evidence on that point in the trial court "due to a misunderstanding by trial counsel as to the necessity of such proof." But now Finerty was prepared to present factual evidence showing that non–poll tax payers were "systematically barred from both the grand and petit juries in Pittsylvania County." Based on these facts Finerty planned to seek a writ of habeas corpus in the Virginia courts "to determine whether, thereby, Waller has been denied his constitutional right of equal protection of the law, both under the Constitution of Virginia and the Constitution of the United States." If he failed in the Virginia court, Finerty stated that he would immediately apply "to the Supreme Court of the United States for the review of any such refusal."[69] This was a position that interested Dabney, who responded on the same day with an editorial calling it "manifestly improper and illegal that the poll tax should be made prerequisite to jury service in Virginia." He did indicate some doubts that this had been the practice in Pittsylvania County, but he concluded that it was desirable to have the matter decided by the courts.[70]

The evidence concerning jurors and the poll tax that Finerty referred to was uncovered as a result of the investigation undertaken in September 1941 by Martin A. Martin of Danville and Hilliard Bernstein of Richmond at the request of the WDL.[71] From the records in the office of the clerk of the Circuit Court of Pittsylvania County, Martin checked the names of those on the grand jury and on the entire panel from which petit juries had been drawn during the year of Waller's trial. He then compared these against the list of poll tax payers for the years 1938, 1939, and 1940. There were seven persons on the special grand jury that had indicted Waller. All had paid their poll taxes for all three years, except one who had paid his poll tax for 1937 only. The entire petit jury list that was drawn on February 15, 1940, for the year ending February 15, 1941, contained 318 names. All had paid their poll taxes at one time or another within the three-year period, but 27 had not paid for 1940. (However, the poll tax for 1940 was not yet due at the time the petit jury list had been drawn). Every member of the petit jury at Waller's trial had paid his poll tax for the years 1938, 1939, and 1940. Martin could not discover whether all of the persons on the jury lists were registered voters. Two members of the grand jury were black, as were a number of others on the entire petit jury list and the *venire facias* from which the petit jury had been drawn.[72]

Later Martin went back to the clerk's office to obtain similar information for earlier jury lists. This time, however, the clerk, E. E. Friend, denied him access to the records, claiming that he did so on the instructions of Judge Clement and that he would not let him see the list unless he got an authorization from the attorney general. Martin wrote to the clerk and told him that he was going to go to the attorney general. He sent a copy of this letter to Clement, who replied that he had not given such an order to the clerk. Finally Martin did speak to Assistant Attorney General Joseph L. Kelly, Jr., who told him that he could not give an opinion on the matter unless the request came from an officer of the state.[73] Whether Judge Clement actually instructed the Pittsylvania County Clerk to deny Martin access to these records cannot be determined from the available evidence. But it was clear that Martin had been given the runaround and prevented from seeing public records that he had every right to examine. It was also clear that there had been at the least an extremely high probability that members of any petit jury in Pittsylvania County in 1940 would have been poll tax payers.

Nevertheless, Judge Clement continued to insist that there had been no connection between the poll tax and jury duty. "I selected the grand jury which indicted Waller," he wrote to Dabney, "and at no time did the thought of poll taxes enter my mind." He also insisted that the jury commissioners "had no thought of poll taxes in their mind" when they drew up the list of jurors. He acknowledged, however, that the "substantial and intelligent citizens" they wanted for juries were "the type of men who usually pay their taxes as well as other debts."[74] Dabney asked Clement for permission to publish his letter, but Clement refused on the grounds that it would be "a little out of keeping with judicial ethics for a judge to be drawn into a newspaper controversy, and especially with the type of men who are representing Waller."[75]

The information uncovered about the payment of poll taxes and jury service in Pittsylvania County had given Waller's defense some grounds for hope, and, as Finerty noted, the basis for a new appeal in the courts. Despite their obvious differences, Finerty and Stone cooperated in preparing their next legal move. The NAACP too promised its continued support of the Workers Defense League in its efforts to save Waller.[76] The Revolutionary Workers League, however, ever suspicious of any who did not share its ideologically shaped view of the case, repeated its denunciations of the WDL and asserted that the RWL was the group, through its attorney, Stone, that would take the case to the United States Supreme Court.[77] On October 13, 1941, Stone wrote to Governor Price requesting a sixty-day stay of execution, citing the facts uncovered by Martin as the basis of his request.[78] A few days later Joseph G. Glass, a member of the WDL legal staff, sent a similar request.[79] Stone wrote again on October 25, giving more details of the results of Martin's investigation. "I am just calling this to your Excellency's attention," he added, "so that you may see that we are not requesting stay for the purpose of delay, but that our contention is based upon weighty grounds."[80] The governor's secretary responded to these appeals with the suggestion that they submit "some tangible evidence that further proceedings are to be had in the courts" in order for the governor to grant another reprieve.[81] Actually the requests were somewhat premature in that a new execution date had not yet been set. But once Judge Clement formally received the mandate of the Supreme Court of Appeals he was quick to act, and on November 11 he issued an order resentencing Waller to death by electrocution on December 12, 1941.[82]

The adverse decision by the Supreme Court of Appeals had reawakened broader public interest in the case, and a substantial volume of letters and petitions, many from out-of-state, requesting reprieve or commutation began to flow into Governor Price's office.[83] With an execution date only a few weeks away, the sense of urgency grew. The attitude of the RWL at this point was, perhaps, predictable. Under a headline, "Waller Sentenced to Burn Dec. 12," *The Fighting Worker* wrote:

> Already Waller has been saved from the electric chair for over a year despite the hostility of the courts, the contemptible treachery of Virginius Dabney and his ilk, and the legalistic attitude of the Workers Defense League and the NAACP. What has saved him? Only the mass pressure of the working class elements centered around the Waller Defense Committee.[84]

Fortunately for Waller, Stone did not include the RWL's propaganda in his letters to Governor Price. On November 18, 1941, he again requested a reprieve, this time for a period of four months. Stone noted that he would be submitting a petition for a writ of habeas corpus to the Supreme Court of Appeals of Virginia "on the grounds of the actual exclusion of non–poll tax payers from the grand and petit juries in the Waller case."[85] On the next day, Secretary of the Commonwealth R. L. Jackson telephoned to Stone that Governor Price's term was about to end and that he was "terribly rushed," so Stone should file his habeas corpus petition "at the earliest possible moment." Obviously Price was going to wait until such a petition had been filed before he granted Waller another reprieve. Stone immediately wrote to Finerty, who was drawing up the

ODELL WALLER MUST DIE!

The Virginia Supreme Court has affirmed the conviction of this 23-year-old Negro sharecropper for the self-defense shooting of his white landlord. *His execution has been set for December 12th.*

HERE ARE THE FACTS: Waller, who had been looking for work, returned to find his mother and wife evicted from their shack at Gretna, Virginia. Oscar Davis, their white landlord, refused to give Waller his share of the crop. Davis was himself harassed by the need for money, but Waller was driven into an even worse corner. Would he, a Negro, be able to collect what was due him from a white man? An argument developed, and in self-defense Waller shot Davis, who later died. A jury was chosen made up of ten landowners, one businessman, and one skilled worker—all white, all payers of Virginia's cumulative poll tax. Did Waller, a poor Negro, get what was due him—a fair trial by an unprejudiced jury of his peers? We think not. He got a speedy death sentence.

In 1856 Dred Scott became a symbol for the abolition of slavery. Today another unknown Negro, Odell Waller, like that runaway slave, has in our time become the rallying point for those who would abolish the poll tax and the injustices of the sharecropper system.

"ODELL WALLER MUST DIE"

is the verdict of a Southern court. What is your verdict?

Among the prominent citizens who urge support of the League's work to save Waller's life are:

Alfred Bingham
J. R. Butler
John Dewey
George E. Haynes
Mary W. Hillyer
Paul Kellogg
Freda Kirchwey
A. J. Muste
A. Philip Randolph
Walter White

Your gift to save the life of Odell Waller will mean much in the fight for democracy on the home front.

CARL RAUSHENBUSH,
Chairman,
National Executive Board,
Workers Defense League

<u>YOU</u> can save Waller's life

1. Wire Governor James H. Price, Richmond, Virginia, urging him to grant a stay of execution so that the decision can be appealed to the Supreme Court of the U. S.

2. *Rush funds* to help save the life of sharecropper Waller.

GIVE!!

- -

Dr. George S. Counts, Treasurer,
Workers Defense League
112 East 19th Street, New York City

☐ I subscribe $100. to the fund to save the life of sharecropper Odell Waller.

☐ I contribute $_____ to aid in this work.

Name _____

Address _____

_____

Workers Defense League flier, November 1941, after the Supreme Court of Appeals of Virginia had reaffirmed Waller's conviction.

petition, and suggested that he bring it to Richmond, or if that was impossible, mail it to him so that he could have it signed by Waller and filed as soon as possible.[86] At about that same time Commonwealth's Attorney Joseph Whitehead, Jr. also wrote to Price requesting him not to grant Waller a reprieve yet, "as his attorneys will have ample time to perfect an appeal by December 12, if they so desire."[87] Price waited. On December 3, Stone filed the petition for a writ of habeas corpus. Three days later, on December 6, Price granted Waller his second reprieve, this time until March 20, 1942.[88] It was Waller's 422nd day on death row.

Judge Clement strongly disapproved of the reprieve. In a letter to Price on December 9 he assailed Waller's counsel for raising the question "at this late day . . . that he had been illegally held because his constitutional rights were violated in that he was indicted and convicted by poll tax payers." Ignoring that the defense had presented new data on the jury and the poll tax issue and was no longer contesting that nonpayers had been excluded as a matter of law, Clement wrote that "these questions were raised in the trial court, overruled, and affirmed by the Court of Appeals, and I do not think they should be allowed to delay the execution of the judgment of this court in this manner." Clement then specifically requested the governor to pass his letter on to his successor.[89] Three days later, Clement wrote again to Price and accused Waller's lawyers of deliberately delaying the filing of the petition for a writ of habeas corpus until the end of the court's fall term. Thus the court could not consider the petition until the opening of its next term on January 12, 1942. "You will see," concluded Clement, "that apparently these people have been trifling with the administration of justice."[90]

Governor Price did not share Clement's seemingly nonjudicial eagerness to see Waller sent to the electric chair. As he explained to President Frank P. Graham of the University of North Carolina, "It has always been my policy to let these unfortunate people exhaust their legal rights in an effort to establish their innocence."[91] Price's term as governor would expire on January 21, 1942, however, so his responsibilities in this ever more controversial case would soon end. In the immediate future Waller's fate lay in the hands of the courts. The members of the Supreme Court of Appeals had been unimpressed by the initial appeal. Whether the new evidence concerning the poll tax and Waller's jury would move the same justices in the habeas corpus proceedings remained to be seen.

6
Poll Tax Justice:
Rejection and Appeal,
January–May 1942

As 1942 began, Waller's defenders could look back upon their efforts with mixed feelings. The complete rejection of his appeal by the highest court in Virginia was a major disappointment. Still, their work had not been wholly in vain. Had they not pressed their initial appeal before that court, Waller would surely have gone to his death on December 27, 1940. Had they not continued their fight after the unfavorable decision of October 13, 1941, this time by a petition for a writ of habeas corpus, he would have been executed on December 12, 1941. By the end of 1941, Waller had been languishing in his cell on death row for nearly fifteen months. However horrible that experience must have been, he still had some ground for hope. For one thing the defense had by then uncovered additional information on which to base further appeals. Moreover, his story had been brought to the attention of an ever increasing number of people across the nation, and it was at least conceivable that a big enough public outcry could influence the governor, if not the courts. During the next few months Waller's defenders renewed their efforts on all fronts as they pursued every conceivable legal tactic and a stepped-up public appeal in a last all-out attempt to save his life.

On December 3, 1941, Stone and Martin had filed the petition to the Supreme Court of Appeals of Virginia for a writ of habeas corpus. It was largely the work of Finerty, although he, Stone, Martin, and Shapiro were all listed on it as attorneys for the petitioner, Odell Waller. In it they began by reviewing the arguments regarding jurors that had been made in the original appeal to the Virginia high court. But they now contended that in its decision of October 13 that court had merely held that the constitution and laws of Virginia did not bar nonpayers of the poll tax from grand or petit jury service; it had not ruled on the question of whether nonpayers had in fact been systematically barred from such a jury service.[1] In Pittsylvania County, they argued, persons who had not paid their poll taxes but were otherwise eligible for service on either grand or petit juries had been systematically barred from such service, and this had specifically been the case for the juries that had indicted and tried Waller. They supported this charge with an affidavit by Martin in which he summarized the findings of his investigation of the poll tax and jury lists in Pittsylvania County. They also appended a sworn statement by Waller which asserted that he had not paid his poll taxes and that he was unable to do so because of his economic status.[2]

The defense attorneys did not rest their argument with this factual assertion. Instead, they went on to challenge the validity of the provisions in the constitution and laws of Virginia establishing the poll tax. Their contention here was based on their interpretation of the Reconstruction statute of January 26, 1870, which had readmitted Virginia to representation in Congress. As a condition of readmission, that act stated that Virginia's constitution should never be changed "so as to deprive any citizen or class of citizens of the United States of the right to vote, who are entitled to vote by the constitution herein recognized." The constitution of 1870 had not provided for a poll tax. This had been done in the constitution of 1902 as a result of a constitutional convention whose avowed purpose had been to deprive Negroes, among others, of the right to vote, thus violating the conditions of the 1870 readmission act.[3]

They further held that although the constitution and laws of Virginia, as recently construed by the Supreme Court of Appeals, did not *expressly* make payment of poll taxes a qualification for service on juries, these had "been designed to permit them to be so administered."[4] This was due to "the wide discretion conferred upon judges and jury commissioners, in the selection of grand and petit jurors."[5] Thus, the actual *administration* of these provisions made payment of poll taxes a prerequisite for jury service, and such had been the case for the petit jury that had tried Waller. The fact that the constitution and laws of Virginia did not expressly make "the right to vote, and thereby the payment of poll taxes, a qualification of grand and petit jurors" was, they explained, the result of "an intent to evade the provision of certain Acts of Congress," specifically an 1875 statute prohibiting the exclusion from jury service of any person because of race, color, or previous condition of servitude.[6]

Their final argument in the petition was an assertion that the constitution and laws of Virginia were so administered as to systematically exclude from jury service "a numerous and wide-spread class of citizens otherwise qualified." Thus Negroes and sharecroppers, "because of their similar economic status, constitute a large proportion of the class of persons so barred as grand and petit jurors, and that the petitioner himself is of such economic class so barred."[7] For all of these reasons they concluded that Waller had been denied his right to "a trial by an impartial jury of his vicinage and has been deprived of his liberty, and would be deprived of his life, . . . without the judgment of his peers" in violation of Section Eight of the Bill of Rights of the constitution of Virginia, and that he had been denied due process of the law and the equal protection of the laws in violation of the Fourteenth Amendment to the Constitution of the United States.[8]

Beyond doubt, this petition had raised some troubling questions, and the arguments appeared to be considerably more compelling than those in the earlier petition for a writ of error. This time the defense had presented impressive evidence about the relationship of the poll tax to juries in Pittsylvania County and had established Waller's status as a non–poll tax payer. Whatever the motivation might have been in the selection of the grand and petit juries in the case of Odell Waller, the results had been the creation of juries composed of poll tax payers. On the petit jury this had meant the exclusion of people of his race and class. But even if the defense could convince the court of these facts, it was not clear that they constituted, by the standards of 1940–42, a violation of the Virginia constitution's guarantee of due process and equal protection of the laws of such magnitude as to call into doubt the legality of Waller's conviction and imprisonment and thus win his release on habeas corpus. Stone anticipated that the Supreme Court of Appeals of Virginia might not accept these arguments, for in his requests to Governor Price for a reprieve he indicated his intention to apply to the United States Supreme Court should the petition fail in the Virginia court. That did not take long to happen. On January 22, 1942, the Supreme Court of Appeals denied the petition for a writ of habeas corpus. It did not, however, specifically answer the defense's arguments. Rather, it merely stated that "the court having maturely considered the said petition and exhibits therewith, is of opinion that said writ of habeas corpus should not issue as prayed."[9]

Stone and Finerty immediately began preparations for an appeal to the United States Supreme Court. On February 10 Stone wrote to the new governor, Colgate W. Darden, Jr., to request a stay of execution to May 22 in order to allow adequate time for the new appeal to be heard. Stone hoped to be able to present the petition before March 20. Darden responded promptly. "It is not my desire to in any way close the opportunity for an appeal in this case," he wrote. "On the other hand, it is vital that there be no undue delay."[10] After discussing the governor's reply with Stone, Finerty also sent a letter to Darden explaining the difficulties involved in filing a petition with the Supreme Court of the United States. These included the submission of forty printed copies of the record before the Supreme Court of Appeals of Virginia, as well as any brief in support of the petition, and Stone was having trouble with the printer in getting the work done on such short notice. But the biggest problem was the time needed to prepare an adequate brief. As Finerty explained,

> The question to be passed on by the Supreme Court of the United States is novel, and will require fairly extensive discussion of the long series of cases in which that Court has considered what constitutes equal protection and due process of the law, in the constitution of grand and petit juries. The particular question raised in the Waller case has never been raised before that Court, and its decision will undoubtedly depend on what analogies it may draw from its prior decisions of related questions.[11]

Finerty also pointed out that he was heavily pressed for time because of his involvement in other cases, but he promised that he would do his best to file the brief and petition prior to March 20, and in any event no later than March 29.

Despite his busy schedule, Finerty assumed the leading role in preparing this appeal to the Supreme Court. But it was with Stone's cooperation. Writing to Darden again on February 14, Stone noted Finerty's extensive experience in such matters and insisted "that we are as anxious as the Commonwealth to see the important issues raised in the Waller trial settled at the earliest possible moment. I also wish to assure you that I join Mr. Finerty in being sincerely appreciative of the courtesy displayed both by your predecessor and yourself."[12] Darden continued to take a reasonable but firm position. "I am anxious to safeguard the rights of this individual in every way possible," he replied. "However," he continued, "I do not feel that the other engagements by Mr. Finerty should be allowed to interfere in this important matter," and he pressed Stone for the earliest possible submission of their brief to the Supreme Court.[13] Darden wrote to Finerty in a similar vein. Although he promised to give Waller "every opportunity to exhaust his legal remedies," he made it clear that he did not believe that other cases should come first.[14] Finerty assured the governor that he was giving precedence to the Waller case, except for a hearing before the Interstate Commerce Commission in New Orleans which the ICC had refused to postpone, and that he had "started drafting the petition for certiorari." Finerty worked with the assistance of Stone, Martin, and Shapiro, plus six volunteer lawyers who were doing research for the brief. "All of this effort can only be coordinated through me personally," Finerty insisted, adding that he was "in this case, as in the case of Tom Mooney, Sacco and Vanzetti and similar cases, serving entirely without fees".[15] Darden in turn promised that he would grant a reprieve, provided Finerty filed a copy of the petition with the attorney general of Virginia no later than March 10 and filed his brief with the Supreme Court "shortly thereafter."[16]

During the first three months of 1942 the work that was done by Finerty and others in preparing their petition to the United States Supreme Court was only part of the campaign to save Odell Waller. The WDL also stepped up its efforts to influence public opinion through advertisements and fliers. One of the pieces put out by the WDL was a one-page letter, dated February 13, 1942, that was signed by Alfred Bingham, A. J. Muste, Mary White Ovington, Freda Kirchwey, Frank Kingdon, George E. Haynes, and Carl Raushenbush, all individuals with a record of concern for social justice. Their letter stated: "We are asking the highest court in the land to decide the fate of a 24-year old Negro sharecropper. At the same time, the court will decide the fate of ten million whites and Negroes who, like him, cannot pay poll taxes." Odell Waller has been "sentenced to death for the self-defense shooting of his white farmer landlord." They requested their readers to write or wire to Governor Darden "asking him to grant a stay of execution," and they appealed for contributions to help defray the expenses of the appeal to the Supreme Court.[17] Another WDL publication of about this time was a two-page pamphlet that featured a picture of Annie Waller and an adjoining picture of Odell with the word "DOOMED!" in boldface under it. "Must Odell Waller, doomed to die unless you do something about it, be a sacrifice to an unjust legal and social system?" it asked. The pamphlet also referred to Waller's "self-defense shooting of his white landlord" and stressed the injustice of the sharecropper system, which results in "the total exclusion ten million Americans, white and black, from the democratic processes by the poll tax—79 per cent of the adult citizenry of eight Southern states."[18] Such publicity had an impact. For example, in February the governor's office reportedly received more than one thousand letters and wires from all over the country, many obviously sent in response to WDL appeals, urging commutation of the death sentence or further reprieve.[19]

Unfortunately, the growth of public interest in the Waller case was accompanied by a renewal of the dispute between the WDL and the Richmond Waller Defense Committee. Although Stone continued to cooperate with Finerty in the preparation of the petition to the Supreme Court, he had not abandoned his connections with the RWL. Thus, on February 1 he spoke in Chicago at a meeting of the Waller Defense Committee at which a resolution was passed "which condemned the poll tax, and the role of the Virginia Courts, the landlords, bankers, and their 'liberal' stooges."[20] On March 1, Stone also attended a "National Save Odell Waller Conference" that was held in Richmond under the sponsorship of the RWDC. Despite the impressive name given to the meeting, there were only seven official delegates. Stone was not one of them, although both he and Annie Waller addressed the gathering. The delegates voted to establish a committee to organize a Labor Defense Congress, whose purpose, according to Stone, was "to defend laborers of any type who are being politically persecuted or prosecuted." They then passed a number of resolutions, including ones calling for the release of the American Communist party leader Earl Browder from federal prison, the release of the remaining prisoners in the Scottsboro case, the release of political prisoners in India, and the acquittal of Odell Waller.[21] With typical exaggeration, *The Fighting Worker* asserted that the conference had "laid the basis for extending the fight for Waller's freedom to the U.S. Supreme Court." It also reported that the delegates had agreed with a position allegedly taken by Stone that, while the legal aspects were vital, "organized mass pressure [was] . . . decisive to win the case."[22] Just how such pressure could be used to influence the courts or the governor went unexplained.

The revival of interest in the Waller case by the RWL came as unwelcome news to the WDL which feared that it might endanger their relations with Governor Darden. As soon as he learned of the Richmond meeting, Finerty sent a telegram to Darden, with Shapiro's concurrence, in which he disassociated himself from the Waller Defense Committees and the Save Waller Conference. According to an account in *The Fighting Worker*, Finerty and Shapiro tried to get Stone to sign their telegram to Darden, but he refused, stating that "he was willing to work with all forces interested in Waller's freedom."[23] Frank McCallister also wrote to Darden to express the displeasure of the WDL with "the recent meeting and public statements of the so-called 'Waller Defense Committee' in Richmond."

> We want you to know, Governor, that the Workers Defense League, which is responsible for the defense of Odell Waller, has nothing to do with this committee, disapproves of the attitude taken by them, and so far as we know this group has gratuitously injected itself into this situation without any authorization from Odell Waller and we hope that their infantile antics will not be credited by you as representing the kind of people who are interested in this unfortunate tragedy.[24]

This particular episode had no apparent effect on the governor. On March 12, eight days before Waller's scheduled execution, Darden granted Waller his third reprieve, this time to May 19, on the grounds that the Supreme Court was unlikely to have a chance to act on his petition before March 20.[25]

The news of this latest reprieve was slow in reaching some interested parties. On March 18 the *New York Herald Tribune* published a long letter by a Sarah Cleghorn of Arlington, Vermont, which gave a highly sympathetic account of the story of Odell Waller. The letter, which was dated March 15, ended with an appeal for financial contributions to be sent to the WDL and a request that readers write to Governor Darden asking him "to extend Odell Waller's reprieve from March 20 far enough to let him live to see what the Supreme Court decides."[26] On the same page the *Herald Tribune* published an editorial entitled "A Test of Justice" which noted that Waller was scheduled to be executed on March 20 unless Darden granted him a reprieve. It expressed the hope that the Supreme Court would agree to hear the case and pass on the question of whether Waller was tried by a jury of his peers because of the poll tax issue. If Waller were to be granted a new trial as a result of a Supreme Court decision on this matter, the editorial concluded, at least then doubt about the justice of his trial and punishment would have been removed.[27]

The entry of a major New York newspaper into the public debate about the Waller case was itself noteworthy. And it had an effect. After the publication of the Cleghorn letter and the *Herald Tribune* editorial, letters and telegrams urging a reprieve, mostly from the New York area, flooded into Governor Darden's office.[28] But the fact that the *Herald Tribune* was unaware of the reprieve at the time it published its editorial greatly annoyed Darden. "In view of the gravity of this case," he wrote in a letter to the editor, "I regret that you did not take the trouble to ascertain what had occurred before writing the article."[29] Milgram was also bothered by the newspaper's gaffe, which, he feared, might adversely affect the governor's attitude toward the WDL. So he wrote to Darden and explained that, although the WDL had supplied information of the Waller case to the *Herald Tribune*, it had included a press release on the reprieve. Milgram expressed his regrets at any "inconvenience" the incident may have caused him and his appreciation, again, for the reprieve.[30]

Virginius Dabney was even more put out by the *Herald Tribune's* comments than Darden was. In an editorial entitled "Waller Case Phantasmagoria" he accused the New York newspaper of "going off half-cocked editorially." Not only was he annoyed by its failure to know of the third reprieve, he was upset by the *Herald Tribune's*, and especially Sarah Cleghorn's, understanding of the case. Nowhere, he complained, giving his view of the shooting, did either hint that Oscar Davis had been unarmed and that he had been shot twice in the back. Cleghorn's "outburst is of a piece with numerous others which have been perpetrated by defenders of Waller, among them the Workers Defense League of New York which regularly declares that Waller shot Davis 'in self-defense'. This despite the facts we have already recited. . . . His case is not helped by blasts from persons far removed from the scene who know little or nothing concerning the true facts."[31]

Dabney's response was itself open to criticism, however. As one anonymous letter writer, who claimed to be related to Oscar Davis, asserted, non-Virginians had a right to be critical of the state's judicial process. The writer also accused Dabney of arousing "prejudice against the organization defending Odell Waller, by consistently referring to it as the

'Workers Defense League of New York.'" It was a national organization, he explained, not just a New York one, and it had a southern division with headquarters in Atlanta.[32] Dabney responded that it was the New York headquarters of the WDL that claimed Waller shot in self-defense, so he wanted to distinguish it from the Atlanta division which, he said, was not making such a claim. He also insisted that he did recognize "the justice of the contention that in a case involving economic and social conflict, as this one does, the jury should contain members of both classes of society involved in the conflict."[33]

A few weeks later Dabney published another response to his March 21 editorial, this time from Aron S. Gilmartin, vice-chairman of the WDL. Defending the accuracy of the "overall impression" presented by Sarah Cleghorn's letter, he reviewed the debate over whether Oscar Davis had been unarmed, whether he had been shot in the back, and whether Henry Davis's testimony was reliable. On these points Dabney had sided with the prosecution's interpretation. It was at the center of his disagreement with the WDL and many other defenders of Waller. Gilmartin pointed out, however, that the WDL believed "that the killing was not premeditated" and "that Waller's self-defense testimony is credible according to the facts, whereas the testimony of young Henry Davis that Waller just up and shot Davis without a cross word passing between them, after being promised his wheat, is wholly incredible." Gilmartin emphasized that "the principal question . . . was the right to a trial by jury of one's peers." Had Waller been tried by such a jury, he concluded, the verdict would have been different.[34]

Still, the question remained whether Waller would ever get the chance to be retried by a jury that truly represented the different social and economic classes involved in the conflict. This was central to the objectives of the defense lawyers in appealing to the Supreme Court of the United States. On April 2, 1942, Finerty filed a petition with that court for a writ of certiorari to review the January 22 ruling of the Supreme Court of Appeals of Virginia. He accompanied it with an extensive supporting brief and by a shorter amicus curiae brief prepared by Thurgood Marshall for the American Civil Liberties Union. Finerty's petition summarized the arguments that had been presented to the Supreme Court of Appeals in December 1941 to the effect that the laws had been so administered in Pittsylvania County as to make the payment of poll taxes, and thus the right to vote, a qualification *in fact* for grand and petit juries. The question, therefore, was whether this constituted a violation of the clause of the Fourteenth Amendment guaranteeing equal protection of the laws. That provision, insisted Finerty, was not limited to "denial merely on account of race and color, but must of necessity extend to the systematic exclusion from jury service of an entire economic class such as that to which the petitioner belongs."[35]

In his accompanying brief Finerty developed at some length this interpretation of the equal protection clause and the facts regarding the systematic exclusion of non–poll tax payers from jury service. He also devoted several pages to the argument that the failure of Waller's attorney at the trial to offer any evidence of the exclusion of non–poll tax payers was no valid reason to deny certiorari. The petition, he pointed out, was not to review the October 13, 1941, judgment of the Supreme Court of Appeals; it was to review the dismissal by that court on January 22, 1942, of the petition for a writ of habeas corpus. In the latter instance that court had not contended that its dismissal was based on the failure of the defense to offer evidence of exclusion of non–poll tax payers at the trial. The distinction was important, for the scope of inquiry in habeas corpus proceedings was broader than those for a writ of error. "To hold that a court to which application for habeas corpus is made is confined to the record of the court below, and compelled to refuse competent proof upon habeas corpus of facts showing a deprivation of constitutional rights, would defeat the very purpose of that writ."[36] Thus, to contend that such facts pertaining to the exclusion of non–poll tax payers from jury service cannot now be established, because evidence of them was not presented at the trial, "would mean that the petitioner must be electrocuted, in violation of his constitutional rights, because of the assumed mistake of his trial counsel as to the procedure necessary to establish such violation."[37]

The state of Virginia viewed these issues entirely differently. In his brief in opposition to the petition for a writ of certiorari, Attorney General Staples insisted that there simply was no substantial federal question. He made two points. First, he insisted that, even if the facts alleged by Waller's lawyers "constituted a prohibited discrimination, the existence of such facts cannot be brought in issue for the first time and inquired into in *habeas corpus* proceedings." In particular, he insisted that it was an established principle that objections to the selection of jurors had to be made before a verdict is rendered.[38] Second, Staples scoffed at the notion that the payment of a poll tax of $1.50 drew such a line of cleavage between the residents of Pittsylvania County that would amount to class distinction in the selection of jurors. Some prosperous people failed to pay the poll tax, he claimed, while many of the poorest did pay it. Moreover, in his view the defense had failed to show that Waller was unable to pay the tax.[39] Staples also asserted that many states had prescribed property-owning and tax-paying qualifications for jury duty that had a greater exclusionary effect than the practices the defense complained about in Virginia. Thus, to grant certiorari in this case would cast doubt about the laws and judgments of several states. Finally, Staples even alluded to the war emergency to bolster his argument.

> Propaganda of internal dissension and the activation of latent prejudices are among the most powerful weapons available to enemies of the United States. They could ask nothing more than for this Court to countenance an attenuated theory of economic and racial persecution in a case where no such issue is actually involved. . . . Unquestionably the granting of certiorari by this Court would imply that there is some foundation for the petitioner's absurd theory that he is the victim of discriminatory laws and practices arising out of a conflict between economic classes, to the infinite detriment of public confidence in our government.[40]

Obviously, Finerty and Staples interpreted facts and legal precedents very differently. Both attempted to tailor previous decisions to support their objectives. But behind Finerty's court citations and legal rhetoric one could glimpse a deep concern over the conditions that had overwhelmed Odell Waller and placed his life in jeopardy. Admittedly, Staples had a different responsibility. Still, one cannot help but be struck by the abstractness of his argument and its detachment from human realities. Perhaps neither statutory law nor judicial interpretation provided a ready basis for dealing with the social and economic conditions that had to be grasped if one had any hope of comprehending the broader setting of the Waller tragedy. But Staples appeared to take a Procrustean approach in which human realities had to be trimmed away to fit preconceived legal molds. The result was that he could seriously dismiss as an "absurd theory" the notion that Waller was a victim of discriminatory laws and practices. It was a measure of the gulf that separated his world from that of the poor and dispossessed.

OUTLAW POLL TAX JURIES

Condemned by the Circuit Court of Appeals of Pittsylvania County, Virginia, his appeal for a trial by a jury of his peers rejected by the Virginia Supreme Court and the United States Supreme Court, Odell Waller, Negro sharecropper, is facing execution on June 19.

Tried by a jury from which were excluded all persons unable to pay Virginia's undemocratic poll tax, Odell Waller pleaded self-defense in the killing of his farmer landlord during an argument over crop shares in 1940.   His case was taken to the United States Supreme Court by the Workers Defense League, which presented affidavits proving that over 80 per cent of the population of Pittsylvania County, Virginia, did not pay the poll tax and were thereby barred from both grand and petit jury lists in the county.

SHARECROPPER WALLER

Before the United States Supreme Court, Workers Defense League Attorney John F. Finerty quoted the following from a previous decision of the court in Strauder vs. West Virginia:

"*The very idea of a jury is a body of men composed of peers or equals of the person whose rights it is selected or summoned to determine; that is, of his neighbors, fellows, associates, persons having the same legal status in society as that which he holds.*"

Odell Waller is a sharecropper. Most Virginia families like Waller's earn less than $600 a year, according to a 1941 report, "Rural Poverty in Virginia," by the Virginia Polytechnic Institute. Of the many Negroes in his county, only one in 125 cast a ballot. A citizen would often have to pay more than a week's income in order to vote. There were no sharecroppers on Odell Waller's jury.

In rejecting Waller's appeal for review, without opinion, the United States Supreme Court leaves

it in doubt on which of two grounds it so refused. It seems incredible that the highest court in the land would hold that Waller, or anyone else, can be legally tried by a jury from which his economic peers have been deliberately excluded. It seems even more incredible that the Court would directly hold that Waller must die solely because formal proof was not made in the Trial Court of the undenied fact that there was such deliberate exclusion. The Workers Defense League believes it the duty of the Court to consider whether Waller must die for either reason and, if so, to state which.

Governor Colgate W. Darden, Jr., of Virginia, has granted Waller a 31-day stay of execution to June 19. During this time, the Workers Defense League is presenting a final petition for re-hearing to the United States Supreme Court. Favorable action by the Court would set a precedent for a more democratic method of jury selection in Virginia, and save Odell Waller's life.

There is Still Time to Save Odell Waller!

SEND YOUR CONTRIBUTION NOW. *RUSH IT TODAY TO GEORGE S. COUNTS, Treasurer, WORKERS DEFENSE LEAGUE, 112 EAST 19th STREET, NEW YORK, N. Y.*

Among the prominent citizens supporting the Workers Defense League in its fight to save Waller:

ALFRED M. BINGHAM	GEORGE E. HAYNES	FREDA KIRCHWEY	ARTHUR GARFIELD HAYS
J. R. BUTLER	MARY W. HILLYER	A. J. MUSTE	OSWALD HARRISON VILLARD
MARY WHITE OVINGTON	PAUL KELLOGG	A. PHILIP RANDOLPH	BRUCE BLIVEN
JOHN DEWEY	FRANK KINGDON	WALTER WHITE	REINHOLD NEIBUHR
		JOSEPH SCHLOSSBERG	

FOR MORE DETAILS ON WALLER'S CASE, READ "ALL FOR MR. DAVIS" BY PAULI MURRAY AND MURRAY KEMPTON; PREFACE BY FRANK P. GRAHAM, PRESIDENT OF THE UNIVERSITY OF NORTH CAROLINA. 5c PER COPY, 30 FOR $1.00.

ODELL WALLER MUST NOT DIE

Workers Defense League flier, May 1942.

Unfortunately for Waller, the Supreme Court showed no inclination to attempt to bridge that gap. On May 4, 1942, it denied, without explanation, his petition for a writ of certiorari.[41] It was a stunning blow to the hopes of Waller and his defenders, and it meant that, unless another reprieve could be obtained, Waller faced execution on May 19. Immediately after receiving word of the court's refusal to review the case, Finerty telephoned and wrote to Governor Darden to ask for a reprieve in order to allow him time to apply to the Supreme Court for a rehearing of the denial of certiorari and to appeal to that court for an original writ of habeas corpus.[42] Once again the governor responded favorably. On May 6, Darden granted Waller his fourth reprieve, this time until June 19, 1942.[43] Darden appeared to be willing to give Waller's lawyers ample opportunity to exhaust the legal processes, and for this Finerty was certainly grateful. As he told Virginius Dabney, "I have never experienced such humane and unselfish consideration as Governor Darden has extended to Waller." But Finerty needed all the time he could get as he kept at work "day and night" preparing his petition for a rehearing.[44] It was not a mere delaying tactic; rather it was one based on his deep concern about righting an injustice. As McCallister noted, "Mr. Finerty feels so strong about the principle of the thing that he is risking a possible citation for contempt in applying for a rehearing of the writ."[45]

Despite their failures in the courts, Waller's defenders remained hopeful. To be sure, many in the WDL recognized from the start that his case had its ambiguities and troubling aspects, beginning with the admitted fact that Waller had shot Oscar Davis. Still, they also knew that the conflict between Waller and Oscar Davis was rooted in such obvious social and economic evils that only the most callous could view the killing as a simple instance of premeditated murder. Surely, they seemed to be saying, a just and rational society, when made aware of the circumstances, could not conclude that Waller had been justly condemned or that justice demanded the taking of his life. "We have faith in your ultimate vindication," Milgram wrote to Waller, "as the victim of a system which pits man against man."[46]

The larger issues were by no means lost on Odell Waller. Although his letters showed the limitations of his formal education, they frequently indicated his ability to grasp the main point quickly or to suggest an insight into the broader problems. As the case dragged on, Annie Waller did her best to keep him informed through letters and occasional visits at the prison in Richmond. Milgram and others in the WDL also wrote to him or sent him reading matter from time to time. But Waller knew painfully well that he was just hanging on from reprieve to reprieve. In a letter explaining the latest reprieve, that to June 19, Milgram expressed considerable shock at the refusal of the Supreme Court to review his case, but he also let Waller know that they were keeping up the legal fight.[47] Odell was grateful for the WDL's efforts, but it was not easy for him to remain hopeful. "I was glad to hear from you and to no all of you still have your sholder to the wheel trying to help all you can yes seems like all the bad breaks is against me some how," he replied.[48]

Some of the other reactions to the Supreme Court's rejection of Waller's appeal were very different from those expressed by members of the WDL. Indeed, it came as welcome news to the *Danville Register*, which proclaimed that the court's decision "should convince the public generally that the Negro share-cropper has been given a fair and impartial trial." Thus the *Register* interpreted the decision to mean that "Virginia justice has been given the stamp of approval by the highest court in the land."[49] Virginius Dabney's response was more circumspect. In an editorial in the *Richmond Times-Dispatch* he regretted that the court was unable to rule on the question of whether non–poll tax payers had actually been systematically excluded from jury service in Pittsylvania County. But he erroneously asserted that the court had held that, because the poll tax issue was not raised in the trial, it could not be raised later in a habeas corpus proceeding. As before, Dabney criticized the WDL for its assertion that Waller had shot in self-defense. Although he saw injustices in both the poll tax and the sharecropper systems, he expressed little sympathy for Waller or for the defense's interpretation of his case.[50]

Once again Dabney's editorial provoked Stone, who responded with a long, three-page letter that he hoped would be published in the *Times-Dispatch*. Stone correctly observed that the Supreme Court gave no reason for its decision, and thus it did not directly speak to the question of whether the poll tax–jury issue could be raised in later habeas corpus proceedings. Again Stone argued that the evidence on the self-defense issue was evenly balanced quantitatively between the testimony of Waller and Henry Davis, but qualitatively weighted in Waller's favor, given the incredible aspects of Henry Davis's testimony. Finally Stone defended himself at length against the charge that he had not raised the poll tax issue at the trial. Stone was correct on this point. It was not that he had failed to raise the poll tax issue at the trial, as Dabney's editorial seemed to imply. Rather it was his failure to offer proof that the jury had been selected from poll tax payers. Compared with some of his earlier letters to Dabney, Stone wrote with restraint. Still, he concluded with the declaration "that this case is a class struggle between the exploited and the exploiters of the countryside. But you stand on the side of the exploiters, and I on the side of the exploited. . . . But, it seems to me that ordinary human decency would dictate that you do not continue to use the editorial columns of your paper against a helpless prisoner without at least giving his counsel opportunity to correct your, shall we say misunderstandings."[51] Dabney dismissed Stone's letter as a "characteristic tirade" and refused to publish it.[52]

Frank McCallister was also displeased by Dabney's editorial, but his response was quite different from Stone's. "In order to understand what probably happened," he wrote to Dabney, "we must face realistically the status of a Negro to his white landlord and take into account that when Negroes get swindled and protest, they know they are protesting, in many cases, at great personal risk and this I think accounts for Waller's arms." Given the doubts in the case, McCallister did not believe that the death sentence was justified, and "I don't believe a jury drawn from all sections of the population in that community including sharecroppers and possibly Negroes would render such a verdict."[53] McCallister was on friendly terms with Dabney, and it is possible that his polite and careful comments may have influenced Dabney's thinking about the Waller case in ways that all of Stone's bluster could never have achieved. But McCallister was well aware of the difficulty of changing Dabney's opinion, and, he wrote to Milgram, "God knows, if we can't get people like Virginius Dabney on our side on an issue of this kind, we have a fat chance with the average southerner."[54]

Another concern of the WDL was the continuing need to raise money to support the league's publicity campaign and legal maneuvers. Even with the lawyers donating their services, the court proceedings were a steady financial drain. In May the WDL again called upon Annie Waller to assist with the fund raising. At the beginning of the month it brought her to New York for a week or more of speaking engagements in that area. On May 9 she left for a tour of several cities in the East and Midwest, with special attention on Chicago from May 11 to 16 and Detroit from May 17 to 19. As Pauli Murray was then attending law school, Mrs. Waller was accompanied on this trip by J. R. Butler, a former president of the Southern Tenant Farmers' Union who had just joined the staff of the WDL as a field secretary. In addition, Frank McCallister made himself available for speaking appearances in the Washington-Baltimore area.[55]

NATIONAL HEADQUARTERS

WORKERS DEFENSE LEAGUE

NATIONAL
EXECUTIVE BOARD

The Officers and:

IRVING ASTROW
J. R.-BUTLER
GRACE CARLSON
PAUL R. CHRISTOPHER
FRANZ DANIEL
MAX DELSON
JOHN F. FINERTY
MARY D. HAPGOOD
FRANCIS HEISLER
SIDNEY HERTZBERG
JULIUS HOCHMAN

BELLA KUSSY
ALFRED B. LEWIS
PAULI MURRAY
WALTER PASNICK
RALPH G. ROSS
JOSEPH SCHLOSSBERG
WILLIAM STERN
MORRIS SHAPIRO
TUCKER P. SMITH
ISABEL TAYLOR
JAMES WECHSLER

LOUIS YAGODA

112 EAST 19TH STREET • NEW YORK • ALgonquin 4-4954

OFFICERS

CARL RAUSHENBUSH_____Chairman
ARON S. GILMARTIN_____Vice Chairman
LAURENCE T. HOSIE_____Vice Chairman
LAYLE LANE_____Vice Chairman
GEORGE S. COUNTS_____Treasurer

STAFF

MORRIS MILGRAM_____National Secretary
J. R. BUTLER_____Field Secretary
ALICE DODGE_____Administrative Secretary
MARY R. SCHNEIDER_____Research Director
HENRY G. BABCOCK_____Church Com. Secretary
   242 E. 14th St., N.Y.C. ALgonquin 4-2361
MILTON KRAMER_____Midwest Secretary
   180 W. Washington St., Chicago
MARY GALLAGHER_____West Coast Secretary
   474 S. Hartford St., Los Angeles
FRANK McCALLISTER_____Southern Secretary
   313 Palmer Bldg., Atlanta, Ga.

Emergency Appeal!

May 15, 1942

Dear Friend:

The United States Supreme Court just refused, without opinion, to review the case of Odell Waller, young Negro sharecropper who now awaits execution in Virginia for shooting his farmer landlord in a dispute over crop shares. As the enclosed leaflet makes clear, this is a case of deepest concern to every person interested in maintaining American democracy.

The jury that tried Waller was composed entirely of white poll tax payers. Every man too poor to pay a poll tax was systematically excluded from both the grand and petit juries.

Governor Colgate W. Darden, Jr., of Virginia has most humanely granted a stay of execution to June 19, so that the United States Supreme Court may act on a petition for rehearing now being prepared by Workers Defense League attorneys.

Odell Waller's life must be saved.

The United States Supreme Court must be persuaded, if possible, to decide squarely whether a trial by a jury of his peers is the constitutional right of every accused American citizen.

In its two-year battle for Waller's life, through state courts to the highest court in the land, the Workers Defense League has been put to heavy expense. Now the case is at its most crucial stage. Your help is needed urgently.

Your dollars may save Odell Waller's life and will help strengthen democracy on the home front. Act now. Send your contribution to George S. Counts, Treasurer, Workers Defense League, 112 East 19th Street, New York, N. Y.

Sincerely yours,

Alfred M. Bingham   Bruce Bliven   John Dewey   George E. Haynes   Arthur Garfield Hays

Adolph Held   Frank Kingdon   Freda Kirchwey   Maynard C. Krueger   Bishop Francis J. McConnell

Reinhold Niebuhr   Mary White Ovington   A. Philip Randolph   Joseph Schlossberg   Oswald Garrison Villard

The "Emergency Appeal!" of the Workers Defense League, May 15, 1942.

On May 15 the WDL issued an "Emergency Appeal" for the contributions to cover the heavy legal expenses involved in Finerty's efforts for a rehearing. "Odell Waller's life must be saved," the appeal declared. "The United States Supreme Court must be persuaded, if possible, to decide squarely whether a trial by a jury of his peers is the constitutional right of every accused American citizen." The appeal was signed by an impressive array of prominent citizens, including John Dewey, Arthur Garfield Hays, Reinhold Neibuhr, A. Philip Randolph, and Oswald Garrison Villard.[56]

Shortly afterwards John Dewey again played a useful role by writing a letter on the Waller case that was published in the *New York Times* on May 19. "Once more," he began, "our colored citizens, already deeply aroused over discrimination against them in the armed forces and defense industries, have been presented with a grievance." Referring to the Supreme Court's decision of May 4, Dewey claimed that "colored people regard this unexplained refusal as just one more evidence that when white people speak of fighting to preserve freedom, they mean freedom for their own race." Dewey then gave a short summary of the case that was sympathetic to Waller's claim of self-defense. He also noted that "the Virginia Constitution makes the payment of a $1.50 poll tax for three consecutive years the test of a citizen's qualification to vote." Dewey acknowledged that strictly as a matter of law such a poll tax payment was not a prerequisite for jury service. But he insisted that if payment of the poll tax was *in fact* a condition of jury service, as the defense has proved, then the argument about the requirement in law was "obviously technical and irrelevant." And he was right on the mark when he asserted that Waller, "a colored man disenfranchised by poverty, was convicted by a jury of white voters, ten of them farmers employing sharecroppers." It was vital, insisted Dewey, "that the Supreme Court either grant the petition for a rehearing or state its reasons for refusing." If it does not, "the effect will certainly be to weaken the faith of the poor—and especially poor Negroes—in the democratic process." Dewey observed "that both the slayer and the slain were victims of the economic forces which for some decades have exerted terrible pressure on both the white and colored farmers. . . . In dealing with this profoundly tragic issue we must invoke something better than the law of 'an eye for an eye and a tooth for a tooth.' It calls for compassion—for mercy." He ended with the hope that, should all legal appeals fail, Governor Darden would commute the sentence.[57]

Coming from a person of such stature, Dewey's eloquent letter certainly had an impact. For example, it prompted Nobel Prize–winning novelist Pearl S. Buck to submit her own letter to the *Times* a few days later in which she wrote that "Odell Waller has ceased to be an individual, he has become a personification of all those to whom democracy is denied in our country."[58] It also was a factor in Eleanor Roosevelt's decision to write another letter to the governor (she had previously written to Governor Price). Justice Felix Frankfurter called her attention to Dewey's letter and suggested that if the Supreme Court rejected the appeal it would be appropriate for her to write to Darden to urge clemency and to enclose Dewey's letter.[59] At about the same time, A. Philip Randolph asked her to meet with a number of black and white leaders who hoped to enlist her "humanitarian interest in this outrageous miscarriage of justice.[60] Mrs. Roosevelt did not grant Randolph's request, but on June 2 she did send a rather circumspect letter to Darden. In it she noted that she had received "a great many letters about Odell Waller," and that the woman who made the original investigation (Pauli Murray) felt strongly that he should not be executed. She enclosed a copy of Dewey's letter and observed that "if the facts as stated by Dr. Dewey are true, I hope very much that you will be able to go over the case very carefully as it has created a great deal of feeling among both white and colored people and it may have not only national but international implications."[61]

If Governor Darden paid any attention to such a letter it was undoubtedly due to the prominence of its author, not its contents. Mrs. Roosevelt's caution was also shown by her rejection of all efforts to get her further involved in the case at that time. She refused to meet with Morris Shapiro, who wished to discuss with her steps to aid Waller, nor would she even allow her letter to Darden to be made public.[62] Nevertheless, when the Danville *Bee* discovered that she had written to the governor it immediately published an angry editorial attacking her "gratuitous intrusion" into "matters which really do not concern her." It warned that if the president didn't restrain his wife's "sociological impulses" he risked losing the support of the people of the South.[63]

Although Mrs. Roosevelt's modest letter hardly merited such a response, the *Bee*'s reaction was typical of that of many white Virginians in the face of the public criticism, especially from outside the state, of the case of Odell Waller. And by the middle of May national interest in the case, most of it highly critical, was more widespread and intense than ever before. To that extent the WDL's campaign was having an effect. Ultimately, however, its efforts to save Odell Waller depended not on the degree of popular interest in his case but on its success in the courts, or in the last instance, its ability to sway the opinion of Governor Darden. By the beginning of June there were only a few legal options left for the defense lawyers, although they were determined to pursue every possible approach. First was the petition to the Supreme Court for a rehearing, but an attempt to influence the governor was very much a part of the defense's tactics.

7

"To Vindicate Virginia Justice":
June 1942

For Waller's defenders June 1942 became a month of accelerated activity and crucial decisions. All phases of their efforts—from the courtroom, to fund raising, to public relations, to petitions and appeals—took place more or less simultaneously. Within a two-and-a-half-week period the defense lawyers argued their case before the whole gamut of federal courts, from the Supreme Court back to the District Court to the Court of Appeals, and then back to the chief justice. Thanks largely to the efforts of the WDL the case of Odell Waller had become a cause célèbre not only in Virginia but throughout much of the nation. For many blacks, certainly, it was a symbol of the limitations of American democracy, the continuing blight of racial discrimination and poverty. The campaign to defend Odell Waller had helped call attention once again to these problems, but as the end of the month neared it had still not achieved its primary goal. The battle to save Waller's life was not yet over.

As the month of June began, the immediate attention of Waller's defenders was focused on the petition to the Supreme Court for a rehearing of its denial of certiorari. Finerty had filed the petition on May 25. At the request of Waller's pastor, the Reverend Robert Gilbert of the Fairview Baptist Church in Gretna, the Baptist Ministerial Alliance and the International Ministers Alliance, which represented black churches in the New York metropolitan area, voted to appoint Sunday, May 31, as a day of prayer—prayer that Waller would be granted a new trial by a jury of his peers.[1] Assistance of a more tangible sort was offered by the many organizations and individuals who signed an amici curiae brief, prepared by Arthur Garfield Hays and Thurgood Marshall, in support of the petition for a hearing. Signers included the WDL, the NAACP, the National

Urban League, the ACLU, the Union for Democratic Action, the Brotherhood of Sleeping Car Porters, the Negro Labor Committee, the United Transport Service Employees of America, and the Southern Tenant Farmers' Union. Signing as members of a citizens committee were Bruce Bliven, Van Wyck Brooks, Henry Sloan Coffin, John Dewey, Harry Emerson Fosdick, Frank P. Graham, John Haynes Holmes, Freda Kirchwey, Francis J. McConnell, and Oswald Garrison Villard.[2]

As the Supreme Court had given no explanation for its denial of Waller's appeal, it had left a number of important constitutional questions unanswered. For example, in the selection of members of grand and petit juries, was the equal protection clause of the Fourteenth Amendment limited to a prohibition against a systematic exclusion solely because of race and color? If it were not so limited, did it extend to the exclusion of an entire economic class to which Waller belonged? And if it did extend to the latter, must a petitioner die "solely because of the error of his trial counsel as to the procedure necessary to establish the undenied and undeniable facts of such exclusion?"[3] As Layle Lane, vice-chairman of the WDL and head of its Harlem branch, declared: "The high court decision on Waller's case is a blow to Negro rights. But it is also a slap at every poor man, white or Negro, who asks for real democracy in America. We think we have a right to know whether the Supreme Court's refusal to hear the case means that the court thinks it is perfectly all right to bar poor people generally, or any other group of people from jury service."[4] Many Americans shared these sentiments.

In his petition for a rehearing, Finerty requested the United States Supreme Court either to order the Supreme Court of Appeals of Virginia to issue a writ of habeas corpus or to "expressly recognize petitioner's right to obtain a writ of habeas corpus either from the United States District Court for the Eastern District of Virginia or from this Court itself."[5] At the same time, Finerty also submitted a motion for leave to file an original petition for a writ of habeas corpus and a petition for a writ of habeas corpus.[6] He included these because of the narrow time constraints he then faced. May 26 was the last date of that term when the Supreme Court would accept motions. If the court denied his petition for a rehearing, and if the Federal District Court and the Circuit Court of Appeals also denied petitions for a writ of habeas corpus, there would then have been no time to act before Waller's scheduled execution date of June 19.[7]

Finerty's multiple petitions suggested that he was far from being confident that the Supreme Court would reverse itself and show sympathy for Waller. But he and many others certainly hoped that they could at least elicit some sort of an opinion or explanation from the court. As *The New Republic* warned, "Whatever the Court's decision in this instance, failure to explain it with an opinion will be a grave blunder, for this case has gone too far for silence."[8] A. Philip Randolph, the head of the Brotherhood of Sleeping Car Porters and the organizer of the March on Washington movement, expressed a view widely shared among black Americans. "The Waller case is a test case for American democracy. If the Supreme Court once more refuses without explanation—as it did on May 4th—to review this case, its action will be interpreted by colored citizens as a refusal to concern itself with that denial of their Constitutional rights which keeps them in the category of second class citizens. . . . For the sake of justice, for the sake of American democracy, Odell Waller must not die!"[9]

Such pleas again went unanswered. On June 1, 1942, the Supreme Court, without opinion, denied both the petition for a rehearing and the motion for leave to file a petition for a writ of habeas corpus.[10] The court's summary rejection of both motions, again without any explanation, outraged and frustrated Waller's defenders. The WDL promptly issued a statement of protest that was signed by those groups and individuals who had signed or endorsed the amici curiae brief:

> This case not only involves justice for Waller; it involves the whole Southern practice of creating a second-class citizenship by means of the poll tax. At this moment, when America is embattled to defend the 'four freedoms', the Supreme Court has twice evaded this vital and inescapable issue. Twice it has, in effect, condemned Odell Waller to die in the dark. It is difficult to understand how the Court can remain silent on an issue which affects millions of Americans, both white and colored.[11]

Others agreed. An editorial in *Opportunity*, the journal of the National Urban League, warned that "the faith of the Negro in the American Democracy is being stretched to the breaking point. . . . Added to the indefensible and shameless segregation and discrimination in the armed forces and the widespread and cruel exclusion of Negroes from defense industry has now come the crushing disappointment in the refusal of the United States Supreme Court to grant the application for rehearing in the case of Odell Waller." The editorial particularly lamented the failure of the court to issue an opinion. "From the legal standpoint . . . [this omission] may be perfectly proper. From the social standpoint in this crucial period it cannot be said to have been the way of wisdom."[12] *The Nation* came to a similar conclusion and condemned the refusal to review the case as "a shocking evasion of an issue the court should face." It also quoted with approval the statement issued by the WDL.[13] A. Philip Randolph's reaction was similar, if predictable. "The second unexplained refusal of the U.S. Supreme Court to consider Waller's appeal for equal protection of the laws only serves to deepen our sense of injustice and strengthen our resolve to save this victim of 'poll-tax' justice." Randolph pledged his continued support of the Workers Defense League in its fight for justice for Waller. "Poll-tax justice may be good enough for the Supreme Court. It is not good enough for the colored citizens of America. And it is not good enough for American democracy."[14]

Such sentiments, no matter how deeply felt and passionately expressed, had no effect on the stark reality confronting Odell Waller. The options left to his defenders had been severely narrowed. If they could find no relief in the courts, then their last hope would be to seek a commutation of the death sentence from Governor Darden. In the meantime, however, Finerty prepared to file a petition for a writ of habeas corpus with Judge Robert N. Pollard of the United States District Court in Richmond. This was done on June 10. Finerty was assisted by two Virginia attorneys who were new to the case, Edmund M. Preston and Francis V. Lowden, Jr., of Richmond. Stone and Martin, who had continued as Waller's counsel through the petitions submitted to the Supreme Court on May 25, no longer participated. Of these two new lawyers, Preston played the more important role. A respected local attorney, Preston had experience as a trial lawyer, a corporation counsel, and a specialist in labor relations problems. According to Pauli Murray, Preston agreed to help defend Waller only after Stone's withdrawal from the case. Like Stone, Preston provided the necessary Virginia bar affiliation, but he was distinctly different in prestige, manner, and ideology. He proved to be an able and committed counsel during the final weeks of the struggle.[15]

In his argument in support of his petition for a writ of habeas corpus, Finerty held that there had been two distinct violations of Waller's con-

stitutional right of due process and equal protection of the law. The first
was that Waller had been indicted and tried by juries from which non-
payers of poll taxes had been systematically excluded and that Waller
was a member of a widespread class of people in Pittsylvania County
who, because of their economic disabilities, were unable to pay the poll
tax. Thus they were debarred in law from voting and in fact from jury
service. Finerty had, of course, used the same argument in seeking a writ
of habeas corpus from the United States Supreme Court. It had also
been part of his argument when he sought a similar writ from the Supreme Court of Appeals of Virginia. But he now added a second ground,
one that he called an "important variation." This was "the refusal of the
Supreme Court of Appeals of Virginia and the other courts of Virginia to
grant us a remedial judicial process for such violation by the Circuit
Court of Pittsylvania of petitioner's constitutional rights."[16]

In developing this second argument, Finerty began by conceding that
it was an established principle that habeas corpus could not be used to
correct the errors of counsel. However, because the Supreme Court had
"held that the constitutional rights of an accused could not be waived
except by the express and intelligent consent of the accused . . . in my
opinion they could not be waived by the unintelligent non-assent in this
case of counsel because counsel . . . seasonably raised the constitutional
question." The record was indeed clear that Stone had objected at
Waller's trial to the drawing of the grand jury exclusively from poll tax
payers and to the exclusion of non–poll tax payers from the petit jury
panel. The problem had been that Stone had not presented evidence to
prove the facts of such exclusion. Now, however, Finerty suggested for
the first time that Stone might not have even been guilty of an error
here, because "those facts were and must be known to the Court itself,
because they appear in the records of the Court, and, therefore, that the
Court was chargeable with knowledge of the facts and it would have
been a useless gesture to have proved the facts." Even if Stone had committed an error in failing to prove these facts, "that error of counsel
cannot be the equivalent of express and intelligent waiver of constitutional rights by the accused himself and, therefore, it was the duty of the
Circuit Court of Pittsylvania County . . . to have preserved such constitutional rights and that it was certainly the affirmative duty of the Supreme
Court of Appeals of Virginia, if not on a writ of error, then on a writ of
habeas corpus, to have preserved those rights." By failing to do this,
Finerty concluded, the trial court initially, and the Supreme Court of

Appeals subsequently, had denied Waller due process of law and the equal protection of the law.[17]

Responding for the state, Assistant Attorney General Kelly acknowledged that Finerty had raised some "interesting and academic questions." But "the real point is whether or not there is anything to be accomplished by your Honor granting the writ in this case other than the protraction of the perfectly shocking delay which has already occurred in this case."[18] Kelly would not concede the principal factual contention of the defense that there had been a systematic exclusion of non–poll tax payers from the juries. But even if this had been the case it did not necessarily follow that this would have been "a vicious effort to subjugate and persecute a class." Rather, it could be regarded as a "reasonable classification," not an unconstitutional discrimination.[19] Furthermore, Kelly contended that several other states, including "Mr. Finerty's New York," placed heavier property qualifications for jury service than Virginia's $1.50 poll tax payment, yet convictions in criminal cases from those states have been upheld by the Supreme Court.[20]

Finerty, of course, believed that the effect of the poll tax was indeed to discriminate against Negroes and the poor. In 1940, he noted, the average cash earning of Negroes in Pittsylvania County was between $145 and $200. Of these people, 80 percent had not paid the poll tax, and most of them, like Waller, could not pay the tax.[21] Kelly did not agree. At the very least, he said, the defense would have to prove that Waller belonged to that class which was allegedly discriminated against, and he would not concede that this had been proven. Indeed, Kelly asserted that Waller "was neither unable to pay the poll tax nor a sharecropper." The basis for this astonishing statement was the fact that at the time of the shooting Waller "was working on a salary in Baltimore."[22] By playing on such a technicality, Kelly demonstrated his ability to equate superficial form with underlying substance. But he also revealed once again the huge gulf that existed between the state's and the defense's understanding of economic and social conditions in Pittsylvania County.

Most of Finerty's oral presentation was a carefully worded, finely drawn argument that was designed to show, through his analysis of statutes and recent court decisions, that Waller's constitutional rights had indeed been violated. But this was far more than an intellectual exercise for him, and at times his emotions showed as he departed from his main lines of argument. Particularly revealing was his attack on Stone's handling of the case at the trial. It was the first time he had made such criticism in public. "I do not agree that Waller should be hanged for the errors of his counsel," he stated, "and the errors of his counsel in the trial court did not stop with the failure to prove the facts of exclusion. They included baiting the judge and, most of all, they included a complete failure to cross-examine the State's witnesses on the most salient questions, a complete failure to cross-examine the medical witnesses on the incidence of wounds, and so forth." Although this criticism was not relevant to his petition for a writ of habeas corpus, Finerty's frustration was evident, and it bolstered his belief that the trial was botched. "No one, on the record before the Circuit Court of Pittsylvania County, can reach an intelligent conclusion as to whether he was guilty or not and, therefore, so far as the merits are involved here Waller certainly has not been convicted by a record beyond a reasonable doubt."[23]

Oral arguments were concluded on June 11. Later that same day, Judge Pollard issued a decision rejecting Finerty's petition. After summarizing the various stages of the appeals that had been followed since Waller's trial, he stated that

> an examination of the allegations of the petition convinces me that the petitioner is not entitled to have a writ of habeas corpus issue. In other words, the allegations of the petition, if proven, would not entitle the petitioner to be released from prison.
>
> The gist of the petitioner's complaint is that the grand jury which indicted him and the petit jury which tried petitioner were selected by a method which discriminated against a particular group, namely, non-payers of poll taxes, the basis for such charge of discrimination being that the grand and petit jurors were selected from persons who had paid their poll taxes, while petitioner was a non-payer of poll taxes. These facts, if proven would not, in my opinion, amount to a discrimination in the trial procedure of the State of Virginia which is forbidden by the Constitution of the United States. It would be a violent presumption to conclude that the petitioner who had not paid his poll taxes had been denied equal protection of the law because the officers charged with the selection of jury lists had selected only those who had paid their poll taxes.[24]

In short, the effort of the defense to convince the courts that there had been an economic and class discrimination in the selection of the juries that had amounted to a violation of the due process and equal protection of the laws clauses of the Fourteenth Amendment had failed.

In addition to denying the writ of habeas corpus, Pollard also rejected Finerty's request that he certify that there was probable cause for an appeal to the United States Circuit Court of Appeals. Finerty tried hard to get Pollard to change his mind on this point, claiming that without such a certificate it would place a great burden on him, as he would have to apply to each judge individually, and that there was a great time pressure with Waller scheduled to be executed on June 19. But Pollard was adamant, insisting that Finerty's right to apply to a judge of the Circuit Court was an adequate procedure. There was enough time, he said, because the Fourth Circuit Court of Appeals would be sitting in Asheville, North Carolina, on Monday, Tuesday, and Wednesday of the next week, June 15 to 17.[25]

Finerty immediately met with Governor Darden and asked for another reprieve. But, after consulting with Attorney General Staples, Darden announced, on the evening of June 11, that he would not grant Waller a new reprieve. There was still "ample time," he claimed, for the defense to present its case to the United States Circuit Court on Monday, June 15.[26] Although pressed by other legal engagements, Finerty, accompanied by Preston, traveled to Asheville to present the application for a certificate of probable cause for the allowance of an appeal with the Circuit Court. It was an exercise in futility. On June 16 the three-judge court denied the application. After summarizing the legal steps that had taken place in the Waller case, the judges held "that all of the questions raised by the petitioner herein have been repeatedly and maturely considered by the courts hereinbefore mentioned . . . and found to be without merit" and that they too believed "that the petition filed is entirely without merit."[27] For Waller's defenders, such a flat rejection of the petition, with the assertion that the issues had been maturely considered, was close to a mockery, given the failure of the United States Supreme Court even to issue an opinion on the case.

By the next day, June 17, there were less than forty-eight hours remaining before Waller's scheduled execution. In one more desperate legal maneuver, Finerty and Preston decided to apply to Chief Justice Harlan Fiske Stone of the United States Supreme Court for permission to appeal to the United States Circuit Court of Appeals. After making arrangements to see Stone, who was then staying at the Homestead in Hot Springs, Virginia, they chartered an airplane to fly them from Asheville to Hot Springs. But at the last minute their plane was commandeered by the United States Army, so, accompanied by a police escort, they sped the 360 miles by automobile. They arrived late in the evening and discovered that a wartime blackout was in effect, so they had to argue their case in Stone's darkened hotel room with only one small bed light allowed. Although Stone was sympathetic, he rejected their request. Finerty then asked for a stay of execution in order to permit him to apply to the full Supreme Court for a writ of certiorari. This too Stone rejected.[28] Shortly afterwards, Finerty and Preston issued a statement that explained Stone's reasons for denying these requests:

> As Waller's counsel understand it, the Chief Justice felt that the Federal Court in habeas corpus proceedings could not consider whether Waller's constitutional rights had been violated because of the error of Waller's trial counsel in failing to offer evidence at his trial in State Court of the fact of such violation. Thus the Federal Courts are held powerless, because of the error of Waller's trial counsel, to prevent Waller's execution even if his constitutional rights have in fact been violated. Counsel do not believe this doctrine in this case consistent with fundamental justice. Their only remaining hope is that under such circumstances Governor Darden will act to prevent Waller's execution.[29]

Stone's decision should have come as no surprise, for Finerty had spoken to him some two weeks earlier, on June 3, at which time the chief justice stated "that the court did not feel it could undertake in habeas corpus to correct errors of counsel." Obviously Finerty failed to convince Stone, just as he failed with the United States District Court on June 10-11, to accept his argument "that error of counsel is not the equivalent of the express and intelligent waiver of constitutional rights by the accused."[30]

With no apparent legal options left to the defense, it appeared that the struggle had at last come to an end. Unless the governor intervened, Waller would die on June 19. In these critical moments Darden received numerous appeals to commute the sentence to life imprisonment or to grant an additional reprieve. To the surprise of some, on June 18, Darden announced that he was granting Waller another reprieve—his fifth—this time until July 2, 1942. At the same time he issued a statement explaining that he was doing this, at the request of Waller's counsel, in order to hold a special commutation hearing on Monday, June 29.[31] It was an extraordinary procedure, and one that, on its face, suggested that

Darden was still troubled by some feature of the case. Thus the defense was to be given one more opportunity to save Odell Waller, with the final life-or-death decision resting in Darden's hands.

Until that time, the WDL and other Waller defenders were determined to continue their public appeals in hopes that these might ultimately have some effect on the governor. The results of their efforts of May and June were impressive, as telegrams, letters, and petitions flooded into the governor's office in unprecedented numbers. Indeed, by June 1942 the Waller case had become one of the most celebrated causes in recent Virginia history.[32] Darden could not help but be impressed by this outpouring, and in letters replying to several of those who wrote to him he promised that he would "give the case the most serious consideration."[33] But he remained noncommittal as to what his final decision would be.

The appeals to Darden came from all sections of the country, but especially from the Northeast. Most were from ordinary citizens, but they also included many from prominent educators, clergymen, journalists, and other well-known people. These were no accident, for the WDL sought out many prominent individuals and urged them to write to the governor or to give them a brief quotable statement.[34] Most of those writing to Darden argued, in one way or another, for the commutation of Waller's sentence. A few even urged a pardon. Many insisted, like A. J. Muste, executive secretary of the Fellowship of Reconciliation, that he had not been afforded a trial by a jury of his peers. Others, like F. Ernest Johnson, executive secretary of the Federal Council of Churches of Christ in America, simply stated that Waller's execution "would be a miscarriage of justice."[35] Others stressed the perception that had arisen throughout the country that Waller had been treated unjustly and that if he had been white he would not have been given the death penalty. Thus, as one correspondent put it, if Waller were to be executed, "thousands of American citizens will have their faith in the justice of the American courts badly shaken."[36]

In its continuing efforts to influence public opinion and to encourage people to write to Governor Darden on Waller's behalf, the WDL made considerable use of the case of Robert G. Siddle, which it came across towards the end of May 1942. Siddle was a white man from Pittsylvania County who had been acquitted of the murder of his black sharecropper. In early June the WDL put out a flier that summarized the cases of Waller and Siddle in two parallel columns, one entitled "When the Black Man Shoots," and the other, "When the White Man Shoots." It explained that Tom Denson, a Negro with a wife and eight children, had gone to work for Siddle (misspelled "Sittle" here) as a sharecropper in November 1940. In July 1941, Siddle ordered Denson off of his farm and took all of the crops. Denson went to court and got an order forcing Siddle to permit him to return to the farm to complete the harvest and to release his share of the crops. On October 20, 1941, after Denson's truck broke down near Siddle's house, Siddle shot and killed Denson. Tried for murder in November 1941 before Judge James T. Clement in the Circuit Court of Pittsylvania County, Siddle and his wife were found not guilty by a jury that deliberated a mere fifteen minutes. In January 1942, Mrs. Denson sued Siddle for twenty thousand dollars for the unlawful killing of her husband. This suit was also tried before Judge Clement, and again the jury delivered a verdict in Siddle's favor.[37] In short, a comparison of the Waller and Siddle cases seemed to provide additional, dramatic evidence that the poor and the black were unlikely to be afforded equal justice, at least not in Judge Clement's court in Pittsylvania County.

The WDL version of the Siddle case was open to question, however, and it engendered a minor dispute in itself. Thus the account of the shooting that was published in the *Danville Register* at the time the Siddles were charged was substantially different from that presented by the WDL. The shooting, the newspaper declared, was preceded by a dispute between Mrs. Siddle and Denson, who, she claimed, was digging potatoes belonging to the Siddles as well as his own. Denson returned to the Siddle yard later in the day and allegedly declared, "I'll fix 'em." Siddle only shot after he had warned Denson not to approach any further.[38] At his trial, on November 19, Siddle claimed that his trouble with Denson began after Denson had quit during the busy season, not that he was thrown off the farm. Witnesses also claimed that Denson was a "dangerous character" who had served a sentence for murder. Siddle pleaded self-defense and testified that Denson was advancing toward him and had his hand in his pocket as if to draw a knife.[39] According to the account in the *Danville Register*, the jury deliberated only eight minutes before finding Siddle not guilty.[40]

Whatever version one looked at, however, the contrast between the treatment of Waller and Siddle was striking, and it colored much of the subsequent discussion of the Waller case. This was seen, for example, in an editorial entitled "Odell Waller: A Test Case" that was published in the *New York Times* on June 11. Much more was involved than the guilt or innocence of one man, it said. The responsibility involved the poll tax system, the sharecropping system, the exhausted soil that kept farmers poor, and even the crop restrictions placed by the federal government. "The faith of colored people in their country," and that of many whites, was "deeply involved in what happens to Odell Waller." Moreover, the *Times* added, "in a comparable and subsequent case, tried before the same judge, the defendant was acquitted. He was a white man, his victim a Negro."[41] The editorial infuriated Judge Clement. Throwing judicial discretion to the winds, he wrote a long letter to the *Times* which was published on June 19. Clement insisted that "the cases were not similar but just the reverse." He called Siddle "a feeble old man," referred to Denson as a "dangerous Negro" who had served time for murder, and concluded that the jury "very properly" acquitted Siddle "on the ground of self-defense." Clement then gave a review of the Waller case that read like a prosecutor's summary. Waller, he said, "was a vicious and dangerous Negro," and he dismissed Waller's interpretation of the events at the time of the shooting as "incredible." He also denied that there had been the exclusion from the jury of non–poll tax payers, either in law or in practice. Clement concluded by charging the *Times* with having "been misled by the false and vicious propaganda that has been spread practically all over the United States, especially in the North and West, by these Northern societies, who apparently are backed by communism."[42]

Clement's letter could not resolve the disagreements over the Siddle case. Indeed, the WDL found that it was very difficult to reconstruct the facts in the case as no record was kept of the testimony at the trial. Furthermore, although a transcript was made of the civil case, this had been destroyed. Nevertheless, Finerty claimed that from "best information obtainable" he found that the evidence in the Waller and Siddle cases was "startlingly alike" and that the comparison was pertinent.[43] Many people remained troubled by the apparently different standards that seemed to be applied in the Circuit Court of Pittsylvania County, depending on whether one was black or white. Similarly, others found in Clement's letter additional evidence for their belief that Waller had been tried in a less than impartial atmosphere.

Virginius Dabney, however, leaned toward the prosecutor's interpretation of the Siddle case and believed that the WDL used a "distorted version" of it in its literature.[44] As late as June 9, he wrote that "few things have annoyed me more than the highly colored publicity which has been distributed on a nation-wide scale concerning the Odell Waller case." But he then added that he had "some little doubt as to whether the killing was premeditated, although I am inclined to think it was."[45] Despite his distaste for much of the publicity in the Waller case, some of the arguments seemed to have moved him away from the skeptical, even hostile, stand he had taken earlier. This shift was important, for on June 14, 1942, Dabney published an editorial entitled "To Vindicate Virginia Justice" in which he called upon Governor Darden to commute Waller's sentence to life imprisonment if his lawyers did not succeed in getting the federal courts to order a new trial. Dabney continued to express his irritation at the "misleading propaganda" that some sources had put forth in this case, but he stated that "long and careful study" had convinced him that "too much doubt surrounds the justice of the verdict that he was guilty of murder in the first degree." He also now believed that "what appears to be extenuating circumstances . . . doubtless could be brought out, if there was another trial." Beyond that, Dabney acknowledged that "whether we like it or not, Waller's fate has become a *cause celebre*, with national, even international implications. Incredible as it may appear to some, the execution of this humble Negro sharecropper might lessen the chance of the United Nations to win the war." In this regard he noted the extensive national criticism of the verdict and the need for the support of "the colored races" in the war effort. Dabney insisted, however, that he favored commutation not because of this widespread agitation for clemency, but because he believed "that justice should be done, irrespective of the consequence."[46]

Dabney's editorial created a stir. Once again Judge Clement responded publicly, this time in a letter to the *Times-Dispatch* which was published on June 19, 1942. Calling the shooting of Davis "the most dastardly and cold-blooded murder that ever came under my observation," Clement stated that it was incredible that Dabney could reach the conclusion that Waller was not guilty of murder in the first degree. Waller "was not a humble Negro," Clement insisted. "He was a vicious, lawless and dangerous Negro, with whom the officers had had considerable trouble." There was also "no point in the contention that poll-tax payers and sharecroppers happened not be on the jury," as the trial court's judgment had been upheld by the highest state and federal courts. Clement was confident that Governor Darden would not "yield to the pressure of agitators."[47] Thus twice within the same week Clement expressed views in print that were harshly critical of Waller and the defense's position. McCallister observed shortly afterwards that "almost every lawyer in Richmond is of the opinion that Judge Clement's letter to the Times-Dispatch (they did not see the one in the N. Y. Times) shows that he is not fit to sit on the bench."[48]

On June 17 the *Danville Register* published an attack on Dabney's editorial that was even more biting than Clement's. Asserting that Virginia justice had been vindicated by the rejection by the various courts of all the appeals, the editors went on to attack the propaganda of the Workers Defense League as "a mass of falsification intended to prejudice men of good will against Virginia white citizens, against respectability, against legal justice," and it listed a number of prominent people, including Frank Graham, president of the University of North Carolina; John Dewey; Virginius Dabney; "and others with reputations ranging from liberals to revolutionaries" who had come to its support. They in turn "have a motley crew as fellow travelers," including the NAACP, the National Urban League, the American Civil Liberties Union, the Union for Democratic Action, the Brotherhood of Sleeping Car Porters, the CIO, and the Southern Tenant Farmers' Union. "Not all, but several of these organizations are known to have Communistic or Nazi nuclei. The others are dedicated to erasure of the existing color line in Virginia and throughout the South."[49]

Dabney fired back an indignant reply to the editor of the *Danville Register*, accusing him of making "libelous insinuations" in regard to the association with Communists or Nazis, of being "totally inaccurate" in regard to his attitude toward the color line, and of wrongly implying that he was under the banner of the Workers Defense League. He insisted that he had no desire to break down the color line and called attention to his recommendation for state-supported "segregated regional universities for Negroes in the South" in his recent book, *Below the Potomac*.[50] Thus was Dabney placed on the defensive as a result of his cautious efforts to secure justice for Odell Waller.

Although the *Danville Register* published Dabney's reply, it accompanied it with another editorial blast at the Richmond editor. "He does not know the kind of man then on trial. Yet he sits at Richmond and pontificates," despite the fact that "the state and federal courts have found 'no merit' in the contentions of Waller's counsel." His "greatest error, however, was his own 'flagrant misrepresentation' of Odell Waller as 'an humble Negro sharecropper.'" It then noted Waller's previous convictions, and labeled him "one of the most vicious criminals ever to be sentenced to Virginia's electric chair."[51] Dabney limited his response this time to the brief observation that he had used the word "humble" not as the editor assumed, but in the sense of "lowly."[52] Dabney's dispute with the *Danville Register* was, of course, a minor incident in the history of the Waller case. But it well illustrated how sensitive some people in the Pittsylvania County area could be over any criticism of the manner in which the Waller case had been handled and how difficult it was to take a moderate position in a controversy that involved racial relations.

In contrast, the members of the WDL were elated by Dabney's change of position. McCallister immediately wrote to commend him for his "splendid editorial" and to express the thought that it would "have a profound effect on the Governor's ultimate decision in the Waller case." McCallister also noted that Finerty had called the editorial "absolutely magnificent."[53] Many others agreed. One particularly interesting response came from Thomas Sancton, a New Orleans–born, Louisiana-bred reporter who was then managing editor of the *New Republic* and living in New York. Sancton "was profoundly thrilled" by the editorial. "I know in my bones that this case can become a tremendous Southern victory if Governor Darden commutes the sentence to life imprisonment." He agreed that the case could have an effect upon the war effort, but "the ultimate question is one of justice." Sancton claimed that his first reaction to the Waller case had been similar to Dabney's. But,

> really, Mr. Dabney, our first view of this case was the narrow one; perhaps this great emotional current now in motion among the negroes is based in part on other old injustices not related to the Waller case, but it is too important a thing now for a narrow view of evidence to deflect; my own first view was swept aside; I studied the case and its background at greater length and came to a number of the conclusions that you reach in your editorial; but remembering all the miscarriages of justice against negroes which I saw as a police reporter in New Orleans and in Jackson, Miss., I think I feel even more strongly than you do that many of the real words, many of the curses, many of the threatening gestures that passed in those moments when Waller

shot and Davis fell dying, were not brought out in the trial to the benefit of Waller as they would have been if he were a white man and Davis the negro. As to the testimony of the Negro boy Davis, I have lived with negroes too long and too closely to know that any negro boy who lived with my family would testify to anything we told him to say.[54]

Dabney responded warmly to Sancton's letter. "I have gone through quite a lot of mental torture over this business," he wrote, "and did not finally make up my mind until last week. . . . The thing which influenced me very definitely last week was the discovery of new evidence as to the attitude of some white people in Pittsylvania." He did not state what this new evidence was, however, but he was confident that Governor Darden would decide the case fairly. He reported that one of the reporters covering the case believed that the odds were two to one in favor of commutation.[55]

Despite the hopes of the WDL that Darden might be influenced in Waller's favor by the many letters, telegrams, and petitions sent to him, it was a tactic that involved some risk. Too much outside pressure could provoke an adverse reaction. By mid June the WDL decided to try one other nonjudicial approach by preparing a petition to President Roosevelt asking him to appoint a commission of inquiry to investigate the case. The petition was signed by many of the same people who had earlier contributed their names to the amici curiae brief in support of the petition for a rehearing of the case by the Supreme Court. It stressed the blow to Negro morale produced by the refusal of the court to review the case and how this would be used by America's enemies "to hold up American democracy to scorn before the colored races of the world." If, it argued, the court's refusal to review the case was based on the failure of the defense counsel to offer proof of the exclusion of non–poll tax payers at the trial, "then Waller is dying because of a technicality." There was precedent for such presidential intervention, it claimed, noting Wilson's actions in the Tom Mooney and Joe Hill cases. "We believe it will be a national catastrophe if Waller goes to his death, when millions of his fellow citizens are convinced that he was not tried by a jury of his peers."[56]

The WDL hoped to get as many prominent people as possible to add their names to the petition, which was sent to Roosevelt on Monday, June 15. By that time it had obtained 169 signatures. Within a few days,

several hundred more signatures were forwarded to the president.[57] Legally, of course, President Roosevelt had no authority over the case. But
the WDL assumed that, should he appoint such a commission, Governor
Darden would feel obliged to postpone Waller's execution pending its
deliberations and, at best, follow a recommendation for clemency. Ultimately, however, this effort was to no avail. It was not surprising. The
petitioners, after all, had requested an extraordinary presidential intervention into a jealously guarded area involving a state's criminal jurisdiction. Moreover, unlike the Hill and Mooney cases, the problem was compounded by the emotional issue of race. On the whole, Roosevelt's
concern for blacks had been reflected most clearly in his support for
economic programs which included them to an unprecedented degree,
not in a sensitivity over civil rights. Wary of alienating powerful southern
politicians, he had tended to avoid direct involvement in sensitive issues,
such as proposals for a federal anti-lynching law or attacks on disfran-
chisement. Waller's controversial case had even less appeal, especially as
it came at a time when he was hard pressed by the demands of the war.
Thus he consistently refused to get involved.[58]

Roosevelt's apparent indifference to Waller's plight was, for many
blacks, only another illustration of the low order of priority that the administration placed on civil rights. To be sure, in recent years there had
been some progress, as when Roosevelt established the FEPC in June
1941 in response to A. Philip Randolph's threat to organize a march on
Washington. But the lesson for Randolph was that blacks had to keep up
the pressure if they were to hold on to and advance beyond the gains
that had been made. One way to apply pressure was to show that the
March on Washington movement was not dead. Thus Randolph decided
to organize a mass rally of blacks at Madison Square Garden in New York
City on June 16. It provided an opportunity to combine a plea to spare
Odell Waller, who was then scheduled to be executed in only three days,
with a protest against Jim Crow generally and against the continuing
segregation of blacks in the armed forces, defense industries, and federal government bureaus. As an additional statement he called for a
blackout of all homes and stores in Harlem during the evening of the
rally. Thus Randolph hoped to stage an event that the administration
could not help but notice. To a degree he succeeded. Some eighteen
thousand to twenty thousand blacks crowded into Madison Square Garden and listened to five hours of speeches and songs. Huge "Save Odell

Honorable Franklin D. Roosevelt
The White House
Washington, D.C.

Dear Mr. President:

    We respectfully urge and petition you to appoint a Commission
of Inquiry to investigate the case of Odell Waller, Negro sharecropper
of Gretna, Virginia, sentenced to die June 19.

    We exercise this sacred right to petition, because the welfare
of our beloved country is involved. The morale of our Negro fellow
citizens, already badly shaken, was given another shock by the second
silent refusal of the Supreme Court to review the case of one who, as
Miss Pearl Buck says, "has become a personification of all those to
whom democracy is denied in our country." Here is further evidence
for America's enemies, who seize every opportunity to hold up American
democracy to scorn before the colored races of the world.

    Waller, disfranchised by poverty, was convicted by a jury of
white poll-tax-payers. Through misapprehension of his counsel at the
trial, an objection without proof was made to the systematic exclusion of non-poll-tax-payers from jury service. This proof was presented at subsequent habeas corpus proceedings. If this failure of
counsel to offer proof of his contention to the Trial Court is the
basis for refusal by the United States Supreme Court to review the
case, then Waller is dying because of a technicality.

    In an amici curiae brief filed with the United States Supreme
Court, and signed by leading pro-democratic organizations in the
country, a 1942 decision of the Court in Glasser vs. U. S. is cited
as follows:

        "the proper functioning of the jury system, and indeed
        our democracy itself, requires that the jury be a 'body
        truly representative of the community,' and not the organ
        of any special group or class."

    As you know, presidential intervention in a case of this kind
is not without precedent. President Wilson acted in the cases of
Tom Mooney and Joe Hill.

    We believe it will be a national catastrophe if Waller goes to
his death, when millions of his fellow citizens are convinced that he
was not tried by a jury of his peers. Your intervention will help
restore the badly shaken faith of our Negro minority in American
democracy.

                        Respectfully yours,

Bishop Francis J. McConnell	John Dewey	Freda Kirchwey
Oswald Garrison Villard	Bruce Bliven	A. Philip Randolph
John Haynes Holmes	Frank P. Graham	Maynard C. Krueger
Arthur Garfield Hays	Charles Clayton Morrison	

(Please add, with identification and address, names of leaders in
your community)

Petition to President Roosevelt, June 15, 1942.

Waller" banners were draped from the rafters. Near the end of the rally, Randolph introduced Annie Waller to a cheering audience. The meeting also endorsed by a rising vote the petition calling for a presidential commission of inquiry into the case.[59] The rally was an impressive illustration of the degree to which the Waller case had become a matter of concern well beyond Virginia. There is no evidence, however, that it had any direct effect on Governor Darden or that it was related to his decision two days later to grant another reprieve and hold a commutation hearing.

Still, the letters and appeals to spare Waller's life continued to appear. "The American Negro neither asks nor expects more than justice," declared the *New York Herald Tribune.* "But in an hour when national unity is a first concern of every one, it seems fitting to urge that no possible chance of injustice be done this Virginia citizen in the name of the law."[60] Praising Darden's decision to hold a commutation hearing, the *New York Times* observed that "the Waller case transcends sectional issues. The plight of the Negro is a national problem. We cannot be self-righteous about the opportunities the Negro has in our own city, for decent living, for health or for employment. We do believe that, North or South, the justice done him ought to be above suspicion and beyond doubt."[61] Meeting in Durham, North Carolina, on June 18, the delegates to the General Council of the Congregational Christian Churches unanimously adopted a plea to Governor Darden to put off Waller's execution.[62] On June 23, leaders of the ACLU sent a request to Darden to grant another reprieve, should he not favor commutation, to allow one more effort to take the case to the Supreme Court.[63]

Those who were convinced of Waller's guilt were quite unmoved by such appeals. Some, like Judge Clement or the editors of the *Danville Register,* for example, were quick to find subversive or communist influence among those who were defending Waller or who had sought clemency for him. With a few exceptions, the evidence simply does not sustain this charge. Organizations such as the NAACP and the ACLU, both of which had come to Waller's defense, had, of course, long been subjected to red-baiting assaults from the right, but, aside from the unfairness of such attacks, these organizations played only a relatively minor role in the case. The most important organization defending Waller, the WDL, had been associated with American Socialists from the start, but it was staunchly anti-Communist. It was clearly responsible for many of the telegrams and letters sent to Darden, although there were also hundreds from individuals with no obvious affiliation with any group. The bona fide radical support for Waller was largely limited to that provided by the RWL, and this, of course, was a factional group of Trotskyites that was bitterly opposed to the Communist party, although the distinction between such radical organizations was likely to be lost by most of the residents of Pittsylvania County.

Unlike two of the best-known civil rights and civil liberties cases from the 1930s, that of the Scottsboro boys in which the defense was led by the Communists' International Labor Defense (ILD), and that of Angelo Herndon, in which the defendant was himself a Communist who received the support of the ILD, there was little public involvement in the Waller case by Communists or Communist-associated groups, and most of that came late in the struggle. Near the end of June 1942 the left-wing National Lawyers Guild sent a three-page statement to Governor Darden urging him to commute Waller's death sentence. Such an act, it argued, "would constitute a great contribution to the cause of national unity of races." It would also "serve to mitigate a grave injustice and strengthen the people's faith in our institutions."[64] The statement also indicated that the guild planned either to appear at the governor's clemency hearing or to submit an amicus curiae brief. Although it was not a Communist organization, the National Lawyers Guild was controversial. Founded in 1937, it was a product of the Popular Front era, and it included a variety of members holding liberal to left views. It would certainly not have been welcomed by Darden and conservative Virginians. Thus, Morris Shapiro was alarmed at this unwanted intervention, which he felt could only hurt matters, and he immediately sent a letter to the guild asking it not to come to the hearing and not to file a brief.[65]

The Communist party itself, at both the national and local levels, had shown little interest in the Waller case. Conceivably, party leaders had been put off by Waller's defense having been precmpted from the start by the RWL and the WDL and supported by such a prominent anti-Communist as A. Philip Randolph. Later, after the German attack on the Soviet Union on June 22, 1941, the first priority of the Communist party became, in a celebrated reversal of its position, the defeat of the Nazi invaders, to the neglect, as some people complained, of other matters, including concern for the rights of blacks.[66] But on June 19, 1942, three days after the Madison Square Garden rally, the party's newspaper, the *Daily Worker*, published a story under the headline: "Let Gov. Darden Know Before Tonight: Waller Must Not Die." The article had obviously been written before receiving word of the reprieve of June 18. Significantly, it stressed the need to unite the Negro people in the war against fascism. "The best of the American people . . . realize that Hitler and his fascists are the enemy they must destroy, and not Negro sharecroppers who are occasionally goaded into killing in defense of their own lives." After reviewing the history of the case, the article concluded that "it is the old and shameful story of Negro oppression and legal lynching. . . . Odell Waller's case was grabbed up and has been exploited by the Trotskyites, the Lovestoneites and the Norman Thomas 'socialists' for their own questionable purposes. But the very fact that this breed of nondescript defeatists and fifth-columnists profane the Negro's just grievances impels decent Americans to shout their protests against the threatened Virginia outrage."[67] On June 26 the *Daily Worker* carried another story on Waller. "Urgent protests to Gov. Darden are needed to prevent Waller's execution," it argued. Furthermore, "labor and all progressive citizens should let President Roosevelt know that the attempt to execute Waller is a threat to national unity and the war effort."[68]

It was perhaps significant that this belated interest by Communists in the Waller case came at a time when the RWL had ceased to play a prominent role in the defense efforts. It also came at a time when the degree of national publicity over Waller made the case very difficult to ignore. Such was the view of the Trotskyite Socialist Workers party, which had at least written about the case and supported the WDL's efforts from the start. Thus an article in its newspaper, *The Militant*, angrily denounced the hypocrisy and "treacherous role" of the "Stalinists," who for nearly two years had "remained as silent as the tomb" in regard to the case. The Communist party's new interest in Waller, it complained, was only to gain the support of blacks in the war effort.[69] Although the writer in *The Militant* denounced his Stalinist enemies with characteristically strong language, it is difficult not to conclude that he had a valid point. Whatever private views some Communists may have held, Waller's fate remained a matter of minor and only passing concern to the Communist party.

Inevitably, the campaign to save Waller also attracted the attention of his opponents. Thus some complained to Governor Darden about the long delay in carrying out the death penalty or denounced Waller as a vicious individual. A number of such letters came from residents of Pitt-sylvania County. Langhorne Jones, an attorney from Chatham and a former associate of Darden in the General Assembly, wrote that "in my sixteen years of practice I have never heard of a more aggravated case of first degree murder tried in our county, and I think the jury was not only justified in their verdict, but rightly so."[70] J. T. Clark, also of Chatham, warned: "We have been having some minor trouble with the negroes here in Chatham, and I think it has been caused by the newspapers in this case, and if Waller's sentence is commutted [*sic*] I am afraid we will have trouble, and the next time we may have a lynching."[71] Preston Moses, a member of the House of Delegates from Chatham and pub-lisher and editor of Chatham's weekly newspaper, the *Pittsylvania Tri-bune*, took a similar position. If the sentence is commuted, the Negroes' "respect for law and order will be lowered." They "will take a commuta-tion as something to gloat over, and with the growing unrest brought about [by] the much agitation [*sic*], the commutation will add an explo-sive to a dangerous situation here."[72] Another local resident, John C. Roach, wrote a long letter praising Judge Clement, Commonwealth's Attorney Joseph Whitehead, Jr., the members of the jury, and Oscar Davis, and concluded: "When the electric chair erases Waller exzistance [*sic*], it will have done the community in which he lived and the negro race in general a great favor."[73] Methodist Bishop James Cannon, Jr., was another Virginian who opposed commutation. Cannon sent Darden a copy of a long statement that he had prepared for press distribution. Virginia justice, he said, was under attack, largely by outsiders who were not well informed. Claiming to have read the record of the case, Cannon defended the trial and the sentence. "I abhor lynching," he wrote, but he warned that the failure "to give adequate punishment for rape and murder will almost inevitably incite to lynching." Cannon endorsed Clement's view that "if Waller is not given the electric chair, no one should."[74] Not all white residents of Pittsylvania County agreed, and a few even wrote to Darden urging him to commute Waller's sentence. Still, there was at least some truth to the assertion by the *Pittsylvania Tribune* that the "people of Pittsylvania and those who know the true facts in the case all think that the murder was cold-blooded and the death sentence should be imposed."[75] But the important opinion at this stage was that of Governor Darden. Since his inauguration on January 21, 1942, the case of Odell Waller had been one of his continuing concerns. He had followed its progress through the courts and had granted Waller three reprieves. In May and June, more letters, telegrams, petitions, and other appeals for clemency were sent to the governor than, reportedly, at any other time in Virginia history. By calling for a special commutation hearing for June 29 he tacitly acknowledged that this was no ordinary case, and he demonstrated his willingness to give Waller's attorneys every opportunity to explain their position. Whether they could persuade him to accept their view of the shooting was an open question.

8

The Governor's Choice: Hearing in Richmond

Whatever his personal feelings may have been, Governor Darden was careful not to discuss the Waller case publicly despite the numerous appeals directed at him and the intense publicity that the efforts of the WDL and others had generated. Like many southerners, he was sensitive to any real or implied criticism of his state, especially by outsiders from the North, but he was willing to listen to Finerty and Waller's other WDL lawyers, and he treated them with respect. On several occasions Finerty, in turn, expressed his appreciation for the governor. "I have never experienced such humane and unselfish consideration as Governor Darden has extended to Waller," he wrote to Virginius Dabney on May 16.[1] Still, as the time for the commutation hearing drew near, Waller's defenders could not help but be concerned about the ideas and judgment of the man on whom so much depended. What was the best way to present their case? Would he really listen and understand arguments that, no matter how tactfully presented, necessarily were critical of deeply rooted racial, economic, and social practices in Virginia?

Colgate W. Darden, Jr. was no ordinary Virginian. Born in Southampton County on February 11, 1897, he spent his boyhood in the area, attending public school in nearby Franklin. After two years of study at the University of Virginia he left college and enlisted in the French Ambulance Corps during World War I. Because of illness resulting from constant action, he was given a discharge and the Croix de Guerre for valor. After his return to the United States he became a pilot in the Naval Aviation Corps. Subsequently he transferred to the Marine Corps and again went abroad, this time as a Marine Corps bomber. Injured in a crash, he had to undergo a long recuperation before his health was restored. Darden then completed his B.A. degree at the University of Virginia by attending summer session while he studied law at Columbia University during the academic year. He was admitted to the Virginia bar in 1922, but, having been awarded a Carnegie Fellowship in International Law, he spent the next year studying at Christ Church College, Oxford University. In 1924 he began the practice of law in Norfolk, Virginia. Three years later he married Constance du Pont, the daughter of Irénée du Pont of the Delaware chemical-company family. Darden got interested in politics in the 1920s and became a supporter of the Democratic governor and later senator, Harry F. Byrd, whose political organization soon came to dominate the Virginia political scene. He served two terms in the Virginia House of Delegates, from 1929 to 1933, and three in the United States Congress between 1935 and 1941. Unlike Byrd, Darden strongly supported Roosevelt's third-term campaign in 1940, although he kept his ties to the Byrd organization. In 1941 he was elected governor of Virginia, succeeding James H. Price. As a delegate and congressman, Darden supported education and became known as a mild progressive on some issues, despite his wealth and basically conservative inclinations. An energetic and conscientious governor, Darden was a patrician whose relatively cosmopolitan background might well enable him to rise above the parochial as he pondered the case of Odell Waller.[2]

For members of the WDL, some of the signs—Darden's relations with Finerty, for example—seemed favorable. Another was the report that Darden had apparently referred to John Dewey's letter to the *New York Times* as (in the words of Frank McCallister) "a very fair presentation of the case." On the other hand, McCallister, who prepared a confidential report on the governor, was concerned about his racial attitudes. Darden had allegedly said, in private, that "racial relations are becoming dangerously inflamed," and that groups like the WDL "are working to get complete social equality leading to final racial amalgamation." McCallister studied the clemency records of the previous five governors, all of whom served for four years. Byrd had granted the smallest number of commutations and Price the most. Unfortunately, McCallister noted, "Darden is a follower and admirer of Byrd and is likely to follow his lead in this connection." He was also known to believe that Price had been "much too lenient."[3]

Although these signals about Darden's attitude may have been mixed, it was clear that, as the campaign on behalf of Odell Waller intensified, Darden made an effort to get as much information as he could about the case. The sources he turned to, however, were often likely to be slanted against Waller. For example, he sought out the opinions of a number of people in Pittsylvania, such as that of Langhorne Jones, his former colleague in the General Assembly. But Jones was also a partner of Commonwealth's Attorney Joseph Whitehead, Jr., and, predictably, he took a strongly anti-Waller position.[4] It was not surprising that Darden believed that many people expressing opinions about the case were misinformed. On June 17, he wrote to Senator Byrd that "the situation which has developed as a result of the widespread circulation of erroneous information about the case of Odell Waller is dangerous, and I am fearful what may ultimately happen."[5] The next day one of Darden's old friends, John Archer Carter, reported that in New York City there was growing skepticism and concern about the state's handling of the case among many people, including those who were not "Greenwich Village left wingers, or even big city Yankee liberals."[6] Darden replied that "unfortunately, the news stories, particularly the pamphlets which have been circulated by the Workers Alliance [*sic*], have not accurately set forth what happened."[7] This may have been true for some of the first statements put out by the WDL. But it was important to recognize that a major defense contention was that there was a legitimate dispute over a number of key facts in the case. This was especially evident when one considered the disparity between Henry Davis's and Waller's version of the events at the time of the shooting. Darden did not indicate exactly what he thought was inaccurate in WDL material. However honest his intentions, such a comment, coming before the commutation hearing had taken place, might suggest that his own objectivity was open to question.

On Monday, June 22, Darden made an unannounced visit to Pittsylvania County to get a firsthand view of the scene of the shooting and to talk with some of the witnesses. Among others these included Ethel Davis, widow of Oscar Davis; Henry Davis; Archie Waller; and Raleigh Tucker, a neighbor of Oscar and Ethel Davis. Darden attempted to visit the area incognito, and when he spoke to the witnesses he did not introduce himself as governor. He did not let the press know of his visit until Tuesday, June 23, and refused to express an opinion about the case.[8]

Others, particularly Waller's opponents in Pittsylvania County, felt no such inhibitions. Thus, after Darden's visit, Sheriff Overbey issued a statement attacking some of the news articles written by people who allegedly did not know the facts. In particular Overbey objected to the sympathetic portrait of Waller that left the impression that he "was a poor, ignorant and oppressed Negro, and that advantage had been taken over him by Oscar Davis." Instead, claimed Overbey, "Waller was above the average Negro in intelligence, had been to school, wrote a good hand, and made social engagements with Negro school teachers." Moreover, Waller had "a fair and impartial trial before an intelligent jury from this county."[9] In a similar fashion the prosecuting attorney in the case, Joseph Whitehead, Jr., attempted to inform the public of "the true facts" in a letter published in the *Richmond Times-Dispatch* on Sunday, June 28, the day before the commutation hearing. After giving his version of the shooting, Whitehead described Waller in terms similar to those used by Judge Clement in his letter to the *Times-Dispatch* of June 19 and in the editorial in the *Danville Register* on June 23. "This man Waller is a dangerous character, having been convicted of reckless driving, transporting illegal whisky, convicted of carrying a concealed weapon and of threatening an officer, convicted of violating the State game laws, transporting illegal whisky the second time, twice convicted for driving an automobile after his license had been revoked."[10] There were obvious problems with any description of Waller that ignored or denied the social and economic forces by which he and his family had been victimized. Similarly, the recitation of his "criminal" record, without explanation or clarification, was highly misleading. Such statements tell us less about Waller than they do about the desire of Waller's opponents to counter the large volume of material sympathetic to him and to influence public (and possibly the governor's) opinion in the other direction.

On Saturday, June 27, two days before the commutation hearing, Finerty applied again to Chief Justice Stone for a stay of execution in order to permit him to file a new appeal to the United States Supreme Court, which was in recess until October. Again Stone turned him down. Finerty then made the same request successively to Justices Black, Jackson, and Frankfurter, the only other members of the Supreme Court then in Washington. Each refused to grant the stay. Justice Frankfurter held that "the underlying questions . . . [were] precisely those which were before the Supreme Court of the United States in three separate applications—the petition for certiorari to review the dismissal by the Court of Appeals of Virginia of the applications for habeas corpus, a petition for rehearing of such denial and a motion for leave to file a petition for habeas corpus. Although no opinions were filed in the dispositions of these three applications, the questions now urged were fully considered. . . . As a federal judge I am unable to find any justification for summary interference with the orderly process of Virginia's administration of justice."[11] With this chilling rejection there were no justices, judges, or courts left to which Finerty could turn.

On that same day, nineteen prominent Virginians sent a petition to Darden requesting clemency for Waller. The petition was the work of the WDL, which had been soliciting signatures for a number of days. Some agreed to sign with the understanding that the petition would not be given national publicity. Signers included Virginius Dabney; John Stewart Bryan, president of the College of William and Mary; the Right Reverend H. St. George Tucker, bishop of the Diocese of Virginia and presiding bishop of the Protestant Episcopal Church of the United States; the Reverend John M. Ellison, president of Virginia Union University; and other respected business, labor, religious, and educational figures. The petition listed five reasons to support clemency: (1) the widespread belief that the death penalty should not be imposed, (2) the opinion of careful students of the case that it was impossible to determine intelligently that Waller was guilty of first-degree murder, (3) the error of Waller's trial counsel having led the higher courts to rule that they were powerless to consider if his constitutional rights had been violated, (4) their having been "informed by those in whom we have confidence that important facts were not brought out at the trial," and (5) the fact that "an act of mercy by your Excellency at this time would allay public concern."[12] Their reasons were not new, but in this case the petitioners could not be dismissed as a group of radical outsiders. Indeed, McCallister had been careful to limit the signers to Virginians. Similarly the WDL wanted only Virginians to testify at the hearing. As McCallister explained to Milgram: "We must give the Governor the face-saving device of yielding to pleas from people within the state and not to pressure exerted from outside. Anyone coming in here from the outside at this stage, especially from New York, would certainly do harm and might upset what chances we have."[13]

Dabney's willingness to endorse the petition was consistent with his position on the Waller case since his editorial of June 14, and it represented a tactical, if belated, victory for the WDL, which had sought his support since November 1940. Although he was not confident of the outcome of the hearing, Dabney respected Darden. "He has been utterly conscientious about the whole Waller case and I shall not be disposed to criticize whatever he does," he wrote on June 26. He also noted, however, that "right now my distinct impression is that he will not commute the sentence, but I hope I am wrong."[14] In his lead editorial in the *Times-Dispatch* on Monday, June 29, Dabney argued cogently for commutation. "Pertinent facts . . . were not brought out in the trial," he insisted. Furthermore, to say that the federal courts "found nothing in Waller's trial record to justify intervention is misleading, since Chief Justice Stone refused on the technical ground that the constitutional issue had not been properly raised in the lower court." In addition, Dabney argued "that the atmosphere surrounding the trial was not conducive to an objective hearing of the evidence," as the role of the Revolutionary Workers League "was calculated to prejudice the jury from the start," and that the crucial testimony of Henry Davis was unbelievable. Finally Dabney noted "the far-reaching character of this case" with its effect on the morale of colored peoples throughout the world and how the Axis could use Waller's execution "with particular effect in China and India, and throughout the Arab world." Thus, he concluded, Governor Darden would be justified in commuting the sentence, not only because of the lack of "altogether convincing evidence" but also "by virtue of the fact that a commutation will strengthen the Allied front, not only here but beyond the seas."[15]

Dabney was an influential editor, but it was unlikely that most Virginians, certainly not most whites in Pittsylvania County, shared his views. On that same day, for example, a group of some 150 citizens from the Chatham area sent a telegram to Darden in opposition to commutation: "We respectfully request that you not disturb the jury verdict in the Waller case. Commutation would cause serious trouble between whites and blacks."[16] Just what was implied by the latter comment was not specified. In any event, it is doubtful that these arguments had any significant effect on Darden.

The public hearing, which was held in the old Senate chamber at the Capitol, went on from 9:30 in the morning to 8:00 in the evening on Monday, June 29.[17] This was considerably longer than the trial held on September 26, 1940, and the procedure produced an extensive review of the case. Waller was not present at the hearing, but the case for commutation was skillfully presented by Finerty and Preston. Stone did not participate. Twelve witnesses appeared, including Annie Waller, Henry Davis, and Sheriff Overbey, along with the lawyer, Martin A. Martin, and some others who had not testified at the trial. Virginius Dabney had intended to testify but was unable to attend because of a death in his family.[18]

In some opening remarks to the defense counsel, Darden stated that the purpose of the hearing was not to retry the case but "to hear any testimony that you think bears on the point of executive clemency." Preston replied that their purpose was "simply to bring before you essential evidence that was not in the trial."[19] Darden also made emphatically clear at the beginning of the proceedings that he would not be swayed by statements suggesting that, if commutation were to be granted, lynchings would supersede the orderly judicial process.

> My mind is made up on the matter of lynching. Should anybody at any time, any man or group of men, attempt to take a prisoner away from the officers of this Commonwealth I am going to resist it with all the force at my command. There is not going to be any temporizing on that point. They are never going to be surrendered as long as I have the authority to stop them.[20]

Annie Waller was the first important witness. In more sympathetic surroundings she was able to speak at far greater length than had been possible at the trial, where, she pointed out, she had been "cut off" by the judge.[21] Obviously a caring mother, she described Odell as having been a helpful boy and a good worker. She then went into her troubled relationship with Oscar Davis, a man she described as being occasionally good to work for but who was often moody and difficult, a man who refused to pay money owed to her, who evicted them from the house they lived in, who mutilated Odell's dog, and who withheld the shares of wheat belonging to them.[22] Questioned about what she saw and heard at the time of the shooting, Annie Waller testified that she was standing on the running board of the parked truck, looking at Odell and Oscar Davis. Odell asked Davis for his wheat, and "Mr. Davis—he curses and he says, 'Hell, you are not going to get a damn grain,' and he throwed his hand back here and when he throwed his hand back there Odell shot him."[23] This description of these crucial moments differed in important ways from what she had said at the trial. At that time she had testified: "After I got down there I guess I was as fur as from that thing in the corner, I was, when Odell got out and spoke to Mr. Davis. Then I heerd the firing of the gun—like to scared me to death. That's all I know about it. The last time I see it was in the car in the shed. That's the last time I seed it."[24] On cross-examination at the trial she had then been asked about the pistol and shooting. The dialogue went as follows:

> Q. You heard it when it was fired?
> A. Yas, sir, one time.
> Q. One time? You did not hear it but one time?
> A. No, sir.
> Q. And you did not see anything at all?
> A. No, that boy left firing of the gun one time.[25]

Preston picked up this discrepancy in his questioning of Annie Waller, commenting that "you didn't say that when you testified in this trial." But she did not back down. "You know the reason I didn't? I was cut off." The following exchange then took place:

> Preston: You were not cut off before you told about that.
>   You said you didn't see what happened at all.
> Annie Waller: No, Sir, I didn't.
> Preston: Go along anyway.[26]

It seems a little curious that Preston, as a defense counsel, would discuss the differences in Annie Waller's testimonies in such a fashion, and he was not necessarily correct when he said that she had testified that she "didn't see what happened at all." It is not clear from the record of the trial testimony at that point as to what she was referring to. She might have meant simply that she did not see what happened *after* the shot was fired. In her testimony at both the trial and the hearing she stated that she had been badly frightened by the noise of the shot. Thus she must have been in an emotional state that made careful observation unlikely. Moreover, it is not unreasonable to assume that she had been inhibited to some extent by Judge Clement's intimidating manner at the trial. He had, after all, abruptly interrupted Stone shortly after he had begun his questioning of Annie Waller.[27] Another problem at the trial had been Stone's failure to pursue his witnesses with much vigor. Many questions were left unasked. Thus it is at least conceivable that Annie Waller might have brought forth more details had Stone been more persistent in his questioning of her. At the trial, for example, Stone did not ask Annie Waller about Oscar Davis's relations with his sons or whether he carried a gun. But at the hearing she testified that he had had a quarrel with his son Edgar and that afterwards he carried a gun. "I seed that. He carried it back here in this pocket."[28] Thus Annie Waller's testimony at the hearing included a number of details that supported the defense's version of the shooting. But it was an open question whether Governor Darden would find her believable.

The next witness, Martin A. Martin, testified about his investigation into the relationship between the payment of poll taxes and the selection of the grand and petit juries. Martin also stated that he had tried to get Odell's cousin, Robert Waller, to appear at the hearing. He had

Annie Waller testifying at the governor's commutation hearing, June 29, 1942. *Seated on the right* are Edmund Preston and John F. Finerty. Courtesy of the Archives of Labor and Urban Affairs, Wayne State University.

wanted Robert Waller's testimony because he had understood him to have stated that Oscar Davis had cursed him at the time of the wheat threshing about a week before the shooting when Robert Waller had asked Davis to set aside one sack of wheat in four for Odell Waller. On the Tuesday before the hearing, Robert Waller had promised to come, but a few days later he backed off. When Martin asked him about this, Robert Waller said that Langhorne Jones, Joseph Whitehead, Jr., Sheriff Overbey, "and a number of other people had been there to see him." He denied, however, that there had been any intimidation, but he did change his mind about appearing as a witness after their visit.[29]

The longest and most interesting part of the hearing centered upon the testimony and questioning by Preston and Finerty of the prosecution's principal witness, Henry Davis. In describing the moment of the shooting, Davis testified as follows:

> the truck come on down to the house and stopped by the front yard, a little ways from the front yard, and Odell got out and come down and spoke to me and spoke to Mr. Davis and he told Mr. Davis that he came there for his wheat and Mr. Davis told him they was threshing the neighbor's wheat and when they finished down there he would let me bring it down on the wagon and Mrs. Davis called to breakfast and Mr. Davis told me, "Come on, Henry, let us go to breakfast," and I turned—me and him did—and started to the house when he did he shot him and he shot him the first time in the arm.

Q. Which arm?
A. In his left arm and Mr. Davis turned around and said, "Odell, you shot me without a cause."
Q. Were those his exact words?
A. Yes.
Q. He grabbed his arm and said, "Odell, you shot me without cause?"
A. Yes, and then he shot him up beside the head here.
Q. Which side of the head?
A. His own left, I think.[30]

Henry Davis then testified that, after the shooting, Odell pointed the gun at him and that he "fell down behind the bush and run off on all fours around the house." The gun then went off "when he throwed the gun up," and then I "run in the kitchen door and come out to the front door. The door wasn't shut, nothing but the screen there, and he shot him—walked over him and shot him twice and went on back."[31]

Preston and Finerty questioned Henry Davis at length about the exact location of the truck, the distance between it and Oscar Davis and the others, the distance between Odell and Oscar Davis, and other details of the shooting. What was clear was that the version of these events that Henry Davis presented at the hearing differed greatly from his testimony at the trial. Indeed, Finerty went so far as to assert: "There is not a word that you testified here the same as you testified in the last trial." Governor Darden took exception to this, and Finerty corrected himself: "I don't want to be flippant. There are some of the same words used."[32] But Finerty insisted that the "sense" of what Henry Davis was saying was entirely different. In particular he pointed out that the statement attributed to Oscar Davis, "Odell, you shot me without cause," was entirely missing from the trial testimony. Finerty noted that these were words in Oscar Davis's dying declaration as presented at the trial by Frank Davis. "I submit," he concluded, "that the entire thing is a fabrication made on the basis of Frank Davis's testimony."[33]

The defense lawyers noted other discrepancies. For example, in the hearing Henry Davis repeatedly stated that Odell Waller shot Oscar Davis in the left arm and the left side of the head. He did not so specify at the trial. Dr. Risher testified at the trial that Oscar Davis had been shot in the right side of his head, in his arm, and twice in the lower part of the back.[34] Finerty pointed out that the hospital record said "that he was shot on the right side of the head, in the right arm and once in the hip."[35] The discrepancies between the hospital record and the testimony of Dr. Risher were never adequately explained. But in any event they showed clearly the unreliability of Henry Davis's testimony, which, Finerty insisted, "is not to be believed.[36] Finally, Preston and Finerty both ridiculed Henry Davis's statement about running around the back of the house after the first two shots and then going through the house to the front door and watching Odell shoot Oscar Davis twice in the back as he lay on the ground. "It isn't conceivable" that it happened that way, insisted Preston. Henry Davis supposedly ran in mortal fear of Odell, yet he returned through the house and observed the final two shots. There had to be a noticeable lapse of time between the first shots and the last two for Henry Davis to have done this. Yet Mrs. Davis had testified that she heard shots and ran to her husband. She did not hint at any interval between the shots.[37] Finerty also hammered away at the fact that until the hearing "we never heard a word out of Henry Davis that Odell Waller shot Oscar Davis on the ground—not one word. He was the eye witness and where did he get that? He got it from the same dying declaration."[38] Addressing Governor Darden, Finerty said: "What I am pointing out to you is the question of the credibility of Henry Davis."[39] Indeed it is impossible to study Henry Davis's testimony at the trial and at the hearing and not to end up with serious, even overwhelming, doubts about its reliability from start to finish.

None of the other testimonies at the hearing was crucial. Preston read a statement submitted by Percy Dalton, the contractor who had hired Odell Waller for work in Maryland. Dalton gave a favorable description of Waller as a worker and asked for commutation.[40] Another witness was David George, the director of the Southern Electoral Reform League and an ally of the WDL in the fight against the poll tax. George took an interest in the case for personal reasons as well, as three of his cousins had been married, in succession, to Oscar Davis. Nevertheless, George testified that he had asked a "kinsman" about the case and was told that "Oscar Davis didn't treat that nigger right."[41] Another witness was a neighboring farmer, Ed. L. Johnson, who testified that he had gone to Oscar Davis's house shortly after the shooting and was present while Dr. Anderson attended to Davis's wounds. Curiously, although Johnson was interviewed by the assistant commonwealth's attorney, neither he nor Dr. Anderson was called to testify at Waller's trial.[42] But now Johnson quoted Davis as saying to the doctor and himself, "'That nigger ought to be killed for,' he said, 'he shot me without a cause.'"[43] Once again, therefore, the phrase that Finerty characterized as a "slogan adopted by the prosecution"[44] was quoted at the hearing. Johnson's credibility as a witness was open to question, however, given his not having testified at the trial and his never mentioning this alleged remark by Oscar Davis until the hearing. As with Henry Davis's belated use of this quotation, it appeared likely that it had been picked up after the fact from the dying declaration as reported at the trial by Oscar Davis's sons.[45] Johnson claimed that Oscar Davis had been a good neighbor, but he said nothing else of significance about the actual shooting.[46]

The final witness at the hearing was Pittsylvania County Sheriff A. H. Overbey, a man who had first questioned Henry Davis shortly after the shooting. Overbey testified that Henry Davis told him at that time "substantially, I might say—materially the same story" that he testified to at the hearing earlier in the day, although he added that "whether he said he shot him without a cause or left out some word, or something like that, or some sentence, I didn't pay much attention to that."[47] Finerty later asked: "If the Governor commutes this sentence will it create a dangerous situation in Pittsylvania County?" Overbey replied: "I think it will." When pressed for what he meant by this, Overbey explained that he meant racial trouble because the "negro people . . . would have a feeling that they had won a battle or won recognition and would probably take more liberties and all than they have." Finerty pressed Overbey to explain what this might mean, but Overbey only suggested that they might celebrate their victory "by crowding on the streets and having gatherings there, unlawful gatherings."[48]

Shortly before the hearing recessed for lunch, Finerty attempted to clarify the issues under consideration. The question, he said, is not whether Waller shot Oscar Davis. "That is admitted. The question is whether he shot him premeditatedly." Finerty did not believe that the evidence was sufficient to come to that conclusion. Darden in turn saw matters differently. "There is only one problem I want to settle in this case to my satisfaction and that is whether this man is being electrocuted because he is a negro. That is the only issue in the case, when you strip it of everything else."[49] Preston agreed that that was an important issue, but there were other matters as well that had to be considered. One concerned the variations in the story told by the state's only eyewitness. Another was the character of the judge in the case, a man who would "so debase himself and the judiciary of Virginia that he is willing to publish in the Richmond Times Dispatch and the New York Times a statement in defense of himself and in which he turned back to being the prosecuting attorney and no longer was the judge." Such a man, a person who "mistreated Annie Waller on the stand," was not "fit to sit on the bench of Virginia." Finally, Preston said one had to consider whether there was a fair trial when Waller was defended by a radical, anticapitalist organization that wanted to use him to serve their own purposes and that hired a lawyer who was negligent in his handling of the case.[50]

Addressing the "race question in this case," Preston observed that hundreds of thousands of Negroes in America regarded it as a test case. But ultimately, he pleaded, "it is a question of whether or not there will be taken into consideration not only Odell Waller himself but the condi-

tions and whether or not people in high places will exercise judgment
that takes into consideration the hopeless tenantry and practical slavery
that men like Odell Waller have been living in for generations past. . . . I
submit to you with all the earnestness I can that any judgment has to
take into consideration those factors which the court can't and, I am
sorry to say, a great many jurors won't."[51] Although Preston's words and
manner frequently suggested that he shared many of the conventional
racial stereotypes about blacks held by many privileged whites, he also
had an understanding of aspects of the racial realities that was nearly
completely missing from the minds and consciences of the prosecution.
Thus here, and on a few other occasions, he revealed a more passionate
concern than might be inferred from his discussion of the strictly legal
arguments. But it was not at all clear that he would be able to sway the

Members of the audience at the governor's commutation hearing. *Seated on the right*
are Odell Waller's wife, Mollie, and Annie Waller. Courtesy of the Archives of Labor and
Urban Affairs, Wayne State University.

Governor in this regard. Indeed, quite the opposite feeling was indicated when Darden questioned Dr. J. W. Riley, a black professor from
Virginia Union University, during the early part of the afternoon. Dr.
Riley attempted to explain the attitude and conduct of "sub-marginal
people," especially sharecroppers, and how society is responsible in part
for their condition, including the crime and ill health that pervade their
whole structure. But Darden would not concede that Odell Waller was
such a victim. "I don't believe it represents a case of exploitation," he
stated. "If I thought he was a victim of that I would have difficulty in
arriving at a judgment in this case."[52]

The final part of the hearing was taken up by lengthy summaries presented by both Preston and Finerty. Preston began by reviewing the relations between Oscar Davis and the Wallers. "I don't think there was a
great animosity," he concluded. "I think there was a great deal of injustice."[53] And this included the mutilation of Waller's dog, for it was "certainly one of the things that shows somebody's contempt for the rights
of Odell Waller and his mother." Preston argued that "it takes an awfully
short instant of time for a great many old injustices and unfair treat-
ments to well up in a man's mind, and . . . all of that is bound to have
taken part and be one of the motivating reasons for the action." But,
Preston insisted, the evidence did not show that Waller went to Davis
with the intention of killing him because of these injustices.[54] Next
Preston pointed out that the circumstances were such—a black man being tried in a rural community for the murder of his white employer and
defended by an outside, radical group—as to cast doubt on whether
Waller could have had a fair trial.[55] Added to that were the errors by
Waller's counsel at the trial, particularly his belief that Virginia law required juries to be composed of poll tax payers, and the tactics that an-
tagonized both the judge and the jurors.[56]

Most of Preston's summary was devoted to showing weaknesses in the
testimony of the prosecution's witnesses, particularly Henry Davis. Clearly
Preston believed that Henry Davis had been influenced by the commonwealth's attorney in developing his account of the shooting[57] and that
the story he told at the hearing, about running around and through the
house before seeing the last two shots, was impossible.[58] Especially suspect was Henry Davis's testimony (at the commutation hearing) as to
what Oscar Davis had said to Waller after the first shot was fired. Even
Darden had trouble accepting that story.

Mr. Preston: Can you imagine a man having been shot at from
    behind and having been hit in the arm, turning around and
    saying, "Odell, you shot me without any cause?"
Governor Darden: No.
Mr. Preston: Isn't he lying?
Governor Darden: I should say so.
Mr. Preston: If he is lying then, what proof have you or I that he
    hasn't lied straight through?[59]

In his conclusion Preston argued that, even if you assumed that every-
one in the case testified in good faith, "the result is a perfectly garbled
record and one from which two inferences can be drawn. One is that
there was an unjustifiable homicide. The other is that there was a cold-
blooded murder." But if you accept that it was first-degree murder, you
still had to take into account the circumstances of Odell Waller's life. "I
don't believe that you, with your feeling and your knowledge of circumstances, can say anybody is to blame except all of us, you and me and
every citizen of Virginia and every citizen of the United States." Therefore, Preston believed "that you can't find it in your heart and in your
conscience to send this boy to the chair Thursday. I don't believe it is fair
and I don't believe that you believe it is fair."[60]

Finerty's summary immediately followed. First, he said that he wanted
"to make it clear that in spite of Judge Clement's and Mr. Whitehead's
remarks in the papers, this is not a Communist-supported defense," and
he went on to assert his own anti-Communist views and to suggest that
the Communists would get great pleasure if there was no commutation.[61]
Next, he stated his belief that the case was not an indictment of the state
of Virginia. "I consider it an indictment of our Federal laws." His point
was that federal judges, including four members of the Supreme Court,
had so construed the relations between the federal government and the
states in connection with habeas corpus as to allow "a man to die for the
error of his counsel." This, he insisted, "was a denial of substantial justice."[62] The Supreme Court thus had refused to hear the case on purely
technical grounds, but, Finerty insisted, if the Court had taken the case
there was "little doubt" in his mind that they would have decided the
constitutional question in Waller's favor. Hence, "what is involved here
is a double case for clemency."[63]

Like Preston, Finerty showed the unreliability and inconsistencies in

Henry Davis's testimony, which he concluded "is not to be believed."[64] Moreover, there were numerous other inconsistencies in the evidence. As for the "he shot me without cause" remark, which came from Oscar Davis's dying declaration as recounted by Frank Davis, it "was either coached or an inspiration."[65] Finerty insisted that "there isn't a single fact in this case, a single material fact, other than the shooting, that is beyond a reasonable doubt."[66] A little later he stated that "if the constitutional question were to be decided in his favor and he were freed on habeas corpus and reindicted, under the circumstance of this case I would advise him to plead guilty to involuntary manslaughter."[67] But Waller had been denied the opportunity for a new trial. So, Finerty concluded, clemency was clearly justified because it was impossible to reach a decision beyond a reasonable doubt that Waller had been guilty of premeditated murder.[68]

With the hearing finally at an end, Darden was left with the heavy burden of making a decision that meant life or death for Odell Waller. Although no one knew for sure what he would do, many observers doubted that he would opt for commutation. Throughout the hearing Darden's questions showed that he had become very well acquainted with the facts, and he made an obvious effort to let the witnesses and the defense counsel have as free a hand as possible. Nevertheless, there can be no doubt that Darden had been annoyed and upset by the pro-Waller propaganda in the case, much of which he considered false, and by many of the critical editorials that had appeared in some northern newspapers. He did seem to believe that the honor and integrity of the state of Virginia had been impugned, and this was a slight he did not take lightly. It was not clear, however, that such feelings would influence his decision, one way or the other. Near the end of the hearing, Darden did express a few opinions that gave at least some clues to some of his thinking. One concerned Oscar Davis. Responding to some comments by Finerty, Darden flatly stated: "I don't believe that Oscar Davis was a dangerous character. I don't believe he owned a pistol and I don't believe he carried one around."[69] The implications for Waller's contention that he had acted in self-defense were obvious. Shortly afterward, Darden commented on Henry Davis's testimony, saying that he was "by no means convinced of Henry Davis' story. Part of it is fabrication, either intentionally or otherwise, and I am inclined to think it is otherwise."[70] If that comment may have given some encouragement to the defense, his next could not. "I don't believe that there was an altercation in the yard," he asserted, unconvinced by Finerty's interpretation of the crucial moments before the shooting.[71]

Such remarks must have been at least a bit discouraging to Preston and Finerty. Nevertheless, at the conclusion of the hearing, Finerty addressed Darden and said: "We have confidence in you. We may not agree with what your decision is but we will have confidence that your decision is according to your conscience and your judgment and we will not criticize it." Darden ended the hearing by promising that he would have a decision by the next afternoon or early evening.[72] For the moment, Waller's defenders could do nothing but wait.

9

"An Appalling Blunder": Home at Last

With further judicial appeals apparently foreclosed, the all-day commutation hearing on June 29 had kept alive the hope among Waller and his defenders that the death sentence could be at least reduced to life imprisonment. But this was far from a certainty, for it was clearly not going to be easy for Darden to favor clemency. The long struggle to save Waller's life, however justified, had created its own problems. Virginia's social, economic, and judicial practices had been scrutinized and found wanting, frequently by critics from outside of the state. In a society unaccustomed to rigorous self-criticism, Darden and many of his fellow Virginians necessarily were placed on the defensive by Waller's defenders. Hence there was considerable internal pressure against commutation, for to decide otherwise would imply failings in their beloved Old Dominion that many were not yet able to accept.

Darden could certainly find encouragement for a decision against commutation. The staunchly anti-Waller *Danville Register*, for example, published an editorial on June 30 expressing confidence that he would "arrive at a decision worthy of Virginia." It praised the governor for cutting "through the mountain of exaggeration and propaganda" and reducing the question "to the single issue of whether Odell Waller was sentenced to die because he is a Negro." According to the *Register*, "that is the one issue. All else is simply an effort to confuse. On that lone issue hangs not only the life of a vicious killer, but the reputation of Virginia's judiciary and Virginia's citizenry."[1]

In sharp contrast, the *New York Times* held that the question was whether Waller had been granted his constitutional right to an impartial trial by jury. This, it insisted, was an issue of legitimate concern to people outside of the South, just as southerners had a right to be concerned

about constitutional rights in the North. But it also noted the list of
distinguished Virginians who had appealed to Darden to grant clemency.[2] Others made last-minute efforts to sway Darden's decision in favor of commutation. For example, Walter White of the NAACP, A. Philip
Randolph, and a number of other prominent blacks sent a mid-after-
noon telegram to Darden on June 30 that read:

> IMPOSSIBLE EXAGGERATE HARMFUL EFFECT ON RACE
> RELATIONS EXECUTION ODELL WALLER DESPITE CIRCUM-
> STANCES CAETING [CASTING] DOUBT ON GUILT OF FIRST
> DEGREE MURDER AND FAIRNESS OF TRIAL. WE THEREFORE
> EARNESTLY PETITION THAT YOU COMMUTE SENTENCE.[3]

All such efforts were futile. By the evening of Tuesday, June 30, or perhaps earlier, Darden had reached a decision. It was against commutation. At 9:03 he signed a lengthy statement which was shortly afterwards
given to the press.[4] The document began by reviewing the legal history
of the case from the trial through the numerous appeals and the hearing on June 29. Darden noted that there was no dispute over the fact
that Waller had shot Oscar Davis and that Davis had died as a result, but
thereafter there was "conflicting evidence on almost every other point."
Much of the rest of the statement was devoted to his conclusions about
several key points of conflict. He minimized the disputes between the
Wallers and Oscar Davis in the days and weeks prior to the shooting and
even asserted that the forced removal of Annie and Mollie Waller from
their house on the Davis farm "does not seem to have resulted in great
bitterness or ill-will." He resolved the discrepancies between Annie Waller's
testimony at the trial and her statement at the hearing by rejecting the
latter and accepting the former "because Henry Davis testified at the
trial that she was not present at the shooting." Similarly, he accepted
Henry Davis's testimony that there was no argument between Oscar Davis
and Waller immediately prior to the shooting and that Oscar Davis told
Waller that he would get his wheat after all the threshing had been done.
Darden noted that on the morning of the shooting Oscar Davis and
Henry Davis were preparing, as was the custom, to assist a neighboring
farmer in the threshing of his wheat. In Darden's opinion Henry Davis's
assertion about there being no quarrel had been corroborated by the

testimony of Ed. L. Johnson at the hearing when he quoted Oscar Davis as saying that Waller had shot him without cause.

Another point in dispute at the hearing was whether Oscar Davis had been shot once or twice in the back. Finerty had produced a hospital record which, in contrast to the testimony of Doctor Risher, seemed to indicate that there had been only one bullet wound in the back. Darden called the hospital in Lynchburg on the morning of June 30 and reported that both the nurse who had attended Oscar Davis and the operating room supervisor told him that there had been two wounds in the lower back and that the bullets had lodged in the lower part of the abdomen. For Darden this gave further credence to Henry Davis's testimony. Darden also accepted the testimony of Thomas Younger and John Williams that Waller had threatened to get Davis the day before the shooting. Darden discredited the self-defense argument by simply noting that Davis family members testified that Oscar Davis did not own a pistol and that the uncontradicted evidence showed that he was not armed at the time of the shooting. Finally, Darden observed that "Odell Waller was unquestionably fiery and to a degree lawless," and thus he had shown "the temperament which led to this tragic occurrence." In short, without important exception, Darden ignored or dismissed the numerous doubts that Finerty and Preston had raised about much of the evidence and accepted the main lines of the prosecution's argument.

The question then remaining for Darden was whether he should exercise his power to commute. Commutation, he said, was something that should be done not just for the benefit of the convict but also "for the welfare of the people." It could not be used simply to convince those people who believed that the facts did not justify a death sentence that justice would prevail in Virginia. At this point Darden denounced the "widespread propaganda campaign which has been carried on without any regard for the facts in this case," and which has "misinformed and misled" many citizens. He did not identify the sources of the propaganda to which he objected, but it was clear that he had been angered by the Workers Defense League, and not just by the more extreme groups. Thus he noted with disapproval the WDL's appeals for financial contributions to Waller's defense "to be used for what purpose I do not know since the attorneys representing him" were serving without fee.[5] Darden had obviously been upset by many aspects of the campaign to save Waller, and his criticism of it was the one place where his emotions came through in a statement that otherwise was a rather dry recital of events and his interpretations of them. "I regard such propaganda campaigns as extremely detrimental to the public interests," he concluded. "The only possible effect is to sow racial discord at a crucial time when every loyal citizen should strive to promote unity."

Near the end of his statement, Darden briefly addressed the critical question of the poll tax and the class and economic differences between the Wallers and the members of the jury. But he had no sympathy for the argument that such differences prevented Waller from having a fair trial by a jury of his peers. "I do not believe that the payment of this small tax of $1.50 per year has the effect of dividing the people of the Commonwealth into economic classes. Many persons do not pay the tax though well able to do so. I am convinced that the rights of the accused were not prejudiced by the class of persons from which the jury was drawn." Darden then quoted the concluding part of the decision by the Supreme Court of Appeals of Virginia, which stated that "'the accused has had a fair and impartial trial, by an impartial jury; he has been convicted upon evidence adduced by members of his own race, which upon its face bears the impress of truth.'" Therefore, he said, "I have come to the conclusion that I should not interfere with their judgment."[6]

Reactions to Darden's decision were predictable. Waller's defenders were appalled. The Reverend Laurence T. Hosie, acting chairman of the WDL, declared that it signaled "the complete breakdown of American democratic processes so far as one Negro sharecropper—Odell Waller— is concerned."[7] Frank McCallister struggled to be fair. "I give Governor Darden credit for arriving at his decision honestly," he wrote to Eleanor Roosevelt, "but for the life of me I can't see how anyone could sit through the commutation hearing he did and then permit this boy to go to his death. Certainly there was enough reasonable doubt to permit commutation. . . . I can't understand his decision."[8] Pauli Murray felt "that his real reason for refusing to grant clemency was his resentment of the broad interest in the case, which brought Virginia's system of justice and his own role under public scrutiny."[9]

In contrast, Virginius Dabney accepted Darden's decision without protest, despite his recent support of clemency for Waller. In an editorial published on July 1, he stated that he had "never seen a fairer-minded or more conscientious inquiry than the Governor made in this case, and

whether or not one agrees with his conclusions, they should be acqui-
esced in by all." He added, however, that "the conditions which brought
forth this killing remain. Poverty, tenancy and sharecropping . . . are
blights upon our American civilization" which will not be solved by the
execution of Odell Waller.[10] The *Richmond News Leader* published a long
editorial on the decision that similarly praised "the dispassionate thor-
oughness of the Governor's decision," but, lacking any sense of the ambiguities in the case, its tone was different from Dabney's. Much of the
editorial was devoted to countering what it believed was the misrepresentation of facts by Waller's defenders. "Never has there been in Virginia so vigorous, so persistent and so intelligent an effort to create a
cause célèbre. . . . In the background all the while was an agitation one-
tenth for Waller and nine-tenth for radicalism, 10 per cent for the man
and 90 per cent against the poll-tax." Noting the rejection of the defense
arguments by the various courts, the *News Leader* concluded that "Darden
has acted most properly" and that the "execution of Waller will be . . . a
vindication and not a defeat of justice."[11] The *Danville Register*, which
probably reflected prevailing white sentiment in the Pittsylvania County
area, expressed a similar view but came to even more extreme conclusions. An editorial entitled "Justice Prevails" had high words of praise for
Darden but added, in an obvious attack on Virginius Dabney, that "his
decision and the accompanying statement should put to shame the pussy-
footing Virginia editors who counselled a cowardly course in the name
of social justice." The editorial concluded, with what Waller's defenders
would regard as perverse reasoning, that Darden "has restored dwin-
dling faith in Virginia justice. . . . He has made it possible for men, regardless of color, to continue receiving a fair and just trial in Virginia."[12]

One of the most thoughtful criticisms of Darden's decision came from
Thomas Sancton, the managing editor of the *New Republic*. Writing to
Virginius Dabney on July 2, he expressed his disappointment but added
that "the Governor, I am sure, did everything a conscientious man could
do to make a decision. So one may criticize his reasoning, but one can
hardly accuse him of having been hasty or casual in this very important
case."[13] A week later Sancton wrote a much longer, emotional letter to
Dabney in which he tried to relate the Waller case to the long history of
the abuse that blacks in the South have suffered at the hands of whites in
positions of authority. "I do not want to give you the impression that in
my own feelings I sentimentalized Waller's case. . . . But I would rather

make a mistake on that side, in writing or in my own innermost thoughts, than upon the side of cynicism, of prejudice, of smallness, or politics. I do not know Governor Darden, but from his background, which I have gone to the trouble of looking up, I felt that his decision was inevitable. Columbia and Oxford mean little, little more than veneer, in the thoughts and in the soul of a politician."[14] In an analysis of the Waller case published in the *New Republic* on July 13, Sancton continued his criticism of the courts, officials, and Governor Darden for failing to comprehend the elements that lay just below the surface of the evidence. "It was not the handouts of the Workers' Defense League, as Governor Darden believed, which turned this killer into a symbol. It was the Negro's racial memory of injustice." Darden decried the propaganda that could only lead to "racial discord," but, continued Sancton, "the Governor was incapable of any concept of unity on the white man's terms. . . . It is sahib unity, the unity of Burma, the unity of India, the unity of Java. Poll-tax unity." Relating the case to the struggles throughout the world of dark-skinned peoples against white oppression, Sancton concluded that "it was in Governor Darden's hands to win a truly great victory for Virginia, indeed for the whole South. Instead, he chose to interpret this case in the strict, unheroic spirit of a crossroads magistrate."[15]

Sancton's eloquent words, those of the liberal white southerner, represented the thinking of only a small minority in 1942. But they were relevant and insightful commentaries on the attitude of the governor and the other officials and judges involved in the Waller case. Thus Darden chose to ignore the enormous obstacles that confronted Waller in seeking justice, both before and after the shooting—the near impossibility of finding relief in the courts for his grievances against Oscar Davis, the attitude of the trial judge, the evidence that suggested coaching of prosecution witnesses by the authorities, the mistakes of his trial counsel, the gulf that separated the white jurymen from the poor black sharecropper. But as Sancton suggested, it was possible for Darden, and others, to ignore the social and political realities that separated whites from blacks, landlords from tenants, and the upholders of the established order from the poor and powerless, precisely because they would not, or could not, look below the surface and distinguish between form and substance. Odell Waller had killed Oscar Davis. The forms of the judicial process had, presumably, been followed. Therefore Waller must die.

Even after Darden's decision against commutation, however, Waller's defenders refused to abandon their efforts. On the evening of June 30, A. Philip Randolph suggested that a group of Negro leaders go to Washington on Wednesday, July 1, in hopes of meeting with President Roosevelt so that they might try to convince him to intervene. Pauli Murray, who was then in New York, worked all night to round up a delegation. Besides Randolph and Murray, the group consisted of Dr. Channing Tobias of the National Council of the YMCA; the Reverend William Lloyd Imes, pastor of St. James Presbyterian Church in New York; Frank R. Crosswaith of the Harlem Labor Center; Mary McLeod Bethune, director of the Division of Negro Affairs of the National Youth Administration; Layle Lane of the WDL and vice-president of the American Federation of Teachers; Anna Arnold Hedgeman, regional director of race relations, New York area Office of Civilian Defense. They were joined in Washington by a few others, including one white person, Albert Hamilton of the WDL. They hoped that they could convince Roosevelt to make a public appeal to Governor Darden to put off the execution and to appoint a commission of inquiry to examine the case on the grounds that Waller had not been tried by a jury of his peers and that Negro morale would be adversely affected unless there was an impartial examination of the issues. Their effort was a total failure. For more than eight hours they were given, in Layle Lane's bitter words, "the run around" by mostly courteous but largely insensitive officials. Unable to secure an appointment with Roosevelt, they met with Wendell Berge, the assistant attorney general of the United States, Criminal Division, and Victor Rotnem, chief of the civil rights section of the Justice Department. Afterwards they tried to see Vice-President Henry A. Wallace, but they were only able to confer with his secretary, Mr. Young, who, although friendly, seemed primarily determined that they did not disturb the vice-president. While waiting outside Young's office they saw Wallace enter and walk towards his office. When Wallace saw the group, he tried to avoid them. Mrs. Bethune, who knew Wallace, ran after him, but he dismissed her curtly with the observation, "I can do nothing, it is out of my jurisdiction."[16]

That evening the group was summoned to meet with Elmer Davis, the director of the Office of War Information, after Mrs. Bethune had informed Davis's office that the delegation had discussed forming a picket line around the White House. Although Davis listened politely, and even showed some awareness of the problems Negroes faced, he warned that the proposed picketing would cause trouble and please Mr. Goebbels. He did say that he would try to reach the president, but by then it was apparent that the day's efforts had been in vain.[17]

In addition to Randolph's delegation, others made some last-minute appeals. Both William Green, president of the American Federation of Labor, and Philip Murray, president of the Congress of Industrial Organizations, sent telegrams to Darden asking him to spare Waller's life. His execution, said Murray, "would be a grave miscarriage of justice. The attention of the nation is focused on this case and you have an opportunity to right a grievous wrong."[18] Vito Marcantonio, the American Labor party congressman from New York and president of the International Labor Defense, was among others sending telegrams to Roosevelt denouncing Darden's decision and asking Roosevelt to stay the execution. The *Daily Worker* reported that a delegation headed by Dr. Max Yergan, president of the National Negro Congress, and including John Davis, executive secretary of the National Negro Congress, Paul Robeson, and others, was going to try to meet in Washington on Wednesday evening with Vice-President Wallace or with Marvin H. McIntyre, secretary to the president, in the hope that one or the other could persuade the president to intervene. They were not successful in meeting either Wallace or McIntyre, but they did manage to talk with Attorney General Francis Biddle at his Georgetown home. Their efforts achieved nothing.[19] On that same day, Wednesday, July 1, the Washington *Evening Star* published a full-page advertisement that reproduced the petition that had been signed by many prominent people and sent by the WDL to the president on June 15. The advertisement listed seventy-eight names and noted that more than five hundred others had signed. It asked Roosevelt to intervene in the Waller case and "help restore the badly shaken faith of our Negro minority in American democracy."[20]

After their day of frustration in Washington, Randolph and the other members of his delegation looked to Eleanor Roosevelt as their last hope to save Waller's life. In early June she had written to Darden about Waller, and Murray and others in the WDL continued to send her information on the case. Their persistence must have had some effect, for on that final day, July 1, Mrs. Roosevelt tried repeatedly, through Harry Hopkins, to get her husband involved. But even her efforts were unavailing. Apparently tired of her attempts, the president finally telephoned her to say in unequivocal terms that he was not going to intervene with

Governor Darden.[21] Late that evening she telephoned to Randolph at NAACP headquarters in Washington, where he and the other members of his delegation waited, to report her failure. This distressing news sickened one member of the group and drove others to tears. Still, Murray reported that they tried until midnight to telephone to Darden, but he could not be reached.[22]

In the meantime Finerty tried to obtain a last-minute reprieve in order to give them an opportunity to pursue another appeal to the Supreme Court. After learning of Darden's decision against commutation, Finerty sent him a long telegram arguing that Waller had "an undeniable legal right" to apply to the Supreme Court for a review of the recent adverse decision by the district court and circuit court of appeals in his case. Finerty reminded Darden that he had repeatedly stated he would allow Waller the opportunity to exhaust every legal remedy, and Finerty insisted that Waller had the right to have the entire Supreme Court consider whether he "must die even though his constitutional rights have been violated, solely because of the error of his trial counsel."[23] On Wednesday afternoon, July 1, Darden attended a dedication of some new buildings at the Norfolk Navy Yard, and it was not until evening that Finerty was able to speak to him on the telephone. Predictably, Darden refused to consider any further reprieve.[24] Preparations for the execution, which was scheduled for 8:00 A.M. on Thursday, July 2, went ahead.

While the last desperate efforts were being made to save his life, Waller had to wait helplessly in his death row cell. On Wednesday, July 1, he began his 630th day there. This was reportedly the longest period that any criminal had, to that time, ever spent in a death row cell in Virginia.[25] The strain on him was obviously enormous, and by the end of June it began to affect his behavior. Prison Superintendent Major Rice Youell reported that Waller had become violent and that he had taken to cursing his guards and throwing things at them. As a result, a wire screen was placed in front of his cell. One black newspaper headlined its story "Odell Waller Goes Beserk As Death Nears."[26] Nevertheless, Youell reported that, on the morning of Wednesday, July 1, when Waller was informed of Darden's decision against commutation, he received the news "calmly and quietly."[27]

That afternoon, Annie Waller bid Odell a tearful farewell. "Mama, don't cry, because I know you have done everything you could for me," she recalled him saying. Then "he kissed me twice and said goodbye."[28]

After leaving the prison, Annie remained in Richmond waiting to accompany her son's body back to Gretna for funeral services already scheduled for Sunday, July 5. Waller saw two other outside visitors that last Wednesday afternoon. One was the Reverend E. H. Bouey, pastor of the Mount Calvary Baptist Church in Richmond. The other was one of his lawyers, Edmund M. Preston, who spent "three distressing hours" with him. Waller gave Preston a ten-page statement that he had painstakingly written in pencil earlier in the day. He asked that it be given to the newspapers. "I won't be able to see it, but I want it in there."[29]

Waller's "Dying Statement" is a remarkable document. A number of newspapers, including even the *Danville Register*, printed abridged versions of it. The full text, as released by the WDL, was published in the July 17 issue of *The Commonweal*.[30] In it Waller attempted to explain the difficulties he had gotten into. He reviewed his relations with Oscar Davis and stated that he had seen him carrying a pistol. He admitted that he had made mistakes, but he insisted that others had lied about him and that he had not intended to kill Davis.

> I relize I have't lived so up right in the past with the laws of the good lord and with the laws of the land. As my time comes near each second means I am one nearer my grave. I have asked God to forgive me an I feel that he has. . . . All you people take this under consideration have you ever thought Some people are alowed a chance over & over again then there are others ar alowed little chance some no chance at all. . . . this is Odell Waller speaking I axident [I accidentally] fell an som good people tried to help me Others did every thing they could against me so the governor & the corts [courts] dont no [know] the true facts First I will say dont work for a man two poor to pay you he will steel and take from you in my case I worked hard from sun up until sun down trying to make a living for my family an it ended up to mean death for me[31]

Shortly before 8:30 on the morning of Thursday, July 2, Waller was taken from his death row cell and, accompanied by Reverend Bouey and prison officials, was escorted to the execution chamber. At 8:35 he was strapped into the electric chair. Ten minutes later he was pronounced dead by Dr. C. C. Chewning, Jr., the prison physician. Twelve designated witnesses, including four men from Pittsylvania County, were present at the execution, but neither they nor prison officials would give out any further details, other than to report that Waller had had nothing to say during his final moments. About an hour later, Waller's body was released to an undertaker acting for Annie Waller and the WDL. That evening it was placed on board a train for Danville for return to Gretna and burial on Sunday.[32]

The agony of Odell Waller had at last come to an end. But for his family and his defenders the pain continued and could only be dulled by the passage of time. The period of hope, and repeated disappointments, was over; the search for meaning in the life and death of Odell Waller went on. Perhaps the most unusual feature of his case was the amount of attention that it had attracted, for there was nothing extraordinary about black males in the South being put to death for the killing of a white person. Waller was the 180th person to die in Virginia's electric chair since its first use on October 13, 1908. Although he was the first person to be put to death in over a year, there had been, on the average, between five and six executions annually since that date. The overwhelming majority of these unfortunates, 156 of the 180, or nearly 87 percent, were black males. Only 23 of the total, less than 13 percent, were white males, while one was a black female.[33] During these same years, Virginia's black population had declined from 32.6 percent of the total in 1910 to 24.7 percent in 1940.[34] Obviously, blacks were far more likely to suffer the ultimate punishment in Virginia than were whites.

For those who had struggled so hard to save Waller's life, it was no comfort to know that his fate was not unusual. That was part of the problem. For them his death was the extreme, seemingly inevitable, ending to a case that was rooted in the pervasive racial and economic injustice in America. By fighting for Waller they had hoped to do something about the larger problem. Thus many in the WDL were hit hard by the news that the execution had at last been carried out. On July 3 the WDL issued an anguished statement:

> An appalling blunder had been committed which should sober every American citizen with enough insight to understand the perils facing America and all freedom-loving peoples at this hour. The character of any people is not found in its words but in its deeds. The execution of Odell Waller is a setback to the improvement of race relations which has been going on steadily in the South for the last quarter-century.

The statement then listed four facts, any one of which should have resulted in clemency or at least in the postponement of the execution. First, "Waller obviously did not get a fair trial," especially because of the makeup of the jury. Second, the refusal of the Supreme Court to review the case on a mere technicality "has the effect of saying that a man can die for the technical error of his trial lawyer." Third, "the case had aroused the personal concern of millions of Americans . . . in an effort to protect the judicial process. . . . It seemed inconceivable that their earnest desire to fulfill their responsibilities as citizens should be so seriously affronted." Fourth, "an international problem of truly epochal significance has arisen in the relationship of colored people to the white races. . . . Here . . . was an opportunity to demonstrate that, in America, freedom knows no color."

> These facts prove exactly the opposite of Governor Darden's contention that the type of campaign carried on in behalf of Waller was "extremely detrimental to the public interests" and had the effect of sowing "racial discord at a critical time."
>
> The morale of the American people is based on the conviction that this is *their* government and that no liberty is to be infringed upon save because of military necessity. National unity does not depend upon blind acceptance of injustice but in eternal vigilance in the protection of liberty.
>
> Odell Waller has not died in vain. Around him have gathered Americans from every walk of life who understand more clearly now than heretofore how much black and white men have in common and how essential it is that they work together in creating an America that is free in fact as well as in hopes.[35]

As the WDL was the organization most closely involved in Waller's defense, its distress was understandable and expected. So too was the anger expressed in numerous editorials and stories in the black press immediately after the execution. "Democracy cannot long last with one law for the rich and another law for the poor, with justice for white citizens, and injustice for Negro citizens," cried the *Chicago Defender*, expressing sentiments shared by many other black newspapers.[36] In contrast, the immediate reactions in some of the white press that had shown an interest in the case was surprisingly mild. The *New York Herald Tribune*, for example, reported the execution in its news columns (on page

30) but ran no editorial.[37] The *New York Times* also relegated the story to page 19, although it did publish an editorial stressing the continuing problem in Virginia of "a poll tax system which disfranchises the poor and a system of land usage which wastes the national heritage and inflicts hardship on all involved in it," and expressing the hope that these conditions would be changed.[38] Virginius Dabney focused his editorial comments in the *Times-Dispatch* on a criticism of a requirement in New York that one had to own $250 worth of property to be eligible to serve on a jury, comparing it unfavorably with the practice in some parts of Virginia of selecting jurors from voting lists. "Whatever one thinks of Waller's guilt or innocence, it is not for New Yorkers to argue that the imposition of a $1.50 tax as a prerequisite to jury service is unfair to poor defendants."[39] Thus, in the hours just after the execution, Dabney's principal expressed concern was a defense of the state of Virginia from outside criticism, not the problems that led to Waller's death.

It was otherwise for the twenty-five hundred people who gathered in the sweltering heat for Waller's funeral service at the Fairview Baptist Church on Sunday, July 5. The church was a simple white structure on the edge of a shady grove some five miles southeast of Gretna and about one and a quarter miles southeast of the house that once belonged to Willis Waller and where Odell was born in 1917. Nearby was an old log cabin, the former Fairview School which Waller had attended. A short distance further down the road lay Fairview cemetery, which would soon become Odell's burial place. The little church could hold only two hundred people, so the remainder spread out on the church grounds. Many of the mourners were poor black folks from the surrounding area, ones who had known Odell. Others, some well dressed, came from more distant parts of Pittsylvania County, from Danville, from Altavista, from South Boston, and from other communities, in a gesture of brotherhood. Annie Waller was joined by her brother, Sam Hairston, of Columbus, Ohio, and her sister, Odell's natural mother, Dollie Harris, of Man, West Virginia, who was overcome by grief and had to be assisted by her husband and friends. Missing was Mollie Waller, Odell's wife, who, after testifying at the commutation hearing on the previous Monday, had returned to Washington, D.C., where she was living and working.[40] The only white person present was Morris Milgram of the WDL. The mourners had apparently made it clear that whites, especially local whites, were not welcome. As one black reporter put it, "They did not want 'Odell

Waller family members leaving Fairview Baptist Church after Odell's funeral, July 5, 1942. *In the front row from left to right* are Odell's uncle, Samuel Hairston; Annie Waller; Odell's natural mother, Dollie Harris; and her husband, Carl G. Harris. Courtesy of the Archives of Labor and Urban Affairs, Wayne State University.

Waller's murderers' to look on his face in death."[41] The other representative of the WDL was Layle Lane, one who earlier in the week had been
a member of the group that unsuccessfully sought to obtain Roosevelt's
intervention. Pauli Murray did not attend the funeral. The events of that
last week were all that she could take. As she later explained, "I felt his
death too keenly, and went back to New York instead, where we held a
memorial service."[42]

   Several ministers participated in the service. The Reverend J. R. Redd
of Danville led the mourners in singing "Nearer My God to Thee." The
Reverend I. T. Tunney of Chatham read from the Nineteenth Psalm,
and the Reverend R. H. Miller of Dry Fork "prayed for a better day when
there will be no more 'you're right and I'm wrong.'" Both Milgram and
Lane were called upon to say something to the mourners. Overcome
with emotion, Milgram "stood in silence and wept" before he was able to
speak. Waller had not died in vain, he said, for the case had brought
white and black together in the pursuit of justice. He also expressed
pride in the fact that "Waller's fight for life and his death had awakened
hundreds of thousands to the problem of the sharecropper and other
poor people."[43] Lane too sought out a lesson in Waller's death. As she
wrote a short while afterwards, "His death gave a significance to his living
which has revealed more clearly than ever before the evils of poverty, of
exploitation and of race prejudice. His death will not be in vain if we
take renewed courage to wipe these evils completely out of our national
life."[44] The Reverend R. L. Gilbert, the pastor of Fairview Church, delivered a short sermon "telling how trouble draws men to God." Throughout the service Waller's body lay in an open casket, which was finally
moved out to the church grounds so that it could be viewed by all who
had come to the service.[45] Afterwards Odell Waller's body was buried in
Fairview near the resting place of other members of his family.

   On that same Sunday afternoon another service was held for Waller
in New York City at the St. James Presbyterian Church at 141st Street in
Harlem. Speakers there included A. Philip Randolph, Pauli Murray, and
John F. Finerty. Murray gave a short account of Waller's life, summarized the efforts of the WDL on his behalf, and read from his "Dying
Statement." Finerty told the story of the unsuccessful legal battle to save
Waller's life. Anna A. Hedgeman, who had been a member of the delegation that had attempted to see Roosevelt on that previous Wednesday, described the difficulties her group had had and used the occasion

Pallbearers at Waller's funeral. *In the rear center* is J. H. Hughes, the undertaker from Danville. Courtesy of the Archives of Labor and Urban Affairs, Wayne State University.

to urge continued support for the March on Washington movement. Another member of that delegation, Frank R. Crosswaith, had a similar message about the need of blacks "to harness their power in their fight for complete equality." Similarly, A. Philip Randolph saw the memorial service as an appropriate place to remind blacks that they would achieve their rights only through mass action, and he "promised that if discrimination against the Negro continues, the actual march to Washington will be held." Another speaker, Ludlow Werner, the managing editor of the *New York Age*, brought up the Geyer anti–poll tax bill, which was then stalled in committee, and urged his listeners to vote against the reelection of any New York congressmen who had not signed the petition to discharge the bill from committee. "Let us answer the plea of the mother of Odell Waller and show her that though it was not within our power to

Layle Lane and Morris Milgram in front of Fairview Baptist Church after
Waller's funeral. Courtesy of the Archives of Labor and Urban Affairs,
Wayne State University.

spare the life of her son, it is within our power to strike at the very root of
the evil by defeating those who by their actions show that they favor the
continuance of the poll tax and all its attendant evils."[46]

The service at St. James Presbyterian Church was not the only
memorial gathering for Odell Waller in Harlem on July 5. At about the
same time, the Harlem section of the Communist party held a protest
meeting at the Congress Casino at 132nd Street and Seventh Avenue.
Speakers included James W. Ford, a black member of the national
committee of the Communist party, and Peter V. Cacchione, a
communist member of the city council. Cacchione stressed the

importance of "the colored peoples of the world in the war against fascism" and claimed that Waller's execution would "gladden the Axis." Ford called for the ending of racial inequality and contrasted the Four Freedoms with Jim Crow, the poll tax, and "the execution of sharecroppers." He placed primary responsibility for Waller's death on Governor Darden "and the Bourbons and Negro-baiters of the South." But he also struck out against the "mishandling of the case by the Trotskyites" and urged an investigation of their errors. "The Trotskyites," he said, "want to divide the people and injure the war effort."[47]

Although the *Daily Worker* referred to this gathering as a "mass meeting," it did not indicate how many people attended. It did note, however, that the group sent greetings to the meeting being held at St. James Presbyterian Church and urged united action in both the war effort and in the struggle for Negro rights. But Randolph had no use for the Communists. In response to their overture he complained that for almost two years they had been silent on the Waller case, but now "like vultures they are planning to seize on Odell Waller's dead body by holding a memorial meeting in New York. . . . Their only purpose is to confuse their totalitarianism with the historic fight for liberty which was so well conducted by the Workers Defense League."[48] Randolph's criticism was understandable. The Communists had paid little attention to the Waller case until very near the end, and, however much they proclaimed a commitment to racial equality, their interest in it, once begun, was consistently focused on their position in support of unity in the war against Nazi Germany.

Whatever their ideological intent, however, the concern of the Communists about the morale of American blacks was not misplaced. Many did regard the execution of Waller as a "legal lynching" and related it to a number of incidents of racially motivated violence that occurred shortly afterwards. Within two weeks of Waller's execution, a mob in Texarkana, Texas, lynched Willie Vinson, a young black; and a posse in Flagstaff, Arizona, shot and killed Private Jesse Smith, a black soldier. In Rome, Georgia, Roland Hayes, the celebrated tenor, was beaten by police, and, along with his wife, thrown into a jail cell because he had protested against the abusive treatment his wife had been subjected to by a shoe store clerk when she sat in an area usually reserved for whites.[49]

As a result of such incidents, A. Philip Randolph asked Pauli Murray to write an open letter of protest to President Roosevelt. Her letter, which was signed by the members of the delegation that had gone to Washington on July 1 and published in a number of Negro newspapers, was a long and bitter statement. "We who tried without success to see you on July 1 feel that in refusing to intervene in the case of Odell Waller, the government of the United States has failed us. . . . Waller's electrocution is a 'stab in the back' to a group of people who are asked to defend their country, but whom their government does not intend to defend." By refusing to stop Waller's execution because of "a mere technicality," the letter continued, the Supreme Court had also failed them. Waller "was the victim of a vicious economic and political system perpetuated by the poll tax and racial oppression." Moreover, "a man of Governor Darden's political associations, member of the Byrd-Glass machine, the political beneficiary of the poll tax system in Virginia could not be expected to respond to the broader social issues of the Waller case." They had gone to Washington to ask President Roosevelt to appeal publicly to Darden for a stay of execution, only to be denied an audience and to be "made to feel most poignantly the lack of sensitivity and intelligence with which high administration officials approach the colored man's problems." Waller's execution "was the signal for the barbarous forces in this country to renew the unleashing of their venom of hatred upon the Negro people. . . . These fascist-like brutalities in America are grist for the propaganda mills of the Axis powers. . . . If the colored man is not given his full rights now, then the battle for democracy is lost."[50]

Thus had the tragic ending to the Waller case left Pauli Murray and other concerned blacks frustrated and embittered. Unfortunately, they had little immediate success in channeling this sentiment into constructive protest. Randolph turned to a familiar tactic and called on the March on Washington movement to sponsor a silent protest parade in New York City on Saturday, July 25. Organized by the New York division of the March on Washington movement, it was intended to mourn the execution of Waller and to protest the killing of Willie Vinson and Jessie Smith and the jailing of Roland Hayes. As Dr. Lawrence Erwin, the president of the New York division, explained, there will be more of such incidents "if we let those things go unchallenged. No Negro will be safe anywhere." The intent was to have a massive demonstration. Participants wearing black arm-bands and carrying signs were to begin at 56th Street and Seventh Avenue at 2:30 and march silently to Union Square where a number of speakers would be heard at 4:00 P.M. Unfortunately, the event was not well planned. Randolph appointed Pauli Murray as organizer, but he then went off to Los Angeles for the NAACP convention. Murray and other organizers attempted to get Roy Wilkins, Walter White, or Thurgood Marshall from the national office of the NAACP to speak, but they were all unable to attend. Inadequate attention was given to various black leaders, and friction developed between the WDL, which had planned to participate, and Dr. Erwin. Ironically, the Communist party was one group that threw its support behind the protest parade, despite Randolph's recent rebuff of its offer of united action. Ultimately, in marked contrast to the large rally at Madison Square Garden on June 16, only about five hundred blacks participated in the march. The effect of the protest was lessened even further by the lack of coverage by most of the press.[51] Aside from the organizational problems, the enthusiasm for yet another protest might have been weakened by the realization that the Madison Square Garden rally, as well as the long campaign to save Waller, had failed to have any significant impact on public officials.

At the end of July the WDL finally closed its books on the case of Odell Waller. It had been a long, costly struggle that for nearly two years had overshadowed its numerous other activities. Contributions from all sources totaled $29,545.89. Part of this, $5,655.11, came from various organizations, mainly unions, plus some others such as the Jewish Labor Committee, the March on Washington movement, and the NAACP. But most, $23,890.78, came from the contributions of approximately fifty-five hundred people. Unfortunately, the total expenses were $32,390.39, so the WDL was left with a deficit of $2,844.50. The largest expenditures were for stationery, printing, and postage, followed by the salaries of the WDL's professional workers, clerical and office staff. Although the attorneys—Stone, Martin, Shapiro, Finerty and Preston—had donated their services, they still had significant expenses, mainly travel, for which they were compensated. The financial summary makes it clear why Clendenin proceeded with caution before he recommended commit-ting the WDL to the defense of Odell Waller. Justice in America did not come cheaply.[52]

For many of those who had been involved in the defense of Odell Waller, the weeks after his execution became a time of soul-searching and, in some instances, recrimination. An example of the latter was pro-vided by the Revolutionary Workers League. Little had been heard from that organization during the final months of the struggle. Then on July

15 it published an emotional defense of its position in the case in *The Fighting Worker*. "Now that Odell Waller is dead the 'liberals' and others are attempting to find a scape-goat" in the lawyer Stone and the RWL. It claimed, with considerable exaggeration, that the RWL "supported the Waller case fully 8 months before another organization became interested in it." The RWL had appealed for "a united front" for all defense efforts, it asserted, but the others had refused to cooperate. These involved a faction of Trotskyites with whom the RWL was at odds, as well as the WDL. The article denounced the WDL for entering into "an agreement with the Southern 'liberals,' thru Virginius Dabney . . . not to create any 'disturbances' in that area, i.e. not to organize any mass action in Virginia." Thus the WDL followed a policy of "class-collaboration," and "constantly toadied to the bourgeois state."[53]

The RWL held that Waller was innocent of the crime for which he was charged and should have been pardoned because he shot in self-defense. Davis had died not of gunshot wounds but of a collapsed lung brought on by "the carelessness of the hospital in giving him an anesthetic." The article charged that the WDL had "entered the case only on 'humanitarian' grounds, because he had been denied a fair trial," so it was willing to settle for life imprisonment. The WDL had also "spread rotten illusions about Governor Darden," passing him off as a great humanitarian, when in fact this "son-in-law of the DuPont family remained to the last the representative of financial capitalism and Virginia landlordism." The WDL lied about the RWL and Stone, suggesting that they were "major causes of this tragedy," when in fact without them "Waller would have died in September [*sic*] of 1940."[54] It was not because of mistakes made by Stone that Waller went to his death. Rather, "the capitalist judge, the capitalist court, the capitalist state WAS INTENT on killing Waller because of the CLASS issues involved." Thus, the article concluded, "Odell Waller died an innocent man" while the WDL and the "treacherous 'Southern liberals' . . . [sabotaged] every effort to build a real mass movement to save Waller. . . . They too are guilty, guilty of aiding the real criminal CAPITALISM, to take the life of the young Negro sharecropper, Odell Waller."[55]

The RWL's diatribe reached few beyond the limited number of faithful who subscribed to *The Fighting Worker*. Stone, however, tried to explain his role in the case to a wider audience in a long letter sent to several newspapers and magazines. Stone was understandably sensitive about the charge that he and Byron Hopkins had made errors in the trial that were responsible for the Supreme Court's refusals to intervene. Despite the ruling by the Supreme Court of Appeals of Virginia, he still believed that the language of the law and the intent of the Constitutional Convention of 1902 and of the legislature of 1902–4 had been to exclude non–poll tax payers from juries. But he also pointed out, correctly, that he and Hopkins had been allowed only a few days to prepare a defense, and it had to be done without any help from "the social democratic or liberal organizations or persons who now attack Mr. Hopkins and myself." If they had had some help, he continued, they might have been able to have examined the poll tax and jury lists and present such data at the trial. Stone also protested against the attacks upon the RWL. Professing little knowledge of or interest in its political composition, he nevertheless noted that it was the organization that had hired him and the only one that had supported Waller during the trial and for two months after it. Stone emphasized that, unlike the liberal groups, the RWL contended that "Waller was innocent, and that he did not deserve one day of incarceration." He concluded by claiming that his critics had failed to stress "the original and only crime, that of Oscar Davis when he expropriated Waller, his old mother and his wife of the fruits of their toil."[56]

Stone's letter was strongly argued, but it lacked the ideological vehemence of the article in *The Fighting Worker*. Clearly he had a valid point in noting the limited time he had been given to prepare for the trial and the lack of support from groups other than the RWL during that crucial period. Nevertheless, his letter prompted Pauli Murray to write a lengthy reply and defense of the WDL's efforts. First, she claimed that the WDL *had* taken an early interest in the case. This was shown by the efforts of Francis Heisler to prevent Waller's extradition from Ohio. Heisler had been willing to assist at the trial, but he missed it, she said, because Stone failed to notify him of the correct dates. Most of Murray's letter was a bitter denunciation of the activities of Stone and the RWL in Waller's case. "The early days of Waller's defense were hounded by the unhealthy role which the Revolutionary Workers League and Attorney Stone played." She believed that Edmund Campion's "unintelligent and antagonistic remarks" at the trial were "one of the reasons why the jury returned a death verdict." The WDL, and others such as the NAACP and the Brotherhood of Sleeping Car Porters, delayed in entering the case until the RWL ceased to insist on controlling the defense. It was the WDL that raised the money to carry on the fight for Waller, while most of the RWL publicity was devoted to a criticism of the WDL. Stone, who then represented the WDL, confused matters by speaking at a number of RWL meetings. "The net effect of their agitation was to becloud the issue of the case and make the work of the WDL incalculably more difficult." Real support for Waller in Virginia came only after "Mr. Stone withdrew from the defense in the spring of 1942." Then Preston was willing to enter the case, and Dabney switched his position. Murray's conclusion showed the depth of her feeling.

> Had Mr. Stone and the Revolutionary Workers League never handled the case, Waller would have had a fighting chance at least, though the patterns of Virginia justice would have remained the same. I'm for militancy and uncompromising struggle against racial and economic injustice, but the sooner unscrupulous radical organizations with purely political motives take their finger out of the Negro's fight and let him lead his own struggle the better it will be for all of us.[57]

None of Odell Waller's defenders, aside from his immediate family, had been more emotionally involved and deeply affected by the struggle than Pauli Murray. It was hard for her to let go, and in a sense she never did as she continued to struggle with the problems of racial and economic injustice that Waller had come to symbolize and which remained very much a part of the American scene long after his death.

From the start there was much about the case of Odell Waller that was distressingly commonplace, beginning with these underlying problems of racial and economic injustice. In any given year there were surely innumerable disputes between sharecroppers and landlords, as well as other homicides, that received little or no publicity. Had not Waller's flight and arrest in Ohio caught the attention of a number of national organizations, his case might never have become widely publicized. Even then, however, there were just enough problems about it to cause some potential defenders to hold back their support. Unlike the Sacco-Vanzetti case, for example, on which Finerty also worked and where significant doubt existed about their participation in the robbery and shooting for which they were charged, the fact that Waller shot and killed Oscar Davis was never at issue. Beyond that there was a great deal in dispute, but ultimately sides tended to be drawn according to the extent of one's sensitivity to the underlying economic, social, and racial realities that help account for Waller's actions.

Thus, as Finerty and Preston argued at the commutation hearing, there was more than a reasonable doubt that Waller committed a cold-blooded, premeditated murder. The evidence of his threats to get Davis, allegedly made the day before the shooting, depended on the unreliable, very probably coached, testimony of two black witnesses. The evidence that there was no quarrel or harsh words between Oscar Davis and Waller just prior to the shooting depended on the unreliable testimony of Henry Davis and was contradicted by Odell Waller and later Annie Waller, and on its face appeared inherently improbable. The evidence that Waller deliberately shot Oscar Davis twice in the back was not clear, and, as Finerty showed, the back wounds could be explained by Davis having been spun around by a series of shots from the frightened Waller. There was conflicting testimony as to whether Oscar Davis owned or frequently carried a pistol, but Waller's claim that he believed Davis was armed is credible under the circumstances. Thus, the fact that Waller carried a gun when he went to confront Davis about his wheat can be seen just as readily as an act of self-defense by a frightened young man than as part of a planned murder.

The disputes over the facts surrounding the shooting loom all the larger when one considers whether Waller received a fair trial before a jury of his peers. The white, landlord dominated, poll tax–paying jurors resolved all doubts in favor of the prosecution. A truly representative jury, one that included blacks and sharecroppers, would very likely have reached a different conclusion. Waller's jurors were incapable of comprehending or looking critically at the institutionalized racism and economic injustice that did so much to explain his behavior. This was equally true for the prosecution and the judge. From the start, Judge Clement's attitude was hostile to the defendant and to the defense lawyers, beginning with his unseemly haste in scheduling the opening of the trial only three days after Waller's indictment by the grand jury. Waller's trial difficulties were compounded by the mistakes of his counsel and the prejudice inevitably generated by the presence of representatives of the RWL. Some of Stone's difficulties can certainly be explained by the lack of time he was given to prepare for the trial. Given more time, he might have undertaken an investigation into the jury and poll tax payments, as well as produced evidence that Waller was a non–poll tax payer. Such evidence, introduced in timely fashion at the trial, might have saved Waller's life, for the Supreme Court later said, in effect, that he could be executed for the procedural error of his counsel.

Thus, the circumstances of Waller's trial—the composition of the jury, the attitude of the judge, the inadequate time to prepare a defense, the association of detested radicals with the defense, the quality of his counsel —made it difficult, if not impossible, for Waller to receive a fair trial. A fair trial, that is, according to the standards deemed just in the minds of his defenders. But at the time Virginia's highest court and the federal courts saw things differently. Unwilling or unable to look beyond form to substance, they found no constitutional error sufficient to reverse his conviction or to stop his execution. There was indeed a long way to go before the ideal of equal justice under the law became a reality.

Beyond the forms of the criminal process, however, were other related but more deep-seated issues—ones of poverty and helplessness, of race and power. They involved memories of injustices and wrongs against the poor and the black that regularly went uncorrected. They involved a realistic understanding by Waller, and others like him, of the lines of power and the limits they were held to. They involved Waller's inability to find, or even to conceive of, redress for his grievances through regular, constituted channels. Thus one must recognize the anger and fear that the ugly circumstances must have produced in Odell Waller. These cannot, as Finerty and other defenders acknowledged, excuse the shooting, but they can help us understand it, and see it, correctly, as something other than premeditated murder. The life and death of Odell Waller tell us much about the limits and failings of American society. Those who defended him were correct in relating him to deeper issues and in seeing him as a symbol of the broader racial and economic problems of their time.

For one historical moment, Odell Waller's name had become known, and took on a meaning, for many people across the country. But, except for those who were directly involved in his case, it was soon forgotten, overshadowed by the far greater events of the time, especially World War II. Subsequently, it was lost even to the historians who do not seem to have remembered it even in the proverbial footnote. It deserves to be remembered, however, for it raised important issues, and it can serve as a continuing reminder of some of the obstacles that the American people have had to overcome, and how far they have to go, to achieve a racially and economically just society.

Epilogue

Although the story of Odell Waller quickly became a part of a largely forgotten past, some of the key issues, particularly that of the poll tax, remained very much alive for years to come. Similarly, the life and death of the poor black sharecropper from Gretna had, in varying degrees, a continuing impact on many of those who had been involved in his case. This is easiest to trace, of course, in those who remained in public life. A number of the participants, however, dropped totally out of sight, leaving no available record of their whereabouts or activities.

Among the latter was Mrs. Oscar Davis, from whom little was heard after Waller's trial in September 1940. This was also true of Odell's wife Mollie. After testifying at the commutation hearing on June 29, 1942, she told a reporter that she was going back to Washington, D.C., and that she never expected to return to Pittsylvania County.[1] She left Richmond without stopping to visit Waller in the penitentiary and did not attend her husband's funeral.

Annie Waller also left Virginia. After the funeral she went to live with her sister, Dollie Harris, in Man, West Virginia. She exchanged a few letters with some of her friends in the WDL, but after the summer of 1942 neither she nor her sister was heard from again. In a letter to Morris Milgram she indicated her shock at what had happened, but she expressed her sincere appreciation to him and to the WDL for doing all it could to try to save Odell's life. In closing, she wrote:

> I also hope that Odell is now at rest sleeping in the arms of Jesus Christ. Where he need not fere being harmed as god will sheild him from all harm and danger. And I hope to meet him in the great beyond in the great bye-m-bye if it is god ever lasting will[2]

Judge J. Turner Clement had no regrets. Among the whites in Pittsylvania County and Danville he remained a respected public official, and when he died on November 18, 1944, the *Pittsylvania Tribune* and the *Danville Register* showered him with praise as having been an able and principled jurist. Neither newspaper mentioned the Waller case in its obituary or editorial.[3] The writer of the obituary published by the Virginia State Bar Association, however, stressed the courage and fairness with which Clement had handled cases involving whites and blacks and discussed the Waller case in that context. For that writer at least, Clement was seen as one who withstood mistaken popular pressure in favor of Waller and saw to it that "the case proceeded in an orderly and judicial manner."[4] The fact that the campaign to assist Waller came after the hasty trial was obscured in this obituary.

Governor Darden had devoted a considerable amount of time to the Waller case during the first six months of his administration and had been subjected to extraordinary pressure by both opponents and proponents of commutation. He had certainly been upset by the critics from outside of Virginia and had referred to misleading and false statements in the literature of Waller's defenders. But, when challenged by Pauli Murray to indicate any inaccuracies in the only "pamphlet" put out by the WDL on the Waller case (Murray and Kempton, *All For Mr. Davis*), he declined, stating that he had not seen that document and that his references had been to other "circulars" issued by the WDL. "Whatever may be your desires in the matter it is too late now to attempt to correct them. . . . The truth would never reach the thousands of people throughout the Country to whom the circulars were sent."[5]

Nevertheless, the experience had weighed heavily on Darden, and it stimulated his interest in reform in the state's penal system. One result was the creation of a Pardon and Parole Board that had commutation power; another was the establishment of a new full-time Board of Corrections which was headed by Major Rice M. Youell.[6] But on the larger underlying issues, particularly that of race, Darden remained cautious at best and, at times, unreconstructedly conservative. Although he said he was against the poll tax, he opposed federal anti–poll tax legislation. A Virginian gentleman, he did not engage in race-baiting political tactics, but he defended segregation and refused to back the modest reform championed by Virginius Dabney in late 1943, the repeal of the streetcar segregation laws. Viewed by whites as a genteel reformer who left a progressive record as governor, Darden remained a biased "20th Century Confederate" in the opinion of at least some Virginia blacks. Still, after

Two victims. Gravestones of Oscar Davis in Chatham Burial Park in Chatham and of Odell Waller in Fairview Cemetery near Gretna. In one final error, Waller's death date has been erroneously carved as July 3 instead of July 2, 1942. Photographs by Richard B. Sherman.

he completed his governorship in 1946 he continued to use his undisputed talents to serve the state and nation, most notably as president of the University of Virginia from 1947 to 1959 and briefly as a delegate to the United Nations. Although the first black students at the University of Virginia were admitted during his presidency, Darden was no integrationist. In 1956 he took the position that *Brown* v. *Board of Education* was "such a departure from judicial precedent . . . as to render the decision not truly legal." Darden died on June 9, 1981. A long obituary in the *Richmond Times-Dispatch* did not mention his role in the case of Odell Waller.[7]

Virginius Dabney was a late and reluctant supporter of clemency for Odell Waller, and his concern had been as much or more for the international implications of the case as it had been over the question of the fairness of Waller's trial. Perhaps, therefore, it was not surprising that he accepted Darden's decision against commutation, and Waller's death, with such equanimity. Still, no newspaperman devoted as much time to the case as had Dabney between November 1940 and July 1942. Dabney continued his opposition to the poll tax and, in November 1943, proposed the abolition of segregation on Virginia's streetcars and buses. But in 1942 and 1943 he also feared that the increasingly aggressive tone of blacks demanding improvement in their condition and abolition of segregation would lead to violence and bloodshed.[8] The limits of Dabney's racial liberalism were more clearly demonstrated in the latter 1950s when, in conformity to the wishes of his publisher, he failed to criticize massive resistance. What Dabney saw in the Waller case had been filtered through his understanding of the proper relationship between whites and blacks, and however benign those views may have been, compared to those of the strident racists or even much of the white public, they were very different from the understanding of most blacks, certainly of Pauli Murray, and of those few whites who were truly committed to racial equality. Thus the long-run impact of the case of Odell Waller was very different for him from what it was for Pauli Murray or Morris Milgram. Significantly, Dabney's 1978 memoir, *Across the Years*, does not mention Odell Waller.[9]

Thomas H. Stone's emotional denunciations of Dabney had been excessive and counterproductive, but buried in the overblown rhetoric was a recognition of the distinct limits of such southern liberalism. Not surprisingly, Stone continued to regard himself as an "independent leftist," and he pursued a maverick career that was definitely at odds with Virginia's political and legal establishment.[10] After dropping out of the Waller case in the spring of 1942, he kept on practicing law in Richmond, where hc served both white and black clients. He reappeared one final time in connection with Odell Waller on November 27, 1942, when he participated in a memorial meeting in Richmond sponsored by the National Labor Defense Congress, the organization formed by the RWL in the spring of 1942.[11] Stone's subsequent career never again attracted public attention comparable to that surrounding his role in the Waller case or with the Richmond Unemployed Council in the 1930s. But his activities remained of interest to the FBI, which for years thereafter kept him under continual scrutiny. Stone continued his association with the RWL, for whom he worked as legal counsel, but he claimed that he merely checked articles appearing in *The Fighting Worker* to be sure that they were suitable for transmission through the United States mails. The FBI reports later alleged that Stone sometimes used the alias Thomas F. Harden, a man they identified as being the organizational secretary of the RWL. Although the FBI characterized Stone "as one of the more radical individuals in the State of Virginia," they produced no evidence of any illegal or subversive activity. Stone died in Richmond on June 10, 1963.[12]

Edmund M. Preston also continued to practice law in Richmond, but, unlike Stone, he was associated with the eminently respectable firm of Hutton, Williams, Anderson, Gay & Moore. Some whites from southside Virginia, however, did not forgive him for his vigorous defense of Waller and his attack on Clement at the commutation hearing. On July 7, 1942, the *Danville Register* published an editorial commenting on Preston's criticism of Clement for the letters he had sent to the *Richmond Times-Dispatch* and the *New York Times*. It claimed that Preston had made a serious charge that ought to be heard by a committee of the Virginia Bar Association to determine if it was correct or if "Mr. Preston has unjustifiably disparaged both Judge Clement and the Virginia judiciary."[13] Nothing came of this, but the members of the bar of Clement's Seventh Judicial Circuit passed a resolution that denounced Preston's criticism of Clement as "intemperate, unwarranted, and of such a nature that it properly calls for an apology." At the same time, they expressed their confidence in Clement. They sent copies of the resolution to Preston and Darden.[14] In contrast, the WDL honored Preston at a testimonial dinner in the spring of 1943, at which time they acclaimed his distinguished service in his efforts to protect the constitutional rights of Odell Waller.[15] Outside of Pittsylvania County and vicinity Preston continued to be respected as an able, liberal-minded Virginian, one who showed his commitment to the public good by serving, among other duties, on the executive committee of the Richmond Commission on Interracial Cooperation and on the executive committee of the Southern Regional Council. He lived and worked in a different world from that of Thomas Stone, but his effort on behalf of Odell Waller was consistent with his conception of his own responsibilities to further justice. Preston died at the age of forty-six on March 21, 1945.[16]

John F. Finerty also continued to pursue a career in law and public service that was consistent with his efforts in the Waller case. On September 23, 1942, he testified as a representative of both the WDL and the ACLU in favor of the Pepper anti–poll tax bill at a Senate subcommittee hearing.[17] In his remarks he drew on the Waller case and voting practices in Pittsylvania County to illustrate the baneful effects of the poll tax. In the fall of 1942 the WDL honored Finerty as the recipient of its annual award for distinguished service in behalf of labor's rights. He was selected for his work in defense of Odell Waller and for the abolition of the poll tax.[18] Finerty's distress over the fact "that a man can be executed for the procedural errors of his counsel" did not lessen. In his testimony before the Senate subcommittee he said that he hoped "to have the *Waller case* back before this committee in an effort at a subsequent date to prevent what I consider further indulgence in a barbarous doctrine."[19] This did not happen. Ten years later, in September 1952, he expressed similar sentiments in a letter to Thurgood Marshall, to whom he had sent copies of some of his briefs and petitions in the Waller case.[20] Finerty's affinity for difficult, and often lost, causes was shown again the next year when he labored, without success, to convince the Supreme Court to spare the lives of Julius and Ethel Rosenberg. This was his last big constitutional case. He retired in 1961 and died on June 5, 1967.[21]

Morris Milgram and Pauli Murray were the two members of the WDL staff who were most closely involved in the case of Odell Waller. From his position as assistant national secretary and subsequently national secretary of the WDL, Milgram, then a young man in his mid twenties, assisted in the efforts to save Waller from the beginning to the end. After returning from Waller's funeral, he "resolved to transform the WDL into a new abolitionist agency to abolish all forms of racial discrimination." In this he did not succeed, although the WDL did significantly increase its efforts to fight job discrimination.[22] Milgram continued with the WDL until 1947. He then entered the housing construction business, a field apparently totally unrelated to his earlier endeavors. After spending a few years learning the trade, however, Milgram turned his talents to the decidedly unfashionable business of developing integrated, multiracial communities. His decision was due, at least in part, to the influence of Pauli Murray's epic poem, "Dark Testament," which showed him "that the ghetto's purpose is to preserve the unfreedom blacks suffered under slavery."[23] During the 1950s he began building integrated housing in the Philadelphia area. Before long his work spread to New York, Washington, and other cities, and it continued over the next three decades. Milgram's operative premise has been that racially integrated housing was not only morally right but practical and potentially profitable. Along with James Farmer he founded, and continues to serve as president of, the Fund for an Open Society, a nonprofit mortgage fund dedicated to open housing. Thus the dedication and racial idealism Milgram displayed in his work for the WDL and its campaign to save Odell Waller became guiding characteristics of a lifetime career.

Pauli Murray's life was deeply affected by the case of Odell Waller. More than anyone else among his defenders she seemed to empathize with the unfortunate young sharecropper, and on a number of occasions she reminded him and others that she too had experienced the inside of a Virginia jail. Her work on the Waller case convinced her that she had to study law, and taking up an offer for a fellowship from Leon Ransom, the acting dean of Howard University Law School, she began her studies in the fall of 1941. While in law school she organized a successful sit-in that desegregated a small cafeteria in Washington. After graduation from Howard in 1944 she practiced and taught law until the early 1970s. In an extraordinarily active life she found time to champion the rights of women as well as blacks, and in 1966 she became one of the cofounders of the National Organization for Women. In 1973 she switched careers and, after several years of theological study, was ordained in 1977 as the first black female Episcopal priest.[24] For many years Murray worked on an epic poem of blacks in America called "Dark Testament," the work that had such an impact on Morris Milgram. She completed her first version in 1943. Part 2 drew heavily on her connections to Odell Waller.

> For the same red earth gives rest
> To the white bones of Tom Jefferson
> And the white bones of Odell Waller,—
> Sharecropper and President—in death all men are equal.
>
> For the heart of America is Tom Jefferson
> And the heart of America is Odell Waller.
> Tom wrote it down in words and they made him President.
> Odell wrote it down in words too—in the shadow of the Chair.[25]

She then quoted extensively from his "Dying Statement." "Dark Testament" was first published in 1945 in Lillian Smith's journal, *South Today*. It was a drastically revised version that omitted the second reference to Waller and the quotation from the "Dying Statement," but it retained the phrase, "And the white bones of Odell Waller."[26] A final version was published in 1970, along with a number of her other poems. Milgram wrote an introduction to this collection in which he emphasized the impact of the Waller case on her life and writings. In this version the "white bones of Odell Waller" become the "white bones of Nat Turner."[27] The deletion of Waller was not a measure of the importance of his case on Murray's life; rather it was a response to the obvious, but painful, fact that America had almost entirely forgotten his case. But the underlying lessons were still there to be learned. In her later years Murray was a priest at the Episcopal Church of the Holy Nativity in Baltimore, the city of her birth. She retired in January 1984 and moved to Pittsburgh, where she died on July 1, 1985.[28]

Many of those involved in the Waller case lived to see significant changes in the social, economic, and racial conditions that had set the stage for the tragic events of the early 1940s. But there was no quick, or complete, resolution of all the issues and problems. The defense's innovative argument that equal protection of the laws demanded that a particular economic class not be excluded from jury service did not find favor. Had it been possible to have shown systematic exclusion from the jury because of race, Waller's conviction would certainly have been overturned on appeal. But such was not the argument. Although the Supreme Court has accepted the notion that a jury should be representative of the community, it has interpreted that idea to mean that the jury has to be randomly drawn from a cross-section of the community, not that a particular economic group, or even race, has to serve on a particular jury.[29]

The campaign to abolish the poll tax also proved premature. During the next two decades, Congress was unable to enact a federal anti–poll tax law, although three states, Georgia in 1945, South Carolina in 1951, and Tennessee in 1953, eliminated the tax. It remained in Virginia and four other southern states, however, until the ratification of the Twenty-fourth Amendment in January 1964. This prohibited the poll tax as a prerequisite for voting in federal elections, but it continued to be required for state and local elections in those five states. Arkansas dropped the tax late in 1964. The end finally came in March 1966 as a result of a suit brought by Virginia residents. In the case of *Harper et al.* v. *Virginia State Board of Elections*, the Supreme Court held that the tax was an unconstitutional violation of the equal protection of the laws clause of the Fourteenth Amendment.[30]

The abolition of the poll tax, and the application of the 1965 Voting Rights Act, resulted in substantial increases in the number of blacks voting in Virginia. Similarly, the civil rights movement brought about the abolition of the oppressive segregation laws. The end of the Great Depression and the long period of expansion after World War II also played an important role in altering the economic conditions that had victimized both the Davis and the Waller families. Not everything had changed in Pittsylvania County by the 1990s, however, for poverty had not been abolished, and one could still recognize fairly easily many of the black and white sections. Still, enough had happened by that time to make it possible to believe that a simple repetition of the events of 1940 to 1942 would be very unlikely. Odell Waller may have been forgotten by most people, but there has been at least some righting of the wrongs that his life and death once symbolized.

One final footnote to the story remains. Later in the summer of 1940, after the death of Oscar Davis, Henry Davis delivered to the Waller family the sacks of wheat that had been owed to them.[31]

Appendix
Odell Waller's Dying Statement

Written July 1, 1942. Transcribed from photocopy
of original handwritten manuscript in Finerty Papers.

I relize I havent lived so up right in the past with the laws of the good lord and with the laws of the land. As my time comes near each second means I am one nearer my grave. I have asked god to forgive me an [and] I feel that he has. One thing you cant make a young person out of an ole [old] one an you cant make a ole person out of a young one. it takes time an expernce [experience]. All you people take this under consideration have you ever thought Some people are alowed a chance over & over again[.] then there are others are alowed little chance[.] some no chance at all[.] when a fellow accident [accidentally] falls dont get one [on] him with both feet[.] help him up an when he see another ditch he will walk around it an advise others of the place so they can seen it. if you mash him down he cant advise others of the danger[.] this is Odell Waller speaking I axident [accidentally] fell an som good people tried to help me[.] Others did every thing they could against me so the governor & the corts [courts] dont no [know] the true facts[.] First I will say dont work for a man two poor to pay you[.] he will steel and take from you[.] in my case I worked hard from sun up until sun down trying to make a living for my family an it ended up to mean death for me[.] when the wheat was threshed I was in maryland working 7 days a week 10 to 12 hours per day sending money home to pay for harvesting & thrashing the wheat and had told mother to have Robert to bring my share from the machine when it was threshed Robert hope [helped] measure the wheat an my share was 52 bushels[.] his wagon was there to move my share[.] Mr Davis was too poor to see me have the wheat an wouldnt let Robert cary the [it] to mothers house[.] took it and locked it in his store house[.] I diten [didn't] owe him one penny[.] I should have gave him the wheat if I had to beg for bread and eat out of other people garbage cans[.] now going after the wheat I wasnt thinking of shoting Mr Davis[.] when I left home I put the gun in the truck and the pistol in my parket [pocket] planing on getting of [out of] the truck up at the road coming around the edge of the woods seeing a Rabbit or some thing[.] I told that in cort[.] here is how thomas was at davis[.] his Father an law had cut Curtis Williams an was in jail. Curtis lived on the next farm working with a farmer[.] Thomas said he was going to go over an see Curtis about going to the trial that morning and I will be back an help load the wheat[.] he got off and went down cross the field to Curtis[.] I spoke to Mr Davis & Henry a negro staying with Davis[.] they spoke[.] I told Mr Davis I came after my share of the wheat[.] Henry said you cant carry that wheat all one [on] that truck[.] I said I can make two trips[.] then Davis spoke[.] you ant [ain't] going to carry that wheat away from here[.] I told him I diten [didn't] see why[.] I diten owe him any thing[.] when I said that Davis flue hot [got hot] and began to cursh [curse] about the wheat[.] naturly I got angry and from one word to another[.] Davis thut [thrust] his hand in his pocket in an effet [effort] to draw a gun[.] if he diten have one he was Bluffing[.] he frightened me[.] I pulled a gun an begin shoting not intending to kill him[.] I was frightened[.] I dont no [know] what became of Henry[.] I dont no how many times I shot[.] I thue [threw] the pistol away[.] I no Davis had a pistol for I have seen it in his parket [pocket.] he carried it for his son Edgar[.] they always had trouble and Davis tried to make Edgar leave so he could take his tobacco crop in 39 [1939.] Edgar wouldnt leave[.] he said I fight Dady [daddy] every day before he take my crop[.] Edgar said after this year he can have the farm so Edgar & Frank Davis Both left in 40 [1940.] now here it is a negro have shot a white man[.] Thomas younger was with me[.] got off the truck going over to Curtis Williams[.] naturly the law got them[.] they scared like I would have been or any other negro is liable to say any thing[.] also henry staying there with Davis so they lied like a dog[.] Thomas young [Younger] & Curtis told I said I was going to kill Mr Davis[.] I never told nether one that[.] Henry Eating from Mr. Davis table he had better tell a lie on me for Mr Davis if he new [knew] what was best[.] even the law questioned Archard [Archie] Waller[.] Birk Fitzearlds [Buck Fitzgerald] the boy driving the truck[.] they Diten lie[.] the law came an got my mother and wife an carried them to Chatham[.]

Kept them up ther in the night[.] it wouldnt have surprised me if they hadnt told a lie one me threu [through] fear of the law[.] thank God they diten tell a lie

the good Book sais a lie is the worst thing a person can tell[.] so I no [know] lies was told one [on] me[.] they no they lied and God no they lied so in the great day God will say you fellows lied on Odell Waller[.] so I appreciate every effert [effort] the people put forth to try to save me[.] it is a none [known] fact man is the ruler over Earth but God is the ruler of all[.] man can say Odell you must die at a certen time then God can call man an say you must Die.

Refering to my carictar [character] when I started to violate the laws of the land I was farming working part time day an night trying to make some thing[.] During the year I bought a car[.] One time the end of the year I diten have any thing to pay for it with the man was going to take it back[.] I wanted to keep the car[.] I diten believe in Robin [robbing] & Steeling so I bought 2 Gallons of whiskey from a fellow & gave him $5.00 for it[.] I sold that at 50 or 60 ¢ per pint[.] took that money an bought some more[.] when I sold that I made a little payment on the car[.] I kept on bying an selling paying on cars[.] that got me that rep [reputation.] As the avage [average] boy do I wanted to ride fast[.] I was pulled my permit took[.] I waited the time out and went to the motor vehicle man for another permit[.] he told me I would have to put up a $10,000 Bond before I could get another permit[.] where were I going to get the money[.] Rob A Bank[.] I wasnt thinking of nothing like that so I drove some without a permit[.] I was caught for that[.] One sun day I put a Razor in my parket to carry it to a friends house to have it sharpened[.] I got one [on] a car with some more boys an we went by to see a boy had Been in a fight that saturday night[.] me an some more boys was out there in the yard cutting some fire wood for the sick man during the time Mr. Hubard [Herbert] Bailey & another officer drove up to the house with the boy who cut the sick boy[.] when Mr Baley got out of the car I thought about the razor I had in my parket[.] it was an old car sitting by the wood pile[.] I droped the razor in it[.] the other officer saw m [me.] he said get that gun that fellow put in the car[.] I reached over an grabed the razor out of the car and out Run Mr Baley[.] several weeks after that I was at Chatham to a tent shoe [show.] Mr Baley had told the town law when they caught me up there to lock me up so they did[.] when I was Running across the field I passed a Briar patch and thrue the razor in it[.] Mr Baley could [couldn't] catch me an he went back and got the razor[.] my father was at the trial and told him it was his Razor an why I had it[.] they gave it back to father All Right[.] when I was tried Mr Joseph Whitehead Common wealth attorney called Mr Bailey County Officer to testifie against me[.] this is the last man should lie[.] here is what he said[.] Odell Waller was a bootleger[.] that was true Odell been caught Reckless Driving an after his permit had been taken caught carry a Razor[.] he is a dangerous boy[.] the Judge said what about him dangerous[.] with the best respects to Mr. Baley here is where he lied[.] Odell thruten [threatened] me with the Razor[.] I threten him with gravels from my feet running[.] All of that to make it hard on me[.] All I could do was set there an take it[.] you take big people as the president Governors Judgs their children will never have to suffer[.] they has plenty money[.] Born in a mention [mansion] nothing to never wory about[.] I am glad some people are that lucky[.] The penitentiary all over the United states are full of people ho [who] was pore tried to work and have something couldnt dos [do] that maid [made] them steel an rob[.] look at that fellow here[.] he wanted a bicycle his people was to pore to buy him one[.] to get a bycycle he killed a man wife an Dauter [daughter] to get the money[.] look at the Lees bug [Leesburg] case those fellows killed that Lawyer an took his car[.] they were looking [for] money they were[.] while they are in prison for life thats what happens to the poor people[.] I wont say anymore

—Odell Waller

Notes

Abbreviations

Hearing Transcript of "Public Hearing Before Hon. Colgate W. Darden, Jr.,
Governor of Virginia, In re Odell Waller, Richmond, Virginia, June
29, 1942." Copy in Odell Waller Case Files, John F. Finerty Papers,
Manuscripts Dept., University of Oregon Library, Eugene.

Record Printed copy of trial transcript of *Commonwealth of Virginia* v. *Odell
Waller*, Circuit Court of Pittsylvania County, Sept. 19, 26, and 27, 1940,
in Record no. 2442, *Odell Waller* v. *Commonwealth of Virginia*, submitted
to the Supreme Court of Appeals of Virginia. The Record includes
the defense's "Petition For Writ of Error," and its Bills of Exceptions.
Copy in box 3, OWF.

OWF "Odell Waller File—1942"—15 boxes of MS in Secretary of the
Commonwealth, Executive Papers, Archives and Records Division,
VSL.

RWL Revolutionary Workers League of the U.S.

VSL Virginia State Library, Richmond.

WDL Workers Defense League.

WDLC Workers Defense League Collection, Archives of Labor and Urban
Affairs, Walter P. Reuther Library, Wayne State University, Detroit.
Number refers to box and folder. E.g., box 183, folder 1, is cited as
"box 183-1."

Chapter 1

1. *Richmond Times-Dispatch*, July 1, 1942, 1.

2. "Odell Waller's Dying Statement," photocopy of original, Odell Waller
Files, John F. Finerty Papers, Manuscripts Dept., Univ. of Oregon Library,
Eugene.

3. Commonwealth of Virginia, Dept. of Agriculture and Immigration,
Virginia, comp. and ed. Charlotte Allen (Richmond, [1937]), 221; U.S. Dept. of
Commerce, 16th Census of the United States, 1940, *Agriculture, Virginia*, 1st ser.

(Washington, D.C.: GPO, 1941), 10, 16, 25, 34, 60, 74; U.S. Dept. of Commerce, 16th Census of the United States, 1940, *Population*, 2d ser., Characteristics of the Population, *Virginia* (Washington, D.C.: GPO, 1941), 44; U.S. Dept. of Labor, Bureau of Labor Statistics, *A Statistical Survey of the Danville Area, Virginia*, Industrial Area Statistical Summary no. 18 (Jan. 1943), sec. III, B, 2.

4. 16th Census, *Agriculture, Virginia*, 1st ser., 19, 25; "The Case of Sharecropper Waller," WDL press release, May 25, 1942, 4–5. A federal government study of sharecropping contracts noted that "No Virginia cases have been reported in which the cropper attempted to assert his rights" by suing for breach of contract. See: U.S. Dept. of Commerce, 16th Census of the United States, 1940, *Agriculture: Crop-Sharing Contracts* (Washington, D.C.: GPO, 1943), 37. On the social and economic plight of southern sharecroppers at that time see Arthur F. Raper and Ira De A. Reid, *Sharecroppers All* (Chapel Hill: Univ. of N.C. Press, 1941).

5. Percentages derived from 16th Census, *Agriculture, Virginia*, 1st ser., 28. For the state as a whole, 25 percent of the white farm operators were tenants and 7 percent were sharecroppers while 36 percent of the black farm operators were tenants and 17 percent were sharecroppers.

6. Data derived from 16th Census, *Agriculture, Virginia*, 1st ser., 16. The average value per white farm was $2,857.92; per black farm it was $1,581.93.

7. 16th Census, *Population*, 2d ser., *Virginia*, 44; Luther P. Jackson, *The Voting Status of Negroes in Virginia: 1942* (Petersburg: Va. Voters League, 1943), unpaged; Frederic D. Ogden, *The Poll Tax in the South* (University: Univ. of Ala. Press, 1958), 33; Murray Kempton, Report on Waller Case to Pauli Murray, Dec. [8] 1940, WDLC, 187-25.

8. Commonwealth of Virginia, State Board of Education, *Annual Report of the Superintendent of Public Instruction for the School Year 1939–40* (Richmond: Division of Purchasing and Printing, 1940), 210, 216; Commonwealth of Virginia, State Board of Education, "Annual Reports of Division Superintendents: 1939–1940," Pittsylvania County, VSL.

9. *Annual Report of the Superintendent of Public Instruction . . . 1939–40*, 52, 80; "A Petition to The Pittsylvania County School Board and The Superintendent of Schools [1940]," file "Pi," box 72, James H. Price Executive Papers, VSL. Danville had previously allowed blacks from the county to attend its black high school, but it had recently adopted a requirement that such children had to pay a fee of $5.00 a month. This was a prohibitive expense for large numbers of blacks.

10. Martin A. Martin to Thurgood Marshall, Aug. 10, 1940; Marshall to Martin, Aug. 12, 1940; Martin to Marshall, Sept. 9, 1940, in file "Schools, Virginia, Pittsylvania High," box 47, Group II, B, NAACP Papers, Manuscript Division, Library of Congress.

11. Record, 98, 99; *Pittsylvania Tribune* (Chatham), July 19, 1940, 2; June 26,

1942, 1. Davis was born in Pittsylvania County on October 6, 1893, according to the information in the Voting Book, Pittsylvania County Court House, and the date inscribed on his tombstone in Chatham Burial Park.

12. Record, 98; Hearing, 163; *Pittsylvania Tribune,* July 19, 1940, 2, and July 26, 1940, 8; Index to Marriage Register, vol. 6 (1927–39): 184, Pittsylvania County Court House.

13. Deed Book 153, pp. 184–85, Pittsylvania County Court House, Chatham. On the Shields property rented by Davis see Deed Book 254, pp. 394–95, and Deed Book 264, pp. 553–54. See also Record, 99; Hearing, 234; Pauli Murray, *Song in a Weary Throat: An American Pilgrimage* (New York: Harper & Row, 1987), 154.

14. *Danville Register,* July 18, 1940, 4; Hearing, 242–43. The *Lynchburg News,* July 18, 1940, 8, referred to Davis as a "prominent tobacco planter." Similarly, the *Pittsylvania Tribune,* July 26, 1940, 4, described Davis as "a prominent figure in the community, a good neighbor, and a prosperous farmer." These accounts clearly exaggerated his prominence and prosperity.

15. Thomas A. Davis to Colgate W. Darden, Jr., June 25, 1942, box 4, OWF. Thomas Davis was not related to Oscar Davis. On Davis's bootlegging see Hearing, 37–38.

16. Dr. Ernest D. Overbey to Darden, June 17, 1942, folder on "Gretna and Chatham," box 2, OWF.

17. Hearing, 217–29; Pauli Murray and Murray Kempton, *"All For Mr. Davis": The Story of Sharecropper Odell Waller* (New York: Workers Defense League, [1941]), 5; Murray, *Song,* 154.

18. Murray, *Song,* 154.

19. Record, 116.

20. Record, 116, 119; "Odell Waller's Own Story," a statement by Odell Waller dated Jan. 2, 1941, in *The Black Worker,* June 1942, 2.

21. Dollie Harris kept in close contact with Annie Waller throughout Odell's trial and appeals. See folders 6 to 16 in box 187, WDLC. The reference to Dollie Harris as the former Dollie Jones is in *Richmond Afro-American,* July 4, 1942, 1, 12. Annie Waller's precise birthdate was not listed in any of the available sources. At the time of Odell's trial in September 1940 she was usually referred to as being 65 years old, in which case she would have been born in 1875 and would have been 41 or 42 at the time of Odell's adoption. The news accounts from 1940 to 1942 consistently referred to her as "aged" or "old."

22. Hearing, 10, 22. "The Waller Case," draft of statement prepared for Governor's Hearing, p. 1, in Odell Waller Files, Finerty Papers. Deed Book 120, pp. 10–11, Pittsylvania County Court House; Pittsylvania County Land Book, 1918, p. 79; 1937, p. 332; 1938, p. 346; 1939, p. 359; 1940, p. 377; 1941, p. 385; 1944, p. 412, VSL.

23. Thomas H. Davis to Darden, June 25, 1942, box 4, OWF; Murray

Kempton, Report on Waller Case to Pauli Murray, Dec. [8] 1940, WDL, 187-25.

24. Hearing, 9; *Richmond Afro-American*, July 11, 1942, 13; "Odell Waller's Own Story," *The Black Worker*, June 1942, 2; Murray, *Song*, 154.

25. Thomas H. Davis to Darden, June 25, 1942, box 4, OWF.

26. Langhorne Jones to Darden, June 8, 1942, box 2, OWF; Record, 125–26.

27. The convictions are described in some detail in Hearing, 157–62; see also *Richmond News Leader*, June 26, 1942, 2. Annie Waller commented on the whiskey selling in Hearing, 37. For Odell Waller's explanation of these arrests and convictions see his "Dying Statement" (copy in appendix).

28. Hearing, 154.

29. Record, 116; Murray, *Song*, 154. Odell was married on Jan. 5, 1939. See Index to Marriage Register, vol. 6 (1927–39): 179, Pittsylvania County Court House.

30. Record, 116; "Petition For Writ of Error," in Record, 1–2; Hearing, 43. Wheat was not included in their sharecropping arrangement until 1940. There was no written contract, and the agreement was not presented consistently or clearly in the available sources.

31. Record, 116.

32. Record, 116–17; Hearing, 12, 166. Governor Darden checked with the Agricultural Adjustment Administration in 1942 and reported on the acreage allotment at the Public Hearing, June 29, 1942.

33. Hearing, 153; Record, 117.

34. Hearing, 12, 16–17, 43, 167; Record, 119; "Odell Waller's Dying Statement."

35. Record, 111, 118; Hearing, 13–15.

36. Hearing, 15–16; Record, 111; Murray, *Song*, 155.

37. Hearing, 16–19, 154, 257–60.

38. Hearing, 22, 24, 234; Record, 119.

39. Hearing, 43–44. In a notarized statement presented at the Public Hearing Robert Waller said "208 bushels," but he must have inadvertently misspoken as there are 2.5 bushels in a bag. Thus he must have meant 208 bags. See also the statement by Henry Davis in Hearing, 88. The threshing of Oscar Davis's wheat must have taken place a few days before Thursday, July 11, or Friday, July 12, because Odell returned to Pittsylvania County on July 13 and would not have had time to have received Annie Waller's letter describing these events unless they had occurred earlier. Annie claimed that the threshing occurred "a week before the shooting," which meant it was probably done on Monday and Tuesday, July 8 and 9. See Hearing, 24.

40. Hearing, 44, 154; Record, 119.

41. Record, 85–94, 108–15, 119–24; Hearing, 25–31 and passim. For local newspaper accounts of the shooting see *Danville Register*, July 18, 1940, 4, and *Pittsylvania Tribune*, July 19, 1940, 2. It was also noted in the *Richmond Times-*

Dispatch, July 19, 1940, 9. The caliber of the pistol is given in the FBI's "Odell Waller," file no. 88-131 (7/24/1940), 6. Throughout the trial and appeals no one raised a question about the source of Odell's pistol. Annie Waller later noted merely that "He had one there in the house where we had protection [*sic*]." Hearing, 25.

42. Record, 95. Much later the defense produced hospital records that reported three wounds, one in the left side of the head, one in the left arm, and one in the hip. See Hearing, 103–4, 324.

43. Record, 95–97; Hearing, 134–35.

44. Record, 100; Hearing, 231; *Danville Register,* July 18, 1940, 4; *Richmond Times-Dispatch,* July 19, 1940, 9; *Pittsylvania Tribune,* July 26, 1940, 1.

45. Record, 120.

46. *Ohio State Journal* (Columbus), July 25, 1940, 3; *Pittsylvania Tribune,* July 26, 1940, 1; *Danville Register,* Aug. 10, 1940, 5; FBI, "Odell Waller File," no. 88-131. The *Richmond Afro-American,* July 11, 1942, 12, noted that Annie Waller's brother Sam Hairston lived in Columbus.

47. James Whitehead, Jr., to Governor James H. Price, July 27, 1940, box 115, James H. Price Executive Papers. The requisition documents for Waller are in "July 12 through August 26, 1940" box, Secretary of the Commonwealth, Executive Papers, VSL.

48. Secretary to the Governor [Price] to Governor John W. Bricker, July 29, 1940; Harry M. Miller to Laura H. Allen, July 30, 1940; Laura H. Allen to Joseph Whitehead, July 31, 1940, box 115, Price Executive Papers; *Pittsylvania Tribune,* Aug. 2, 1940, 1; *Ohio State Journal,* Aug. 3, 1940, 2.

49. *Ohio State Journal,* Aug. 6, 1940, 2; *Pittsylvania Tribune,* Aug. 9, 1940, 1; *Danville Register,* Aug. 10, 1940, 5; Murray, *Song,* 151; *They Call It Murder,* Richmond Waller Defense Committee pamphlet (Richmond, 1941), copy in box 4, Virginius Dabney Papers (#7690), Manuscripts Division, Special Collections Dept., Univ. of Va. Library, Charlottesville; Joseph E. Bowman to NAACP, Oct. 3, 1940, in file "Crime-Odell Waller, 1940–41," box 54, Group II, B, NAACP Papers.

Chapter 2

1. Record, 3, 21–22. *Danville Register,* Sept. 15, 1940, 5; Sept. 18, 1940, 3. *Pittsylvania Tribune,* Sept. 13, 1040, 1; Sept. 18, 1940, 1. The preliminary hearing was before Hubert D. Bennett, trial justice of the County of Pittsylvania. There was no transcript of the proceedings.

2. *Richmond Times-Dispatch,* Aug. 14, 1940, 4; *Pittsylvania Tribune,* Aug. 16, 1940, 1. Stone is discussed later in this chapter. Hopkins was a 1932 graduate of Howard University Law School where he had studied with Charles H. Houston.

In 1935 he had worked with Houston in assisting Alice Jackson, a black woman, in her unsuccessful attempt to be admitted to graduate school at the University of Virginia.

3. Sidney Lens, *Unrepentant Radical: An American Activist's Account of Five Turbulent Decades* (Boston: Beacon Press, 1980), 30–42; Daniel Bell, *Marxian Socialism in the United States* (Princeton, N.J.: Princeton Univ. Press, 1967), 154–56, 172, 174; *Writings of Leon Trotsky*, ed. Naomi Allen and George Breitman, 2d ed. (New York: Pathfinder Press, 1974–78), vol. 9: 439, 558 note #360; vol. 10: 50, 339–40, 462 note #56, 490 note #311, 493 note #342; vol. 11: 404 note #232; *The Fighting Worker*, Nov. 30, 1935, 1, 4. This newspaper was published in New York during its first year and in Chicago from November 15, 1936, until November 3, 1947. It usually appeared monthly, but its schedule was sometimes irregular.

4. Article 1, Section 1, Constitution of the Revolutionary Workers League, U.S.: Amended by the Third Convention, Apr. 30–May 2, 1938. (Copy in Library of Congress).

5. Lens, *Unrepentant Radical*, 44.

6. Ibid., 42–62, 89–92.

7. WDL, "Workers Defense League," brochure [1941] in bound volume of WDL pamphlets, Library of the Univ. of Calif., Berkeley.

8. WDL, "The History of the Workers Defense League," mimeographed pamphlet [1941] in bound volume of WDL pamphlets; *New York Times*, May 28, 1936, 24; Harry Fleischman, *Norman Thomas: A Biography, 1884–1968* (New York: Nor-ton, 1969), 159; Frank A. Warren, *An Alternative Vision: The Socialist Party in the 1930s* (Bloomington: Ind. Univ. Press, 1974), 37; Harry Fleischman, "Workers Defense League," in *Encyclopedia of the American Left*, ed. Mari Jo Buhle, Paul Buhle, and Dan Georgakas (New York: Garland, 1990), 848–49; Beatrice Loeffel, unpublished manuscript on the history of the Workers Defense League, copy in office of the Executive Director of the WDL, pp. 1–2. The International Labor Defense (ILD) was formed in 1925. It gave special attention to cases involving blacks. See Charles H. Martin, "International Labor Defense," in *Encyclopedia of the American Left*, 366–67, and Wilson Record, *The Negro and the Communist Party* (Chapel Hill: Univ. of N.C. Press, 1951), 34–36, 86–91. On the Scottsboro case see Dan T. Carter, *Scottsboro: A Tragedy of the American South* (Baton Rouge: La. State Univ. Press, 1969). The Scottsboro boys were nine black teenagers falsely accused of raping two white girls. After a trial in Scottsboro, Alabama, eight were sentenced to death in April 1931. But the incredibly harsh sentences, given the age of the defendants, and the unfair trial aroused widespread public concern. The ILD led a publicity and legal fight on behalf of the defendants. On two occasions, in 1932 and again in 1935, the U.S. Supreme Court overturned the convictions, and none was executed.

But the state of Alabama retried the defendants, and the last was not released from prison until 1950.

9. *Workers Defense Bulletin*, Oct. 1941, 1–4; Summer 1943, 2; WDL, *Press Service*, Sept. 8, 1941, 1; Murray, *Song*, 135, 181. *Yale Obituary Record 1941–1942*. See the poem in honor of Clendenin by Tracy D. Mygatt, *The Black Worker*, Dec. 1941, 4. James A. Wechsler noted that Clendenin gave $8,000 a year to the WDL and worked full-time for it as a "dollar-a-year man." *P.M.*, Sept. 12, 1941, 22, reprinted in *Workers Defense Bulletin*, Oct. 1941, 4.

10. WDL, "The History of the Workers Defense League"; "Workers Defense League," brochure [1941]; Loeffel, history of the Workers Defense League, 1–10; Fleischman, "Workers Defense League," 848; WDL, *"To Establish Justice . . .": Sharecroppers under Planters Law* (New York: WDL, 1940), endleaf; Thomas A. Krueger, *And Promises to Keep: The Southern Conference for Human Welfare, 1938–1948* (Nashville, Tenn.: Vanderbilt Univ. Press, 1967), 22–23. On the STFU see Donald H. Grubbs, *Cry from the Cotton: The Southern Tenant Farmers' Union and the New Deal* (Chapel Hill: Univ. of N.C. Press, 1971). A number of Communist or Communist-led organizations, including the ILD, were present at the Birmingham convention. Frank McCallister, the southern head of the WDL, began a campaign in late 1939 to remove them from SCHW leadership. See Krueger, *And Promises to Keep*, 89–90.

11. Harry M. Miller to Laura H. Allen, July 30, 1940, box 115, Price Executive Papers; unsigned letter to WDL [Aug. 1940], box 184-28, WDLC; Pauli Murray to *Richmond Afro-American*, Aug. 29, 1942, box 184-26, WDLC; Frank McCallister to David L. Clendenin, Aug. 20, 1940, box 187-26, WDLC. Heisler, along with Clendenin and others, had been a member of the original WDL organizing committee headed by Norman Thomas. He had also been a member of the Socialist party in Chicago, which in 1937 had published his study *The First Two Moscow Trials—Why?* See Heisler, "It was a memorable trial . . . ," in *Workers Defense League: A Journal to Mark the 35th Anniversary of the Workers Defense League*, [1971, 7], and *Writings of Leon Trotsky*, vol. 9: 241, 541 note #215.

12. Thomas H. Stone to Clendenin, Aug. 28, 1940, box 186-17, WDLC.

13. Clendenin to Stone, Sept. 3, 1940, box 187-27, WDLC.

14. *Richmond Times-Dispatch*, Dec. 30, 1932, 2; *Martindale-Hubbell Law Directory:1940*, 72d ed. (New York: Martindale-Hubbell, 1940), vol. 1: 999; Alumni Records File, Alderman Library, Univ. of Va.

15. Irving Howe and Lewis Coser, *The American Communist Party: A Critical History (1919–1957)* (Boston: Beacon, 1957), 193–94, 196; Harvey Klehr, *The Heyday of American Communism: The Depression Decade* (New York: Basic Books, 1984), 50–51.

16. *Richmond Times-Dispatch*, Dec. 29, 1932, 1; Dec. 30, 1932, 2; Jan. 8, 1933, 6; Feb. 8, 1933, 1, 5; Mar. 7, 1933, 7; Mar. 28, 1933, 2; Mar. 29, 1933, 6; May 25,

1933, 3; Oct. 27, 1933, 2; Nov. 15, 1933, 5; Dec. 24, 1933, 1, 4; Dec. 25, 1933, 14; Dec. 26, 1933, 7; Dec. 31, 1933, sec. IV, 9. *Richmond News Leader*, May 25, 1933, 33; Nov. 16, 1933, 2; Dec. 23, 1933, 2; Virginius Dabney, "Richmond's Mayor Arouses Radicals," *New York Times*, Feb. 15, 1933, sec. IV, 1; Virginius Dabney, *Richmond: The Story of A City* (New York: Doubleday, 1976), 313–14.

17. *Richmond News Leader*, Oct. 12, 1934, 4; Oct. 13, 1934, 3; Oct. 15, 1934, 11; Oct. 16, 1934, 17.

18. *Richmond News Leader*, July 14, 1934, 2; May 27, 1935, 1, 22; *Richmond Times-Dispatch*, May 28, 1935, 2; Univ. of Va., *Alumni News* 23 (Feb. 1935): 109; FBI, "Thomas H. Stone," file no. 100-6190 (5/19/43), 1, 5, 7. Richmond Waller Defense Committee, *They Call It Murder*. Lens, *Unrepentant Radical*, 92. On legal education requirements see W. Hamilton Bryson, "The History of Legal Education in Virginia," *University of Richmond Law Review* 14 (Fall 1979): 205. Stone's exact connection with the Communist party was a matter of dispute. In an article in the *Richmond News Leader*, Oct. 20, 1934, 11, A. L. Holt, a person who claimed to speak for the City Committee of the Communist party, said that Stone had been expelled from the party in 1929, and when he applied for readmission in 1933 it was denied "due to his past record."

19. *Pittsylvania Tribune*, Sept. 13, 1940, 1; *Richmond Afro-American*, Sept. 14, 1940, 23; *Danville Register*, Sept. 15, 1940, 5.

20. *The Fighting Worker*, Sept. 1, 1940, 4.

21. *Proceedings of the Fifty-sixth Annual Meeting of the Virginia State Bar Association, 1946* (Richmond, 1946), 153–56; *Pittsylvania Tribune*, Nov. 24, 1944, 1, 4; *Danville Register*, Nov. 19, 1944, 2, 6; Philip Alexander Bruce et al., *History of Virginia* (Chicago: American Historical Society, 1924), vol. 6, *Virginia Biography*, 561; Maud Carter Clement, *The History of Pittsylvania County Virginia* (Lynchburg, Va.: J. P. Bell Co., 1929), 267; *Martindale's American Law Directory: 1929* (New York: Martindale, 1929), 994.

22. A. H. Overbey to C. E. Hennrich, Sept. 21, 1940; Hennrich to Director of FBI, Sept. 24, 1940; Hennrich to Overbey, Sept. 24, 1940, FBI, "Odell Waller File."

23. Record, 55–57, 58.

24. Record, 59.

25. Record, 59–60. See also *Danville Register*, Sept. 20, 1940, 1, and *Pittsylvania Tribune*, Sept. 20, 1940, 1. Section Eight of the Constitution of Virginia was part of that document's Bill of Rights. It included the guarantee that in criminal prosecutions a person "shall not be deprived of life or liberty, except by the law of the land or the judgment of his peers."

26. Clendenin to Heisler, Sept. 24, 1940, box 187-27, WDLC. See also Heisler to Clendenin, Sept. 23, 1940, box 187-27, WDLC, and Stone to Heisler, Sept. 20, 1940; Heisler to Stone, Sept. 23, 1940, box 186-17, WDLC.

27. Heisler to Clendenin, Sept. 25, 1940; Hugo Oehler to WDL, Sept. 25,

1940, box 187-27, WDLC.

28. Clendenin to Heisler, Sept. 26, 1940, box 187-27, WDLC; Murray, *Song*, 151. See also Clendenin to Stone, Oct. 3, 1940; Stone to Clendenin, Oct. 4, 1940; Heisler to Stone, Oct. 5, 1940, box 186-17, WDLC.

29. Record, 61–63.

30. Hearing, 268.

31. Record, 63.

32. Record, 64; *Danville Register*, Sept. 27, 1940, 2; *Richmond Times-Dispatch*, Sept. 27, 1940, 17. Stone later claimed that Campion was an American-born doctor of philosophy. He asserted that the description of Campion as one who used broken English was an attempt to suggest that "foreign agitators" were using Waller for their radical purposes. See Stone to Editor, *Richmond Times-Dispatch*, Oct. 21, 1941, copy in box 4, Dabney Papers.

33. Record, 64–65.

34. Record, 67–72.

35. Record, 71.

36. Record, 73.

37. Record, 75.

38. Record, 75–84.

39. Record, 85–86.

40. Record, 87–88.

41. Record, 90.

42. Record, 92.

43. Record, 92.

44. This point was raised in the Governor's Commutation Hearing on June 29, 1942 (see Hearing, 178–79), but it was not brought out by Stone at the trial.

45. Record, 95. On Anderson, see Hearing, 214, 232.

46. Record, 95–97.

47. Record, 98–99.

48. Record, 102, 106.

49. Record, 102–4.

50. Record, 102. This was the statement that Frank Davis made when the jury was out of the courtroom. After the jury returned he said only the first two sentences (Record, 104).

51. Record, 103.

52. Record, 106.

53. Record, 109.

54. Record, 109.

55. Record, 110.

56. Record, 110–11.

57. Record, 111.

58. Record, 112.

59. Record, 114.

60. Record, 116. On Edgar's testimony, see Record, 107.

61. Record, 120, 121, 124.

62. Record, 120.

63. Record, 123.

64. Record, 122.

65. Record, 125–26. See Waller's explanation of the charges made against him in his "Dying Statement," in appendix.

66. Record, 29; *Danville Register*, Sept. 28, 1940, 1, 2; *Richmond Times-Dispatch*, Sept. 28, 1940, 7. The FBI agent at the trial later reported that "there was no demonstration whatever when the verdict was read, the audience remaining very quiet and orderly." "Memorandum For the File," Sept. 27, 1940, FBI, "Odell Waller" file.

67. Judge's instructions, jury's verdict, and judge's sentence in records of clerk of Pittsylvania Circuit Court, Chatham, Va.; *Danville Register*, Sept. 28, 1940, 1, 2; *Richmond Times-Dispatch*, Sept. 28, 1940, 7. The closing arguments by the defense and by the prosecution do not appear in the printed record of the trial.

68. *Danville Register*, Sept. 28, 1940, 4.

69. One of Richmond's major newspapers, the *Times-Dispatch*, carried reports of the shooting of Oscar Davis and of Waller's trial. I could find no mention of the case in the *Richmond News Leader*. The two most important black newspapers in Virginia, the *Richmond Afro-American* and the Norfolk *Journal and Guide*, did not play up the story. The first reference to the case in the *Afro-American* was published on September 14, 1940, when it carried a brief account of the meeting in Richmond on September 12 that had been sponsored by the Revolutionary Workers League. Its next story, one on the trial, was published on October 5, 1940. The *Journal and Guide* first mentioned the case on October 5, 1940, when it noted Waller's trial and conviction. An important black newspaper, the *New York Age*, also reported on the Waller case on that date. It mentioned the efforts by Stone and Hopkins to have the trial postponed to a later date and to get a change of venue as well as the formation of the Richmond Waller Defense Committee. The Waller story did not get picked up by most black newspapers across the country until mid November after the WDL entered the case and began to circulate news stories. See the *New York Amsterdam News*, Nov. 16, 1940; the *Chicago Defender*, Nov. 16, 1940; the *Baltimore Afro-American*, Nov. 23, 1940. The Waller case was not reported in most national publications until much later. The first story on it in the *New York Times* came in the spring of 1942. The *Socialist Appeal*, the official organ of the Trotskyite Socialist Workers party, carried stories about the trial on September 28 and October 5, 1940, and appealed for funds to be sent to the Waller Defense

Committee. The trial was not reported in the *Daily Worker*, the official organ of the Communist party of the United States.

Chapter 3

1. *Pittsylvania Tribune*, Oct. 4, 1940, 1; James T. Clement to Virginius Dabney, Nov. 8, 1941, box 4, Dabney Papers.
2. "Memorandum For the File," Sept. 27, 1940; C. E. Hennrich to Director of FBI, Oct. 8, 1940, FBI, "Odell Waller" file. Copies of the letter and the telegrams accompanied the "Memorandum For the File." *The Fighting Worker*, editorial, Oct. 1, 1940, 1, made a similar protest against the speeding up of the trial.
3. *Journal and Guide*, Oct. 12, 1940, 8.
4. Richmond Waller Defense Committee, *They Call It Murder*. See also statement of facts of Waller case issued by Waller Defense Committee (Provisional), Oct. 3, 1940, box 186-17, WDLC.
5. *The Fighting Worker*, Oct. 15, 1940, 1, 4.
6. *The Fighting Worker*, Nov. 1, 1940, 3. See also *They Call It Murder* and the flier issued by the Provisional N.Y. Waller Defense Committee in file "Sharecroppers: Odell Waller," box 526, Group II, A, NAACP Papers. For some early press releases by the Provisional Waller Defense Committee in Chicago see "Odell Waller Defense Committee," folder 5, box 47, Sidney Lens Papers, Chicago Historical Society.
7. Clendenin to Stone, Sept. 3, 1940; Clendenin to Heisler, Sept. 24, 1940, box 187-27, WDLC.
8. Hugo Oehler to WDL, Sept. 25, 1940, box 187-27, WDLC.
9. Clendenin to Stone, Oct. 3, 1940, box 186-17, WDLC.
10. Stone to Clendenin, Oct. 4, 1940, box 186-17, WDLC.
11. Clendenin to Oehler, Oct. 7, 1940, box 186-6, WDLC.
12. Oehler to Clendenin, Oct. 15, 1940, box 186-17, WDLC; Oehler to Clendenin, Oct. 27, 1940, box 186-18, WDLC; Clendenin to Oehler, Oct. 18, 1940, box 186-6, WDLC.
13. Stone to Heisler, Oct. 2 and Oct. 11, 1940; Heisler to Stone, Oct. 5 and Oct. 14, 1940, box 186-17, WDLC.
14. Morris Milgram to Heisler, Oct. 14, 1940, box 186-17, WDLC; Clendenin to Heisler, Oct. 18, 1940; Clendenin to Stone, Oct. 18, 1940, box 186-18, WDLC.
15. Clendenin to Heisler, Oct. 18, 1940, box 187-28, WDLC. See also Milgram to Heisler, Oct. 14, 1940, box 186-17, WDLC.
16. "Minutes of Conference on Waller Case, Nov. 2, 1940, called by Workers

Defense League," box 186-19, WDLC. See also *Workers Defense Bulletin*, Nov. 1940, 1, and Murray, *Song*, 150–51.

17. "Statement of Facts on the Case of Odell Waller," Nov. 2, 1940, box 183-1, WDLC.

18. NEWS from Workers Defense League, SPECIAL TO NEGRO PRESS, Nov. 7, 1940, box 183-1, WDLC; Clendenin to J. R. Butler, Nov. 4, 1940, box 187-29, WDLC.

19. Murray, *Song*, 1–50. See also *Southern Exposure* 4, no. 4 (Winter 1977): 4.

20. Murray to Clendenin, Nov. 8, 1940; Murray and Gene Phillips, "Memorandum on Waller Case," Nov. 12, 1940, box 187-23, WDLC; Murray and Phillips, "Funds Raised—Waller Defense Fund," Nov. 12, 1940, in folder "Odell Waller Case," box 57, Pauli Murray Papers, Arthur and Elizabeth Schlesinger Library on the History of Women in America, Radcliffe College, Cambridge, Mass.; Murray, *Song*, 153–63.

21. Murray and Phillips to Stone, Howard Davis, and J. Byron Hopkins, Nov. 13, 1940, box 187-23, WDLC; Howard Davis to Murray, Nov. 14, 1940, box 186-19, WDLC. Davis had the same office address in Richmond as Stone.

22. Murray and Phillips, "Memorandum on Waller Case," Nov. 12, 1940; Murray to Clendenin, Nov. 8, 1940, box 187-23, WDLC; Murray to *Richmond Afro-American*, Aug. 29, 1942, box 184-26, WDLC.

23. Murray, *Song*, 158.

24. Murray to Odell Waller, Nov. 15, 1940, box 187-6, WDLC.

25. Odell Waller to Annie Waller, Nov. 15, 1940; Odell Waller to Murray, Nov. 22, 1940, box 187-6, WDLC.

26. Murray, *Song*, 164; Murray to Eleanor Roosevelt, Nov. 20, 1940, box for "Dec. 19–Dec. 31, 1940," Secretary of the Commonwealth, Executive Papers, VSL; Florence Becker, Letter to the Editor, *The Nation*, 151 (Nov. 23, 1940): 516.

27. Flier, in box for "Dec. 19–Dec. 31, 1940," Secretary of the Commonwealth, Executive Papers, VSL.

28. Murray to Eleanor Roosevelt, Nov. 20, 1940; Eleanor Roosevelt to James H. Price, Nov. 30, 1940; Price to Eleanor Roosevelt, Dec. 3, 1940, box for "Dec. 19–Dec. 31, 1940," Secretary of the Commonwealth, Executive Papers, VSL. Pauli Murray first saw Mrs. Roosevelt in late fall 1934 when Mrs. Roosevelt visited Camp Tera, a Federal Emergency Relief Administration camp for women in New York where Murray spent three months. Their first face-to-face encounter came in mid January of 1940 at Mrs. Roosevelt's New York City apartment. Murray had requested an audience in order to ask her to be the speaker at the main dinner in March of the annual National Sharecroppers Week. Mrs. Roosevelt agreed. This was the beginning of a mutually educational association that lasted until Mrs. Roosevelt's death in 1962. Although Murray strongly disagreed with Mrs. Roosevelt on a few occasions, she was deeply

impressed with her from the start and became a warm admirer. See Murray, *Song*, 95–97, 134–37, and passim; Joseph P. Lash, *Eleanor and Franklin* (New York: Norton, 1971), 523–24, 672–75.

29. "Report of the Secretary" (for the December meeting of the Board of Directors), pt. I, reel 6, Microfilm edition, NAACP Papers. *New York Age*, Nov. 23, 1940, 3; Marshall to Walter White, Nov. 2, 1940; Murray to White, Dec. 2, 1940, in file "Crime—Odell Waller, 1940–41," box 54, Group II, B, NAACP Papers; Murray to Roy Wilkins, Nov. 19, 1940; Murray to Marshall, Jan. 7, 1941, in file "Sharecroppers: Odell Waller," box 526, Group II, A, NAACP Papers; "Minutes of the 5th Annual Virginia State Conference of Branches of the NAACP Convening in Richmond, Virginia—Nov. 20, 1940," in branch file "Virginia State Conference, 1940–41," box 210, Group II, C, NAACP Papers. The NAACP's interest in Waller's plight dated from the time of the extradition proceedings in Columbus, Ohio. On September 24, just two days before the trial began, Marshall sent a telegram to Stone asking for a report on the case. Stone replied the next day. But the national office of the NAACP provided neither financial nor legal assistance to Waller's defenders at the time of the trial or immediately thereafter, although Martin A. Martin, an attorney and president of the Danville chapter, did promise to help. After Waller's conviction Stone needed financial aid in preparing the appeal. At Marshall's suggestion he sought assistance in mid October from Dr. J. M. Tinsley, the president of the Richmond branch of the NAACP. See Marshall to Stone, Sept. 24, 1940; Marshall to Tinsley, Sept. 24, 1940; Stone to Marshall, Sept. 25, 1940; Tinsley to Marshall, Sept. 25, 1940; Marshall to Stone, Oct. 14, 1940; Stone to Marshall, Oct. 17, 1940, in file "Crime—Odell Waller, 1940–41," box 54, Group II, B. NAACP Papers.

30. *Journal and Guide* (Norfolk), Dec. 7, 1940, 1; *Workers Defense Bulletin*, Dec. 1940, 2; *The Black Worker*, Dec. 1940, 1. Although he was a committed socialist, Randolph had broken with the Socialist party in 1940 because of his disagreement with its antiwar position. But his support for Waller was consistent with his long record of concern for labor and racial issues. From 1936 to 1940 Randolph had also served as first president of the National Negro Congress, but in April 1940 he refused reelection and broke with that organization after it came under the total domination of the Communists. Becoming militantly anti-Communist, Randolph got the Brotherhood of Sleeping Car Porters to bar Communists from holding office in the union. See Jervis Anderson, *A. Philip Randolph: A Biographical Portrait* (New York: Harcourt, Brace, Jovanovich, 1972), 230–39; Paula F. Pfeffer, *A. Philip Randolph: Pioneer of the Civil Rights Movement* (Baton Rouge: La. State Univ. Press, 1990), 39–44; Mark Naison, *Communists in Harlem during the Depression* (Urbana: Univ. of Ill. Press, 1983), 295–96, 309–12. Members of the Harlem Committee included Lionel C. Barrow, president of the Harlem branch of the NAACP; Edith Ransome, business agent of local #22

of the I.L.G.W.U.; Layle Lane, vice-president of the American Federation of Teachers; Edward Welsh of the American Labor party; and others.

31. Clendenin to Thomas H. Stone, Nov. 18, 1940; Murray to Howard Davis, Nov. 19, 1940, box 186-19, WDLC; WDL, *Press Release*, Nov. 23, 1940, copy in box 4, Dabney Papers.

32. *New York Times,* June 6, 1967, 47; *Time* 40 (July 6, 1942): 16; Roger Nash Baldwin, "The Reminiscences of Roger Nash Baldwin," Columbia Univ.: Oral History Research Office, 1972, vol. 1: 134–35, 227; *Who Was Who in America,* vol. 1, *1897–1942* (Chicago: A. N. Marquis Co., 1942), 397; *Who's Who in America,* vol. 23, *1940–1945* (Chicago: A. N. Marquis Co., 1944), 674.

Tom Mooney was a labor leader who was sentenced to death for the bomb killings in a 1916 San Francisco Preparedness Day Parade. There were many questions about the validity of his trial, and his sentence was commuted to life imprisonment. After a long legal struggle Governor Olson of California pardoned Mooney in 1938. See Richard H. Frost, *The Mooney Case* (Stanford, Calif.: Stanford Univ. Press, 1968), 449 ff., on Finerty's role. See below, chap. 7, note 56.

33. *Workers Defense Bulletin,* Dec. 1940, 1, 2.

34. Murray to Odell Waller, Nov. 24, 1940, box 187-6, WDLC.

35. Odell Waller to Finerty, Nov. 27, 1940, box 186-2, WDLC.

36. Layle Lane to "Dear Friends," Nov. 11, 1940, box 186-1, WDLC; Gene Phillips to Mrs. E. E. Waller, Nov. 23, 1940, box 186-6, WDLC; Adelene McBean to "Dear Friend," Nov. 23, 1940, box 183-12, WDLC; *Workers Defense Bulletin* (Dec. 1940), 1. Murray Kempton published an article on Mrs. Waller in the *New York Age,* Dec. 7, 1940, 3. This was subsequently reprinted as a WDL pamphlet, *Odell Waller's Mother,* copy in box 4, Dabney Papers. The use of a defendant's mother for publicity and fund-raising purposes was not, of course, an original tactic. The International Labor Defense had used the technique extensively on behalf of the Scottsboro boys. In that case, however, there were several defendants, and thus several mothers could be put into service. See Carter, *Scottsboro,* 143.

37. Murray, *Song,* 165.

38. Murray to Odell Waller, Nov. 24, 1940, and Nov. 28, 1940, box 187-6, WDLC; Annie Waller to Sam Hairston, Dec. 1, 1940; Annie Waller to Dollie G. Harris, Dec. 2, 1940, box 187-7, WDLC; Annie Waller to Robert Waller, Nov. 26, 1940, box 187-6, WDLC.

39. "Report of Waller Funds," Dec. 11, 1940, box 183-7, WDLC; Stone to Murray, Nov. 24, 1940; Murray to Stone, Nov. 25, 1940, box 186-19, WDLC; Murray to Odell Waller, Nov. 24, 1940, box 187-6, WDLC.

40. *The Catholic Worker* 8 (Dec. 1940): 1.

41. *The Nation* 151 (Dec. 21, 1940): 635.

42. Murray to Odell Waller, Dec. 7, 1940, box 187-7, WDLC.

43. Odell Waller to Clendenin, Dec. 14, 1940, box 187-7, WDLC. This letter was later published in the *Workers Defense Bulletin,* Jan. 1941, 3.

44. Thomas Stamm to Clendenin, Nov. 9, 1940, box 186-19, WDLC.

45. *Revolt,* Nov. 23, 1940, clipping in box 155, WDLC.

46. Edmund Campion to All Labor, Fraternal, Negro and Liberal Organizations; All Supporting and Sympathetic Individuals and Groups, Dec. 1, 1940, box 4, Dabney Papers, also box 186-20, WDLC.

47. Morris Milgram to Clendenin, Nov. 18, 1940, box 186-19, WDLC.

48. McCallister to Pauli Murray, Nov. 25, 1940, box 186-6, WDLC.

49. Murray to McCallister, Dec. 9, 1940, box 186-6, WDLC. See also Finerty to Stone, Nov. 27, 1940, box 186-19, WDLC.

50. Murray to Dabney, Nov. 27, 1940, box 4, Dabney Papers.

51. Dabney to Murray, Dec. 4, 1940, box 186-15, WDLC.

52. McCallister to Murray, Dec. 8, 1940, box 186-6, WDLC.

53. Finerty to Dabney, Dec. 9, 1940, box 4, Dabney Papers.

54. Dabney to Finerty, Dec. 10, 1940, box 4, Dabney Papers.

55. Murray to Dabney, Dec. 21, 1940, box 4, Dabney Papers; Dabney, "Civil Liberties in the South," *The Virginia Quarterly Review* 16 (Winter 1940): 81–91. Dabney concluded that real progress had been made, but he condemned the frequent violations of civil rights in employer-employee conflicts, the continued instances of peonage, and the poll tax. See also the news item on the WDL's efforts to win a new trial for Waller in *Richmond Times-Dispatch,* Dec. 13, 1940, 15.

56. *Richmond Times-Dispatch,* Dec. 21, 1940, 10. See also Dabney to Finerty, Dec. 21, 1940, box 4, Dabney Papers.

57. "Poll Taxes and Juries—II," *Richmond Times-Dispatch,* Dec. 24, 1940, 6.

58. Murray to Clendenin and Milgram, Dec. 24, 1940, box 187-23, WDLC.

59. Stone to National Administrative Committee, WDL, Dec. 30, 1940, box 4, Dabney Papers.

60. Murray Kempton to Murray, Wednesday [Dec. 4, 1940], box 187-25, WDLC. Throughout November 1940 the WDL's statements on the case had been based largely on information supplied by Stone. Not until his meeting with Finerty and others on December 1 did Stone present the WDL with a copy of the trial record which, of course, revealed the points Kempton complained about. Thus, if some of the WDL's early literature on the case contained some errors or incomplete statements, as Dabney charged, these could be attributed, at least in part, to the summaries Stone gave to the WDL.

A young white man about twenty-two years old, Kempton, like Pauli Murray, was born in Baltimore. He was graduated from Johns Hopkins University in 1939. In 1941 he became publicity director of the American Labor party. Subsequently he went on to a distinguished career as a journalist for the *New York Post* and other newspapers and magazines.

61. Kempton to Murray, Sunday night [Dec. 8, 1940], box 187-25, WDLC. There are twelve pages of his handwritten report in the WDLC files. One or more pages at the end are missing.

62. Kempton, "Waller Case Report," Dec. 9, 1940, box 187-3, WDLC. On Martin see Hearing, 39; "List of Branch Officer—April 1941," pt. I, reel 10, NAACP Papers; *Martindale-Hubbell Law Directory: 1955* (Summit, N.J.: Martindale-Hubbell, 1955), 238.

63. Murray and Kempton, *"All For Mr. Davis,"* 1.

64. Stone to James H. Price, Nov. 30, 1940; Secretary to Governor to Stone, Dec. 4, 1940, box for "Dec. 19–Dec. 31, 1940," Secretary of the Common-wealth, Executive Papers, VSL. See also Secretary to Governor to E. E. Friend, Clerk of Pittsylvania County Court, Dec. 13, 1940; E. E. Friend to Price, Dec. 14, 1940, folder 1, box 8, OWF.

65. Reprieve is in box for "Dec. 19–Dec. 31, 1940," Secretary of the Com-monwealth, Executive Papers, VSL. See also Price to Stone, J. T. Clement, Joseph Whitehead, R. M. Youell, and Odell Waller, Dec. 20, 1940, also in box for "Dec. 19–Dec. 31, 1940," Secretary of the Commonwealth, Executive Papers, VSL.

66. Murray to Price, Dec. 20, 1940, folder 1, box 8, OWF.

67. Flier in box 4, Dabney Papers.

68. RWL, "Press Release," [Dec. 20, 1940], box 186-20, WDLC.

Chapter 4

1. Murray to Annie Waller, Dec. 26, 1940, box 187-7, WDLC.

2. Odell Waller to Murray, Dec. 5, 1940, box 187-7, WDLC.

3. Murray to Odell Waller, Dec. 7, 1940, box 187-7, WDLC. With that letter she enclosed "a Crisis [NAACP], and Opportunity [National Urban League] Magazine, some letters about the conditions among sharecroppers written by high school children in New York City, a folder on National Sharecroppers Week and a pamphlet outlining the cases of other sharecroppers who have come up against the law."

4. Murray to Dollie G. Harris, Nov. 24, 1940, and Nov. 28, 1940; Dollie G. Harris to Murray, Nov. 26, 1940, box 187-6, WDLC; Dollie G. Harris to Murray, Dec. 9, 1940, box 187-7, WDLC.

5. Odell Waller to Annie Waller, Dec. 18, 1940; Murray to Annie Waller, Dec. 26, 1940, box 187-7, WDLC.

6. Murray to Odell Waller, Dec. 28, 1940, box 187-7, WDLC.

7. Murray to Clendenin and Milgram, Dec. 28, 1940, box 187-23, WDLC. Murray sent a copy of this letter to Odell Waller.

8. Murray to Finerty, Dec. 28, 1940, box 186-21, WDLC.

9. Murray to Clendenin and Milgram, Dec. 28, 1940, box 187-23, WDLC.

10. Murray to Clendenin and Milgram, Dec. 31, 1940, box 187-23, WDLC; Murray, *Song*, 166–67. On Jan. 2, 1941, Waller wrote out a short account of his life and the shooting. In it he used the words quoted by Murray. Copy in box 187-8, WDLC. It was printed in *The Black Worker*, June 1942, 2. Afterwards Murray wrote to Captain Brent that she was "impressed with the cleanliness, efficiency, and courtesy" at the Virginia State Penitentiary, in contrast to what she had experienced as a prisoner in the Petersburg City Jail. Murray to Brent, Jan. 3, 1941, box 187-8, WDLC.

11. Odell Waller to Finerty, Dec. 30, 1940, box 187-7, WDLC.

12. Murray to Waller, Jan. 3, 1941, box 187-8, WDLC. See also Murray to Clendenin and Milgram, Dec. 31, 1940, box 187-23, WDLC.

13. Stone to National Administrative Committee, WDL, Dec. 30, 1940, box 4, Dabney Papers.

14. Stone to Waller Defense Committee (Richmond), Dec. 31, 1940, and Stone to National Administrative Committee, WDL, Dec. 31, 1940, box 4, Dabney Papers.

15. Stone to Odell Waller, Dec. 31, 1940, box 186-21, WDLC; draft of proposed letter, Waller to Stone (n.d.), box 186-22, WDLC; Odell Waller to Murray, Jan. 2, 1941, box 187-8, WDLC.

16. Edmund Campion to National Administrative Committee, WDL, Jan. 31, 1941, box 186-23, WDLC; C. B. Cowan to National Administrative Committee, WDL, Feb. 15, 1941, box 186-24, WDLC.

17. Murray to J. Byron Hopkins, Jan. 7, 1941; Hopkins to Murray, Jan. 13, 1941, box 186-22, WDLC. Murray later wrote that "Hopkins refused to continue his association with the defense as long as Mr. Stone remained." Murray to *Richmond Afro-American*, Aug. 29, 1942, box 184-26, WDLC.

18. *The Fighting Worker*, Jan. 1, 1941, 1.

19. Finerty to Richmond Waller Defense Committee, Jan. 3 and Jan. 24, 1941, box 4, Dabney Papers; Finerty to Virginius Dabney, Feb. 26, 1941, box 186-24, WDLC.

20. Finerty to Dabney, Feb. 26, 1941, box 186-24, WDLC. This letter was published in *Richmond Times-Dispatch*, Feb. 28, 1941, 16. See also Finerty to Murray, Feb. 3, 1941, box 186-24, WDLC.

21. Finerty to Dabney, Mar. 3, 1941, box 4, Dabney Papers.

22. *Richmond Times-Dispatch*, Jan. 13, 1941, 6. See also *Workers Defense Bulletin*, Jan. 1941, 1–2, for a defense of the WDL's handling of the Waller case.

23. Dabney to Clendenin, Jan. 13, 1941, box 4, Dabney Papers.

24. Dabney to Editor, Jan. 30, 1941, in *The Nation* 152 (Feb. 8, 1941): 168.

25. Finerty to Editor, Feb. 10, 1941, box 4, Dabney Papers. This letter was published in *The Nation* 152 (Feb. 22, 1941): 223–24.

26. "Poll Taxes and Waller," *Richmond Times-Dispatch*, Feb. 16, 1941, sec. IV, 6.

27. Dorothy C. Stone to Editor, Feb. 19, 1941, box 4, Dabney Papers.

28. Thomas H. Stone to Editor, *Richmond Times-Dispatch*, Feb. 20, 1941, 8. In that same edition there also appeared a response from Pauli Murray in which she requested that Dabney clarify the names of the organizations involved so that the WDL would not be confused with the RWL. The RWL published an attack on Dabney's editorial in *The Fighting Worker*, Mar. 11, 1941, 2, which was headlined: "New Deal Southern Liberal Hopes to White-wash Va. Court in Waller Case." The argument was similar to Stone's.

29. Joseph Whitehead, Jr., to Editor, *Richmond Times-Dispatch*, Feb. 21, 1941, 16.

30. "Poll Taxes and Waller—II," *Richmond Times-Dispatch*, Feb. 20, 1941, 8.

31. C. B. Cowan and Paula Subienne to Editor, *Richmond Times-Dispatch*, Feb. 28, 1941, 16. In early February, C. B. Cowan replaced Edmund Campion as chairman of the Richmond Waller Defense Committee. See Edmund Campion, Paula Subienne, and C. B. Cowan to All Waller Defense Committees; All Supporting Groups and Individuals; The Press, Feb. 14, 1941, box 4, Dabney Papers. For another vituperative letter attacking Dabney as a prejudiced "Southern 'liberal'" and his "attempts to 'legally lynch' Waller," see William Street, Sec'y Prov. Waller Defense Committee, Kansas City, Mo., to Dabney, Feb. 27, 1941, box 4, Dabney Papers.

32. Murray to Frank McCallister, Feb. 19, 1941, box 186-7, WDLC; Memorandum, "Re Waller Defense Committee and Stone," [Feb. 24, 1941], box 186-24, WDLC.

33. Stone to C. B. Cowan, Mar. 14, 1941, box 186-25, WDLC.

34. Record, 20; Stone to WDL (telegram), Jan. 24, 1941, box 186-23, WDLC; Stone to Finerty, Jan. 13, 1941, box 186-22, WDLC; Stone to James H. Price, Mar. 4, 1941, folder 1, box 8, OWF.

35. Martin to Finerty, Dec. 31, 1940, box 187-27, WDLC; Murray to Martin, Jan. 8, 1941, box 186-22, WDLC; Martin to Finerty, Jan. 17, 1941, box 186-23, WDLC.

36. Stone to James H. Price, Mar. 4, 1941, folder 1, box 8, OWF; Stone to Finerty, Feb. 17, 1941, box 186-24, WDLC. The court allowed Stone thirty minutes for his oral argument.

37. Record, 20; Stone to WDL (telegram), Mar. 5, 1941, box 186-25, WDLC; *Richmond Times-Dispatch*, Mar. 5, 1941, 8; *Danville Register*, Mar. 5, 1941, 1; Secretary to Governor Price to Stone, Mar. 5, 1941, folder 1, box 8, OWF. By granting a writ of error the court agreed to review the record and judgment of the trial. The supersedeas order suspended the execution of the sentence pending the outcome of this review.

38. WDL, "THE CASE OF SHARECROPPER WALLER—A STATEMENT

OF FACTS," Feb. 4, 1941, 3, box 183-2, WDLC.

39. Krueger, *And Promises to Keep*, 42–47; *Outside the Magic Circle: The Autobiography of Virginia Foster Durr*, ed. Hollinger F. Barnard (University: Univ. of Ala. Press, 1985), 128–31; *Congressional Record*, 77th Cong., 1st sess. (Jan. 3, 1941), vol. 87: 18; (Mar. 31, 1941), vol. 87: 2698; appendix, 1128.

40. "THE CASE OF SHARECROPPER WALLER—A STATEMENT OF FACTS," 1.

41. *Congressional Record*, 77th Cong., 2d sess., appendix, 3626–27; U.S. Senate Committee on the Judiciary, *Poll Taxes: Hearings before a Subcommittee of the Committee on the Judiciary*, 77th Cong., 2d sess., Mar. 14, 1942, 179. North Dakota was not included in the total.

42. Luther P. Jackson, *The Voting Status of Negroes in Virginia: 1942* (Petersburg: Virginia Voters League, 1943), unpaged pamphlet. See also Moss A. Plunkett, *The Skeleton in Democracy's Closet* (Richmond: Southern Electoral Reform League, n.d. [1940]), an eight-page pamphlet.

43. *Richmond Times-Dispatch*, Feb. 2, 1941, 1; "For War on the Poll Tax," editorial, *Richmond Times-Dispatch*, Mar. 27, 1941, 10; *Workers Defense Bulletin*, Feb. 1941, 1; Murray to Finerty, Feb. 5, 1941, box 186-24, WDLC; *Outside the Magic Circle*, 157, 263. Jennings Perry, associate editor of the *Nashville Tennessean*, was named chairman of the league and Le Roy Hodges was named treasurer.

44. McCallister to Clendenin, Feb. 8, 1941, box 186-7 WDLC. Pauli Murray observed that David George was said to be related to Oscar Davis and that this could have made it hard for him to work with the WDL. Murray to David George, Jan. 31, 1941, box 186-7, WDLC. Each of Oscar Davis's three wives was a cousin of David George. See Hearing, 163.

45. "Poll Tax Repeal Gains Momentum," editorial, *Richmond Times-Dispatch*, Feb. 2, 1941, sec. IV, 6; Murray to Dabney, Feb. 5, 1941, box 4, Dabney Papers.

46. *The Fighting Worker*, Apr. 1941, 2; June 1941, 2, Sept. 17, 1941, 1.

47. Robert K. Gooch, "The Poll Tax in Virginia Suffrage History: A Premature Proposal for Reform" (Charlottesville: Institute of Government, Univ. of Va., 1969), mimeographed report, 6–10, 11, 14, 15, 33, 34; *Congressional Record*, 77th Cong., 2d sess. (Nov. 23, 1942), vol. 88: 9065; *Civil Liberties Quarterly* 45 (June 1942): 38, and 47 (Dec. 1942): 1; Ogden, *Poll Tax in the South*, 201–4; George B. Tindall, *The Emergence of the New South, 1913–1945* (Baton Rouge: La. State Univ. Press, 1968), 640–41; WDL, *Press Service*, Feb. 9, 1942, and Mar. 9, 1942.

48. Memorandum, Murray to Milgram and Clendenin, Jan. 6, 1941, box 187-23, WDLC; *Workers Defense Bulletin*, Feb. 1941, 1. Murray originally expressed some skepticism that the trip would raise more money than it cost.

49. "REPORT—PAULI MURRAY–ANNIE WALLER TOUR," Jan. 7 to Jan. 27, 1941, box 187-23, WDLC. See also Murray to Clendenin and Milgram, Jan.

9 and Jan. 13, 1941, box 188-1, WDLC; Murray to Finerty, Jan. 20, 1941, box 186-23, WDLC; Minutes of Executive Committee Meeting, Chicago Branch— Workers Defense League, Jan. 16, 1941, box 188-2, WDLC; *Workers Defense Bulletin,* Feb. 1941, 1–2; *News* from WDL, Jan. 17, 1941, box 183-1, WDLC; WDL, *Press Service,* Feb. 10, 1941, 2.

50. Adelene McBean, Sec'y Harlem Branch, WDL, mimeographed letters, Jan. 8, Jan. 18, Feb. 5, Mar. 4, 1941; WDL flier, box 186-1, WDLC; WDL, *Press Service,* Feb. 17, 1941, 1–2.

51. Murray to Dollie G. Harris, Feb. 5, 1941; Annie Waller to Murray, Feb. 28, 1941; Murray to Odell Waller, Feb. 18, 1941, box 187-9, WDLC.

52. Dollie Harris to Murray, Mar. 18, 1941, box 187-10, WDLC.

53. Murray to Annie Waller, Mar. 31, 1941, box 187-10, WDLC. The Chicago Waller Defense Committee issued a flier announcing talks by Mollie Waller to be given on Mar. 29, Mar. 31, and Apr. 2. Copy in folder 5, "Odell Waller Defense Committee," box 47, Lens Papers.

54. Murray to Odell Waller, Mar. 31, 1941, box 187-10, WDLC.

55. Odell Waller to Murray, Apr. 4, 1941; Murray to Annie Waller, Apr. 15, 1941, box 187-11, WDLC; Odell Waller to Annie Waller, Apr. 23, 1941, "Odell Waller Case" folder, box 57, Murray Papers. Throughout Odell Waller's long ordeal, his wife Mollie remained very much in the background. There are no letters of hers in the WDLC, and the above incident was one of the few instances when Odell mentioned her.

56. Odell Waller to Clendenin, Apr. 3, 1941, box 186-11, WDLC.

57. Murray to Waller, Mar. 31, 1941, box 187-10, WDLC. On this concern see also McCallister to Stone, Apr. 24, 1941, box 186-26, WDLC.

58. "Statement of Income and Expenditures of the WDL from January 1, 1941, to April 30, 1941," box 188-9, WDLC; "Report of the National Secretary-Treasurer to National Executive Board of Workers Defense League—May 9, 1941," box 185-17, WDLC.

59. "Report of the National Secretary-Treasurer . . . —May 9, 1941."

60. WDL, *Press Service,* Apr. 14, 1941, 1–2.

61. William Allen White to James H. Price, Apr. 14, 1941, folder 1, box 8, OWF.

62. Murray to Annie Waller, Mar. 12, 1941, and Mar. 26, 1941, box 187-10, WDLC.

63. "Report of the National Secretary-Treasurer . . . —May 9, 1941." The folder by the WDL is in bound volume of WDL pamphlets, Library of Univ. of Calif., Berkeley.

64. For correspondence regarding planning of the tour see folders 9 to 12, box 188, WDLC. See also Samuel H. Friedman to Walter White, Mar. 21, 1941,

and Morris Milgram to William Pickens, Apr. 5, 1941, in file "Sharecroppers: Odell Waller," box 526, Group II, A, NAACP Papers.

65. Murray to Milgram, May 26, 1941, box 188-11, WDLC.

66. "Minutes of National Administrative Committee," WDL, May 7, 1941; Murray to Milgram, May 7, 1941; Murray to WDL, May 24, 1941, box 188-9, WDLC; Murray to WDL, May 26, 1941, box 188-11, WDLC.

67. Murray, *Song*, 168.

68. Murray to Ted Le Berthon, June 19, 1941; "Statement of Expenses—Murray-Waller Tour"; "Cash Returns from Murray-Waller Tour," box 188-12, WDLC.

69. Annie Waller to Robert Waller (telegram), June 12, 1941, box 188-12, WDLC; Milgram to Odell Waller, June 13, 1941, box 187-11, WDLC; "Report of the National Secretary-Treasurer . . . —May 9, 1941"; Murray, *Song*, 177–79. Murray's work on the Waller case had stimulated her interest in studying law. During the year she applied to Howard University Law School, and in August she received the news of her acceptance with a tuition scholarship for the session beginning in mid September 1941. See *Song*, 162, 180–81.

Chapter 5

1. David Clendenin to Thomas H. Stone, May 22, 1941; Morris Shapiro to WDL, May 27, 1941; Stone to Clendenin, May 28, 1941, box 186-26, WDLC. They submitted their brief replying to the state's arguments against the case laid out by Stone in his petition for a writ of error in June. See WDL, *Press Service*, June 28, 1941, 2.

2. Morris Milgram to McCallister, Aug. 18, 1941. See also Stone to Finerty, Aug. 12, 1941; Finerty to Stone, Aug. 13, 1941, box 186-27, WDLC. Milgram had also invited representatives from the NAACP (Thurgood Marshall, Walter White, or Roy Wilkins) to attend the conference on August 17, but none was able to attend. See Milgram to White, Aug. 13 and Aug. 25, 1941, in file "Crime—Odell Waller, 1940–41," box 54, Group II, B, NAACP Papers. On September 2, 1941, Pauli Murray, who remained as a member of the WDL's National Executive Board, came back to the WDL's office to help out until she left for Howard Law School on September 15. She also wrote to several Virginia attorneys (Martin A. Martin, Oliver W. Hill of Richmond, Valentine and Cooley in Petersburg) encouraging them to attend the session on September 8. See Murray to McCallister, Sept. 2, 1941, box 186-8, WDLC.

3. *Workers Defense Bulletin*, Oct. 1941, 1–2, 4. Clendenin's decision to step down as national secretary-treasurer of the WDL at the beginning of the summer of 1941 had come as a result of mounting internal criticism of his performance as an administrator. See Milgram to Murray, May 24, 1941, in

folder "Odell Waller Case," box 57, Murray Papers. On Milgram see *Contemporary Authors* (Detroit: Gale Research Co., 1981), vols. 73–76: 433; *Workers Defense Bulletin*, Oct. 1941, 1; Milgram, "When it was my turn to speak . . . ," *Workers Defense League: A Journal to Mark the 35th Anniversary*, [5].

4. Milgram to Odell Waller, Aug. 22, 1941, box 187-12, WDLC.

5. Dollie Harris to Pauli Murray, Aug. 10, 1941; Milgram to Dollie Harris, Aug. 15, 1941; Dollie Harris to Murray, Aug. 31, 1941, box 187-12, WDLC.

6. Milgram to Walter White, Aug. 25, 1941, box 186-13, WDLC; *Richmond Times-Dispatch*, Sept. 9, 1941, 5; *The Fighting Worker*, Sept. 24, 1941, 3; *Workers Defense Bulletin*, Oct. 1941, 2.

7. Condensed from "Petition For Writ of Error," Record, 3–20.

8. "Brief on Behalf of the Commonwealth," *Odell Waller* v. *Commonwealth of Virginia*; "Reply Brief for Plaintiff in Error," *Odell Waller* v. *Commonwealth of Virginia*, copies in box 3, OWF.

9. "Petition For Writ of Error," Record, 10.

10. Record, 58.

11. "Petition For Writ of Error," Record, 10.

12. "Brief on Behalf of the Commonwealth," 13–14.

13. "Reply Brief," 8.

14. "Petition For Writ of Error," Record, 11–12.

15. "Brief on Behalf of the Commonwealth," 14.

16. Record, 76.

17. "Brief on Behalf of the Commonwealth," 17.

18. "Reply Brief," 12.

19. "Petition For Writ of Error," Record, 15–16.

20. "Brief on Behalf of the Commonwealth," 18–19.

21. "Petition For Writ of Error," Record, 16–17.

22. "Brief on Behalf of the Commonwealth," 19–20.

23. "Reply Brief," 13.

24. Hearing, 137. Edmund M. Preston, a Richmond lawyer who joined Finerty in the last stages of the case, later called Stone's argument "one of the silliest things that happened in the trial" and its use before the Supreme Court of Appeals "inane." Hearing, 136.

25. "Petition For Writ of Error," Record, 12. Stone erroneously listed only eight names in his petition, having omitted E. P. Dunn. See Record, 82.

26. *Pierre* v. *State of Louisiana*, 306 U.S. 354.

27. "Petition For Writ of Error," Record, 13.

28. Ibid., 12–14.

29. "Brief on Behalf of the Commonwealth," 16.

30. *Smith* v. *State of Texas*, 311 U.S. 128 at 130. In this case, which was decided on November 25, 1940, the conviction of a black man, Edgar Smith, of rape was overturned because the record showed that there had been the

intentional and systematic exclusion of blacks from grand jury service because of race.

31. "Reply Brief," 11. The defense was unable to show, and did not argue, that there had been explicit and systematic discrimination against blacks in the selection of Waller's jury, despite the trial jury being all white. Had they been able to do so, judicial precedents would have been on their side, and they probably would have won a reversal of the conviction. Stone was correct in viewing *Smith* v. *Texas* as an important decision in enlarging the standards of what constituted a fair cross-section in juries in state trials. But the Supreme Court did not set forth a concept of representativeness that clearly included Stone's ideas of economic class.

32. "Petition For Writ of Error," Record, 5.

33. Record, 59–60.

34. "Petition For Writ of Error," Record, 5–6.

35. Ibid., 8–9.

36. Ibid., 6, 8–9; *Craft* v. *The Commonwealth*, 65 Va. 602.

37. "Petition For Writ of Error," Record, 9.

38. "Brief on Behalf of the Commonwealth," 6.

39. Ibid., 6.

40. Ibid., 8–9; *Booth & al.* v. *The Commonwealth*, 16 Gratt (57 Va.) 519 at 527–28.

41. "Brief on Behalf of the Commonwealth," 10.

42. Record, 60.

43. "Reply Brief," 4.

44. Ibid., 6; "Petition For Writ of Error," Record, 8. At the beginning of the Constitutional Convention of 1902, Carter Glass said: "The chief purpose of this Convention is to amend the suffrage clause of the exiting Constitution. It does not require much prescience to foretell that the alterations which we shall make will not apply to 'all persons and classes without distinction'. We were sent here to make distinctions. We expect to make distinctions. We will make distinctions." Near the end of the convention, Glass was also quoted as saying "that no body of Virginia gentlemen could frame a constitution so obnoxious to my sense of right and morality that I would be willing to submit its fate to 146,000 ignorant negro voters (great applause) whose capacity for self-government we have been challenging for thirty years past." Quoted in "Petition For Writ of Error," Record, 8–9.

45. "Reply Brief," 7.

46. "Petition For Writ of Error," Record, 18–19.

47. "Brief on Behalf of the Commonwealth," 3–4.

48. Ibid., 5.

49. "Reply Brief," 2.

50. The members of the WDL had some hope that the court would agree

with at least some of the defense's contentions in regard to the jury. In contrast, the RWL had no faith at all in Virginia justice. Thus *The Fighting Worker* (Sept. 24, 1941, 3) declared, after the oral arguments on September 8 but before the court had rendered its decision, that "workers can have no more confidence in the 'impartiality' of the boss representatives on the Supreme Court bench than they had in the local landlords on the lower court. Only mass pressure can save Waller." Just how this was to be accomplished was not spelled out.

51. *Waller* v. *Commonwealth of Virginia*, 178 Va. 294 at 299.

52. Ibid., at 301.

53. Ibid., at 303.

54. Ibid., at 304.

55. Ibid., at 305.

56. Ibid.

57. Ibid., at 307.

58. Ibid.

59. Ibid., at 313.

60. Stone to Finerty, Oct. 13, 1941, box 187-1, WDLC.

61. Milgram to Stone, Oct. 14, 1941, box 187-1, WDLC. The WDL appealed to, among other organizations, the Fellowship of Reconciliation, which agreed to send an appeal to people on its membership list. See A. J. Muste to Milgram, Oct. 22, 1941, box 188-13, WDLC. From November 1, 1940, through October 31, 1941, the WDL's Waller Fund had received $7,031.60, but it had disbursed $7,362.28, leaving a deficit of $333.68. See "Statement of Income and Expenditures—Waller Case Funds. First Twelve Month," box 183-7, WDLC.

62. *Richmond Times-Dispatch*, Oct. 14, 1941, 10.

63. Ibid., Oct. 18, 1941, 4.

64. Ibid.

65. *Richmond Times-Dispatch*, Oct. 20, 1941, 20.

66. Stone to Editor, Oct. 21, 1941, box 4, Dabney Papers.

67. Ibid. Stone also sent copies of his letter to the *Richmond News Leader*, the *Richmond Afro-American*, and *The Nation*.

68. Stone to Odell Waller, Oct. 29, 1941, box 4, Dabney Papers.

69. Finerty to Editor, Oct. 27, 1941, and correction dated Oct. 28, 1941, box 187-1, WDLC. It appeared in *Richmond Times-Dispatch*, Oct. 31, 1941, 18.

70. "Poll Taxes and Waller—III," *Richmond Times-Dispatch*, Oct. 31, 1941, 18.

71. McCallister to Hilliard Bernstein, Sept. 4, 1941; Bernstein to McCallister, Oct. 7, 1941, box 186-8, WDLC; McCallister to Milgram, Sept. 23, 1941, box 183-8, WDLC; Martin A. Martin to Finerty, Oct. 9, 1941, Finerty Papers. Martin had done some preliminary work into this in January 1941.

72. Martin to Finerty, Oct. 9, 1941, Finerty Papers; Hearing, 45–58.

73. Hearing, 46–47, 54–56.

74. James T. Clement to Editor, Nov. 5, 1941, box 4, Dabney Papers.

75. Dabney to Clement, Nov. 7, 1941; Clement to Dabney, Nov. 8, 1941, box 4, Dabney Papers.

76. "Report of the Secretary" (for the Nov. 1941 meeting of the Board of Directors), p. 7, pt. I, reel 6, microfilm ed., NAACP Papers; *New York Age*, Oct. 29, 1941, 1.

77. *The Fighting Worker*, Oct. 29, 1941, 1, 3.

78. Stone to James H. Price, Oct. 13, 1941, folder 2, box 8, OWF.

79. Joseph G. Glass to Price, Oct. 20, 1941, folder 2, box 8, OWF.

80. Stone to Price, Oct. 25, 1941, folder 2, box 8, OWF.

81. Ex-Officio Sec'y to Governor to Stone, Nov. 6, 1941, folder 2, box 8, OWF.

82. *Commonwealth* v. *Waller*, Order Resentencing, Nov. 11, 1941, Finerty Papers.

83. See box 8, OWF. Among many others were letters to Price from Mary McLeod Bethune, President, National Council of Negro Women, Dec. 9, 1941, and a telegram from Frank P. Graham, President, University of North Carolina, Dec. 12, 1941.

84. *The Fighting Worker*, Dec. 10, 1941, 1.

85. Stone to Price, Nov. 18, 1941, box for "Nov. 24–Dec. 9, 1941," Secretary of the Commonwealth, Executive Papers, VSL.

86. Stone to Finerty, Nov. 19, 1941, box 187-2, WDLC. The tone of Stone's letter was remarkably cordial, in contrast to his exchanges with Pauli Murray.

87. Joseph Whitehead, Jr., to Price, Nov. 17, 1941, folder 1, box 8, OWF.

88. Price to Stone, Clement, Whitehead, Youell, and Odell Waller, Dec. 6, 1941, box for "Nov. 24–Dec. 9, 1941," Secretary of the Commonwealth, Executive Papers, VSL; WDL, *Press Service*, Dec. 8, 1941, 2; Dec. 9, 1941; and Dec. 15, 1941, 1.

89. Clement to Price, Dec. 9, 1941, folder 3, box 8, OWF.

90. Clement to Price, Dec. 12, 1941, folder 3, box 8, OWF.

91. Price to Graham, Dec. 13, 1941, folder 3, box 8, OWF.

Chapter 6

1. "Odell Waller, Petitioner, against Rice M. Youell, Superintendent of the State Penitentiary, Richmond, Virginia, Respondent, Petition For Writ of Habeas Corpus, Dec. 3, 1941," 5–6. Copy in box 3, OWF, and in box 185-2, WDLC.

2. "Odell Waller, . . . Petition For Writ of Habeas Corpus," 6–8, and Exhibits 3 and 4.

3. "Odell Waller, . . . Petition For Writ of Habeas Corpus," 8–11.

4. Ibid., 11.

5. Ibid., 13.

6. Ibid., 15.

7. Ibid., 15–16.

8. Ibid., 16.

9. Copy of opinion in Finerty Papers. See also *Richmond Times-Dispatch*, Jan. 23, 1942, 4; *Danville Register*, Jan. 23, 1942, 8; WDL, *Press Release*, Jan. 26, 1942.

10. Stone to Colgate W. Darden, Jr., Feb. 10, 1942; Darden to Stone, Feb. 11, 1942, in box for "March 7–April 16, 1942," Secretary of the Commonwealth, Executive Papers, VSL.

11. Finerty to Darden, Feb. 11, 1942, in "March 7–April 16, 1942," box, Secretary of the Commonwealth, Executive Papers, VSL.

12. Stone to Darden, Feb. 14, 1942, in "March 7–April 16, 1942," box, Secretary of the Commonwealth, Executive Papers, VSL.

13. Darden to Stone, Feb. 16, 1942, in "March 7–April 16, 1942," box, Secretary of the Commonwealth, Executive Papers, VSL.

14. Darden to Finerty, Feb. 16, 1942, in "March 7–April 16, 1942," box, Secretary of the Commonwealth, Executive Papers, VSL.

15. Finerty to Darden, Feb. 18, 1942, in "March 7–April 16, 1942," box, Secretary of the Commonwealth, Executive Papers, VSL. In the appeals process the Supreme Court may, as an exercise of discretion, issue a writ of certiorari. By granting certiorari the court is agreeing to review a case, such as one in which a decision by a state court has been called into question on constitutional grounds.

16. Darden to Finerty, Feb. 21, 1942, in "March 7–April 16, 1942," box, Secretary of the Commonwealth, Executive Papers, VSL.

17. Copy in "Miscellaneous File," box 7, OWF. Alfred Bingham was coeditor of the social action–oriented monthly journal *Common Sense* and a member of the National Committee of the WDL; A. J. Muste, a clergyman, labor leader, and peace activist, was executive secretary of the Fellowship of Reconciliation; Mary White Ovington was one of the founders of the NAACP and then treasurer of that organization; George E. Haynes was one of the founders of the National Urban League and secretary of the department of race relations of the Federal Council of Churches; Frank Kingdon, a Methodist clergyman, was former president of the University of Newark and president of the Union for Democratic action; Carl Raushenbush, a professor at New York University, was chairman of the National Executive Board of the WDL; Freda Kirchwey, an active member of the NAACP, ACLU, and other organizations concerned with civil rights and civil liberties, was editor and publisher of *The Nation*.

18. Pamphlet in "Miscellaneous File," box 7, OWF.

19. *Richmond Times-Dispatch*, Mar. 11, 1942, 7.

20. *The Fighting Worker*, Mar. 4, 1942, 1, 3. See also *The Fighting Worker*, Jan.

28, 1942, 3. This was probably the occasion referred to by Stone in an interview with an FBI agent on October 4, 1942, when he acknowledged that he had once been called to Chicago by the RWL in order to discuss the Waller case. See FBI, "Thomas H. Stone," file no. 100-6190 (5/29/43), 7.

21. *Richmond Times-Dispatch*, Mar. 2, 1942, 4; *Richmond Afro-American*, Mar. 7, 1942, 10; FBI, "Committee For The Labor Defense Congress," file no. 10-4891 (7/28/42); "National Save Odell Waller Conference," file no. 100-4890 (7/28/ 42); "The Labor Defense Congress," file no. 100-4891 (10/29/42). Stone's quotation is from the last file.

22. *The Fighting Worker*, Mar. 4, 1942, 1, 3, and Mar. 28, 1942, 2. Subsequently the Committee for a Labor Defense Congress attempted to organize a public protest meeting at Franklin Park in Washington, D.C. See the open letter signed by Allen Willis, May 26, 1942; Thurgood Marshall to Willis, May 28, 1942; and Morris Milgram to Marshall, June 6, 1942 in file "Crime—Odell Waller, 1940–41," box 54, Group II, NAACP Papers.

23. Finerty to Darden, undated [Mar. 1942], box 187-4, WDLC; *Richmond Times-Dispatch*, Mar. 11, 1942, 7; *The Fighting Worker*, Mar. 28, 1942, p.2.

24. McCallister to Darden, Mar. 16, 1942, box 1, OWF.

25. Reprieve is in box for "March 7–April 16, 1942," Secretary of the Commonwealth, Executive Papers, VSL. See also Darden to Stone, Finerty, Clement, Whitehead, Youell, and Waller, Mar. 12, 1942, in the same box. Darden received a copy of the petition to the Supreme Court from Finerty on March 10, and he telephoned to Finerty on that day to tell him that he would grant the reprieve. See Darden to Editor, Mar. 19, 1942, in *Herald Tribune*, Mar. 21, 1942, 10.

26. *New York Herald Tribune*, Mar. 18, 1942, 24.

27. Ibid.

28. *Richmond Times-Dispatch*, Mar. 20, 1942, 13.

29. Darden to Editor, Mar. 19, 1942, in *New York Herald Tribune*, Mar. 21, 1942, 10.

30. Milgram to Darden, Mar. 25, 1942, box 187-4, WDLC. Milgram and Carl Raushenbush of the WDL had previously sent Darden a note of appreciation for the reprieve on Mar. 12, 1942, box 187-4, WDLC.

31. *Richmond Times-Dispatch*, Mar. 21, 1942, 6. Darden approved of Dabney's editorial. See Darden to Evangeline Porter, Apr. 7, 1942, box 188-18, WDLC.

32. *Richmond Times-Dispatch*, Mar. 27, 1942, 14.

33. Editorial, "The Waller Case Again," *Richmond Times-Dispatch*, Mar. 27, 1942, 14.

34. Aron S. Gilmartin to Editor, Apr. 10, 1942, box 183-4, WDLC, published in *Richmond Times-Dispatch*, Apr. 15, 1942, 10. Dabney's editorial prompted McCallister, who was consistently more cautious in his handling of the Waller case than Murray had been, to propose that the WDL should not say that

Waller shot Davis in self-defense. Rather, it should say that Waller *testified* that he shot in self-defense. Finerty and Shapiro agreed, but Finerty wrote "that recently Dabney has been decidedly unfair in his treatment of the Waller case." See McCallister to Milgram, Apr. 1, 1942; Finerty to McCallister, Apr. 4, 1942; Shapiro to Milgram, Apr. 6, 1942, box 188-17, WDLC.

35. "Petition For Writ of Certiorari to the Supreme Court of Appeals of Virginia," in U.S. Supreme Court, *Records and Briefs*, 316 U.S. 679, no. 1097, c.d., microfiche. See also WDL, *Press Service*, Apr. 6, 1942, 1.

36. "Brief in Support of Petition For Writ of Certiorari to the Supreme Court of Appeals of the State of Virginia," 27, in *Records and Briefs*, 316 U.S. 679, no. 1097, c.d., microfiche.

37. Ibid., 30.

38. "Brief For Respondent in Opposition to Petition For Writ of Certiorari," 6, 11, 13, in *Records and Briefs*, 316 U.S. 679, no. 1097, c.d., microfiche.

39. Ibid., 12, 15.

40. Ibid., 2.

41. *Waller* v. *Youell, Superintendent*, 316 U.S. 679.

42. Finerty to Darden, May 4, 1942, box for "May 1–May 29, 1942," Secretary of the Commonwealth, Executive Papers, VSL.

43. Darden to Finerty, Stone, Clement, Whitehead, Youell, and Waller, May 6, 1942, in box for "May 1–May 29, 1942," Secretary of the Commonwealth, Executive Papers, VSL.

44. Finerty to Dabney, May 16, 1942, box 4, Dabney Papers. See also Finerty to Darden, May 8, 1942, box 9, OWF.

45. McCallister to Dabney, May 7, 1942, box 4, Dabney Papers.

46. Milgram to Odell Waller, June 13, 1942, box 187-16, WDLC.

47. Milgram to Odell Waller, May 8, 1942; Milgram to Waller, June 13, 1942, box 187-16, WDLC; Milgram to Waller, May 14, 1942, box 188-19, WDLC.

48. Waller to Milgram, May 14, 1942, box 187-16, WDLC.

49. *Danville Register*, May 5, 1942, 4.

50. *Richmond Times-Dispatch*, May 5, 1942, 8.

51. Stone to Editor, May 6, 1942, box 4, Dabney Papers. The language and tone of Stone's letter provided yet another illustration both of his continued interest in a radical approach to social and economic issues and of why the leaders of the WDL were still uncomfortable with his presence as Odell Waller's "chief counsel." At times Stone was circumspect in his language, and his letters to Finerty, with whom he said he agreed as far as the legal steps in the case were concerned, were cordial. "However, I frankly differ with him on the agitational standpoint," he wrote to Milgram. "I think Waller is not going to be saved unless there is increased and renewed agitation." See Stone to WDL, Apr. 14, 1942; Finerty to WDL, Apr. 18, 1942; Milgram to Stone, May 8, 1942; Stone to Milgram, May 14, 1942, box 187-4, WDLC.

52. Dabney to McCallister, May 12, 1942, box 4, Dabney Papers.

53. McCallister to Dabney, May 7, 1942, box 4, Dabney Papers.

54. McCallister to Milgram, May 7, 1942, box 188-19, WDLC.

55. WDL, *Press Service*, May 4, 1942, 1, and May 11, 1942, 1–2; WDL, *Last Minute News*, May 7, 1942; Milgram to Ethel Polk, Apr. 29, 1942; Milgram to George Loyd, Apr. 29, 1942, box 188-18, WDLC; Milgram to Odell Waller, May 8, 1942, box 187-16, WDLC.

56. WDL, "Emergency Appeal," May 15, 1942, box 2, OWF; also box 185-17, WDLC. Arthur Garfield Hays, a lawyer with a long record of involvement in civil liberties cases, was counsel of the ACLU; Reinhold Niebuhr, the noted theologian, was professor of Christian Ethics at Union Theological Seminary in New York City; Oswald Garrison Villard, a journalist, was one of the founders of the NAACP and former editor and owner of *The Nation*.

57. John Dewey to Editor, May 15, 1942, in *New York Times*, May 19, 1942, 18.

58. Pearl S. Buck to Editor, May 28, 1942, in *New York Times*, May 30, 1942, 14. Buck's interest in the Waller case was first aroused in December 1940 after she read one of the early circulars put out by his defenders. See Buck to Walter White, Dec. 21, 1940, in file "Crime—Odell Waller. 1940–41," box 54, Group II, B, NAACP Papers.

59. Memorandum by Malvina C. Thompson, n.d. [May 1942], folder "F," box 834, Eleanor Roosevelt Papers, Franklin D. Roosevelt Library, Hyde Park, N.Y.

60. A. Philip Randolph to Eleanor Roosevelt (telegram), May 26, 1942; Malvina Thompson to Randolph (telegram) [May 1942], folder "Ra–Re," box 847, Eleanor Roosevelt Papers.

61. Eleanor Roosevelt to Colgate W. Darden, Jr., June 2, 1942, box 1637, Eleanor Roosevelt Papers.

62. Frank McCallister to Eleanor Roosevelt, June 8, 1942; Eleanor Roosevelt to McCallister, June 11, 1942, box 1653, Eleanor Roosevelt Papers; Morris Shapiro to Eleanor Roosevelt, June 10, 1942; Eleanor Roosevelt to Shapiro, June 11, 1942, box 1662, Eleanor Roosevelt Papers. On June 29, 1942, Mary McLeod Bethune wrote to A. Philip Randolph that "Mrs. Roosevelt says in consultation with the President she has given all the help possible in the Waller case. She could do no more through a conference," box 188-27, WDLC.

63. *The Bee* (Danville), June 18, 1942, copy in box 259, WDLC.

Chapter 7

1. WDL, *Press Release*, May 26, 1942; *New York Times*, May 26, 1942, 15; *The Black Worker*, June 1942, 1. See also James Rorty to Milgram, memorandum, May 26, 1942, box 184-31, WDLC.

2. "Brief of Amici Curiae in Support of the Petition for Rehearing," *Waller* v. *Youell*, filed May 25, 1942, in U.S. Supreme Court, *Records and Briefs*, 316 U.S. 679, no. 1097, c.d., microfiche. See also WDL, *Press Release*, May 25, 1942. The WDL had sent letters to many prominent people asking them to sign the amici curiae brief. See box 184, WDLC. Bruce Bliven was a journalist and author and a member of the editorial board of *The New Republic*; Van Wyck Brooks was an eminent literary historian and critic; Henry Sloan Coffin was a Presbyterian clergyman and president of Union Theological Seminary; Harry Emerson Fosdick was a Baptist clergyman, professor of practical theology at Union Theological Seminary, and pastor of Riverside Church in New York City; Frank P. Graham was a historian and president of the University of North Carolina; Francis J. McConnell was senior bishop of the Methodist Episcopal Church. On Freda Kirchwey and Oswald Garrison Villard see above, chap. 6, note 17.

3. "Petition for Rehearing of the Denial of Certiorari to the Supreme Court of Appeals of Virginia," p. 2, filed May 25, 1942, in *Records and Briefs*.

4. *New York Age*, May 16, 1942, 3. Lane, a black woman, was also vice-president of the American Federation of Teachers and Chairman of the Program Committee of the March on Washington movement.

5. "Petition for Rehearing," 23–24.

6. "Petition For Writ of Habeas Corpus," filed May 25, 1942, and "Notice of Motion For Leave to File Original Petition For Writ of Habeas Corpus," in *Records and Briefs*, 316 U.S. 648. The latter was required by the Rules of the Supreme Court.

7. See *Odell Waller* v. *Rice M. Youell, Superintendent*, "Argument On Petition For Writ of Habeas Corpus Before Hon. Robert N. Pollard, United States District Judge, Richmond, Virginia, June 10, 1942," 8, copy in Finerty Papers.

8. *The New Republic* 106 (June 1, 1942): 752.

9. *The Black Worker*, June 1942, 1. This paper was the official organ of the Brotherhood of Sleeping Car Porters. The June 1942 edition was a "SPECIAL ODELL WALLER ISSUE!" and was almost entirely devoted to the case. On May 27, 1942, the Executive Board of the March on Washington movement, which was also led by A. Philip Randolph, passed a resolution regretting the Supreme Court's May 4 refusal to review the Waller case and its failure to issue an opinion. It expressed the hope that the court would now grant the request for a rehearing. See "Resolution Presented by A. Philip Randolph to Executive Board of The March on Washington Movement and Passed on May 27," box 188-20, WDLC.

10. *Waller* v. *Youell, Superintendent*, 316 U.S. 712; *Ex Parte Odell Waller*, 316 U.S. 648.

11. *News* from WDL, June 3, 1942, 2. See also "Report of the Secretary for the June Meeting of Board of Directors," p. 6, pt. I, reel 6, NAACP Papers.

12. *Opportunity* 20 (June 1942): 162.

13. *The Nation* 154 (June 6, 1942): 643–44.

14. WDL, *Press Service*, June 8, 1942, 1–2.

15. *Odell Waller* v. *Rice M. Youell, Superintendent*, "Motion in Support of Petition for Writ of Habeas Corpus," June 10, 1942, and "Argument on Petition for Writ of Habeas Corpus," copies in Finerty Papers.

As far as can be determined from the available evidence, Stone did not explain, either publicly or privately, his reason for stepping aside. The fact that the legal battles at this stage were exclusively focused on constitutional issues, which Stone had agreed were Finerty's responsibilities, may have influenced his decision. Preston had been born in Richmond in 1898 and educated at private schools and the University of Virginia, from which he received his LL.B. in 1921. A member of a prominent Richmond law firm, he had been assistant general counsel to the Richmond, Fredericksburg and Potomac Railroad. In the 1930s he became a specialist in labor law, and he did much pro bono work in cases involving civil liberties and labor relations. Active in civic affairs, Preston was a member of the Richmond Commission on Inter-Racial Relations and later became a member of the Southern Regional Council. See Anne Hobson Freeman, *The Style of a Law Firm: Eight Gentlemen from Virginia* (Chapel Hill, N.C.: Algonquin Books, 1989), 112, 117–18; *Proceedings of the Fifty-sixth Annual Meeting of the Virginia State Bar Association, 1946* (Richmond, 1946), 245–47; *Richmond Times-Dispatch*, Mar. 22, 1945, 17; and Pauli Murray to *Richmond Afro-American*, Aug. 29, 1942, in box 184-26, WDLC.

16. "Argument on Petition for Writ of Habeas Corpus," 13–14.

17. Ibid., 10–14.

18. Ibid., 28.

19. Ibid., 29–31.

20. Ibid., 30, 48–49.

21. Ibid., 76–77.

22. Ibid., 81–82.

23. Ibid., 77–78.

24. Ibid., 88–89. Decision in *Waller* v. *Youell, Superintendent*, 46 F. Supp. 411.

25. "Argument on Petition for Writ of Habeas Corpus," 89–96.

26. *Richmond Times-Dispatch*, June 12, 1942, 8.

27. *Waller* v. *Youell, Superintendent*, 130 Federal Reporter, 2d ser., 486 at 487 (June 16, 1942); *Richmond Times-Dispatch*, June 17, 1942, 1. The judges were John J. Parker, Morris A. Soper, and Armstead Dobie.

28. *Workers Defense Bulletin* (Summer 1942), 3; *News* from WDL, June 19, 1942; *Richmond Times-Dispatch*, June 19, 1942, 1; *Danville Register*, June 18, 1942, 4; Hearing, 315, 320–23; "Opinion of Mr. Chief Justice Harlan F. Stone, June 17, 1942," in file "Crime—Odell Waller, 1940–41," box 54, Group II, B, NAACP Papers; Murray, *Song*, 170.

29. WDL, "Memorandum on the Waller Case," June 20, 1942, box 6, OWF.

30. "Argument on Petition for Writ of Habeas Corpus," 9–12, 43.

31. Darden to Clement, Whitehead, Finerty, Youell, and Waller, June 18, 1942, and accompanying statement by Darden about the commutation hearing, in box for "June 1–July 9, 1942," Secretary of the Commonwealth, Executive Papers, VSL; Finerty and Preston to Darden, June 19, 1942, in file "Crime—Odell Waller, 1940–41," box 54, Group II, B, NAACP Papers; *Richmond Times-Dispatch*, June 19, 1942, 1; *Danville Register*, June 19, 1942, 1; *The Crisis* 49 (July 1942): 228.

32. WDL, *Press Service*, May 11, 1942, 2, June 8, 1942, 1, June 11, 1942, 1. For the correspondence sent to the governor see boxes 9 to 15, OWF. See also Murray, *Song*, 169; WDL flier [June 1942], copy in University Publications of America, *New Deal Agencies and Black America*, frame 797, reel 7, microfilm edition; article by Parke Rouse in *Richmond Times-Dispatch*, June 7, 1942, 16. With law school over for the year, Pauli Murray returned to the WDL in June 1942 and worked full time on the Waller case. See Milgram to Odell Waller, June 13, 1942, box 187-16, WDLC, and material in box 188-22, WDLC.

33. Darden to Bruce Bliven, June 8, 1942, in box 2, OWF. Darden could answer only a few of the many letters that were sent to him, but he made similar comments to several letter writers.

34. There are many such examples in boxes 187 and 188, WDLC. See, for example, Milgram to W. E. B. DuBois, May 14, 1942, box 188-19, and Suzanne LaFollette to Pearl S. Buck, June 10, 1942, box 187-20, WDLC.

35. Muste to Darden, June 10, 1942, box 2, OWF; Johnson to Darden, June 12, 1942, box 9, OWF.

36. Martha R. Ford, Secretary of the Social Problems Club of the First Unitarian Church, Richmond, Virginia, to Darden, in *Richmond Times-Dispatch*, June 13, 1942, 6.

37. WDL flier (June 1942). See also WDL, *Press Service*, June 1, 1942, 2, and June 11, 1942, 2. The WDL obtained reports on the Siddle case from Martin A. Martin and Howard H. Davis. It also obtained a sworn statement by Denson's widow, Pensy, and daughter Leola. See Martin to James Rorty, May 27, 1942, box 184-13, WDLC; Davis statement, box 187-1, WDLC; Denson statement, box 185-3, WDLC.

38. *Danville Register*, Nov. 18, 1941, 3.

39. *Pittsylvania Tribune*, Nov. 21, 1941, 1.

40. *Danville Register*, Nov. 20, 1941, 7.

41. *New York Times*, June 11, 1942, 22.

42. James T. Clement to Editor, June 16, 1942, in *New York Times*, June 19, 1942, 22.

43. Hearing, 200–201.

44. Dabney to Thomas Sancton, July 13, 1942, box 4, Dabney Papers.

45. Dabney to Dr. J. D. Eggleston, June 9, 1942, box 4, Dabney Papers.

46. *Richmond Times-Dispatch,* June 14, 1942, ed. sec., 6. In sharp contrast with Dabney's views were those of his fellow Richmond editor, Douglas Southall Freeman of the *Richmond News Leader.* Although he never showed much interest in the case, Freeman believed that "of Waller's guilt, after a fair trial, there is no question whatever. . . . I think even those Virginians who interested themselves in the case at the outset have been compelled to drop out. Too many Communists have taken it up." See Freeman to Marquis James, June 11, 1942, box 187-21, WDLC.

47. Clement to Editor, *Richmond Times-Dispatch,* June 19, 1942, 12.

48. McCallister to Milgram, Friday June 19, 1942, box 187-21, WDLC. In a draft of a summary on the Waller case prepared for the governor's hearing, Finerty asserted that by his letters Clement had "debased the judiciary of Virginia." "The Waller Case," 17, in Finerty Papers, also box 185-7, WDLC.

49. *Danville Register,* June 17, 1942, 6.

50. Dabney to Marion Saunders, June 18, 1942, box 4, Dabney Papers.

51. *Danville Register,* June 23, 1942, 4.

52. Dabney to the Editor, *Danville Register,* June 26, 1942, box 4, Dabney Papers.

53. McCallister to Dabney, June 15, 1942, box 4, Dabney Papers.

54. Sancton to Dabney, June 16, 1942, box 4, Dabney Papers. A graduate of Tulane University, Sancton had been a reporter for the New Orleans *Times-Picayune* and the Associated Press. In 1941–42 he was a Nieman Fellow at Harvard University. For some of his published ideas on race relations, see his articles, "The South and the North: A Southern View," *American Scholar* 12 (Winter 1942–43): 105–15, and "Segregation: The Pattern of a Failure," *Survey Graphic* 36 (Jan. 1947): 7–11.

55. Dabney to Sancton, June 18, 1942, box 4, Dabney Papers.

56. Petition to Honorable Franklin D. Roosevelt, box 15, OWF; William M. Agar and Laurence T. Hosie to President Roosevelt, June 15, 1942, box 187-19, WDLC; *News* from WDL, June 15, 1942. The initial signers were: John Dewey, Bruce Bliven, Frank P. Graham, Arthur Garfield Hays, John Hayes Holmes, Freda Kirchwey, Maynard C. Krueger, Bishop Francis J. McConnell, Charles Clayton Morrison, A. Philip Randolph, and Oswald Garrison Villard.

Tom Mooney, a California socialist and labor leader, had been convicted of murder in the bombing of a Preparedness Day Parade in San Francisco on July 22, 1916, and was sentenced to death. Concerned about the international uproar over Mooney, Wilson took an interest in the case and in September 1917 appointed a Mediation Commission to look into it. Its report, issued on Jan. 16, 1918, was drafted by the commission counsel, Felix Frankfurter. It concluded that justice had not been done, and it recommended that Wilson use his good offices to get the governor of California to put off the execution until a new trial could be held and Mooney's guilt or innocence definitely established. Wilson wrote a number of letters to Governor William D. Stephens, but they went unanswered. However, on November 28, 1918, Stephens commuted Mooney's sentence to life imprisonment. See Frost, *The Mooney Case*, 282–95, and Curt Gentry, *Frame-Up: The Incredible Case of Tom Mooney and Warren Billings* (New York: Norton, 1967), 229–43. The Mediation Commission report is in *The Papers of Woodrow Wilson*, ed. Arthur S. Link et al., vol. 46 (Princeton, N.J.: Princeton Univ. Press, 1948), 68–74.

Joe Hill was a Swedish-born member of the IWW who in 1914 was convicted of murder in Utah and sentenced to death. Wilson's intervention in this case was limited to two communications to the Utah governor asking him to reconsider the case. Although his execution was temporarily delayed, Hill was put to death by firing squad on November 19, 1915. See Gibbs M. Smith, *Joe Hill* (Salt Lake City: Univ. of Utah Press, 1969), 154–77.

57. William Agar and Laurence T. Hosie to Harold Ickes, June 11, 1942, Office Files of Harold Ickes, R.G. 48, in *New Deal Agencies and Black America*, frame 795, reel 7; WDL, "Memorandum on the Waller Case," June 20, 1942, and accompanying letters dated June 20, 1942, in box 6, OWF; "Petition for Presidential Commission of Inquiry," June 14, 1942, box 187-18, WDLC; *New York Age*, June 20, 1942, 12.

58. On June 27, 1942, Assistant Attorney General Wendell Berge wrote to the WDL that while the Justice Department "would like to be of assistance . . . the matter appears to be within the exclusive jurisdiction of the State of Virginia." See Berge to Laurence T. Hosie, June 27, 1942, box 188-21, WDLC. See also Nancy J. Weiss, *Farewell to the Party of Lincoln: Black Politics in the Age of FDR* (Princeton, N.J.: Princeton Univ. Press, 1983), esp. 240–54. For a different perspective on Roosevelt and blacks, see Harvard Sitkoff, *A New Deal for Blacks: The Emergence of Civil Rights as a National Issue*, vol. 1, *The Depression Decade* (New York: Oxford Univ. Press, 1978).

59. *The Black Worker*, June 1942, 1, July 1942, 1, 4; *New York Age*, June 6, 1942, 1, 6, June 13, 1942, 6, June 27, 1942, 1; *New York Times*, June 17, 1942, 11; *New York Herald Tribune*, June 17, 1942; *The Catholic Worker* 9, no. 9 (July–Aug. 1942): 6; *News* from WDL, June 17, 1942; B. F. McLaurin (MOWM) to Dear Co-Worker, June 2, 1942, box 188-2, WDLC; WDL, Church Committee, press release for June 16, 1942, box 183-5, WDLC; fliers for rally in box 184-5, WDLC; Murray, *Song*, 170; Herbert Garfinkel, *When Negroes March: The March on Washington Movement in the Organizational Politics for FEPC* (Glencoe, Ill.: Free Press, 1959), 78–97; Pfeffer, *A. Philip Randolph*, 51–52, 81.

60. *New York Herald Tribune*, June 18, 1942, 20.

61. *New York Times*, June 19, 1942, 22.

62. *Danville Register*, June 19, 1942, 2; *Richmond Times-Dispatch*, June 19, 1942, 9; *New York Times*, June 19, 1942, 21.

63. Edmund A. Ross, Walter Frank, Arthur Garfield Hays, and Roger

Baldwin to Darden, June 23, 1942, box 6, OWF.

64. "Statement to Governor Darden of Virginia by the National Lawyers Guild In Support of the Application of Odell Waller for Commutation of Sentence," (ca. June 27, 1942), box 4, OWF; press release of National Lawyers Guild, June 29, 1942, in file "Crime—Odell Waller, 1940–41," box 54, Group II, B, NAACP Papers. On the Scottsboro case see Carter, *Scottsboro*; on the Herndon case see Charles H. Martin, *The Angelo Herndon Case and Southern Justice* (Baton Rouge: La. State Univ. Press, 1976).

65. Shapiro to Martin Popper, National Lawyers Guild, June 24, 1942, box 186-3, WDLC. On the National Lawyers Guild see Ann Fagan Ginger and Eugene M. Tobin, eds., *The National Lawyers Guild: From Roosevelt through Reagan* (Philadelphia: Temple Univ. Press, 1988) and *A History of the National Lawyers Guild, 1937–1987* (New York: National Lawyers Guild Foundation), 1987.

66. Record, *The Negro and the Communist Party*, 209–26; James W. Ford, "The Negro People and the New World Situation," *The Communist* 20 (Aug. 1941): 696–704; Ben Davis, Jr., "The Communists, the Negro People and the War," *The Communist* 21 (Aug. 1942): 633–35. The monthly magazine of the Communist party, *The Communist*, did not mention the Waller case editorially or in its articles until Ben Davis made a passing reference to it in the August 1942 article cited above. This article grew out of a response to an editorial in the *New York Age*, June 27, 1942, on "Communism and the Negro" which had criticized the Communist party for counseling silence in the fight for the rights of blacks since June 22, 1941. The Communist party denied the charge in a letter written on June 29 and published in the *Age* on July 11, 1942. The picture was much the same at the state level. Whatever interest the few Communist party members in Virginia may have had in the case, it was not made evident by public activity. Alice Burke, secretary of the Communist party in Virginia and the party's candidate for governor, has acknowledged in a recent conversation with Professor Patricia Sullivan of the University of Virginia that she was not involved in Waller's defense (conversation of author with Professor Sullivan, Sept. 26, 1990). Similarly, Esther Cooper (later Jackson), one of the leaders of the Communist-led Southern Negro Youth Congress (an organization founded in Richmond in 1937 but primarily active in Birmingham and New Orleans in the late 1930s and early 1940s), has said that she can remember having no active involvement in the Waller case (conversation with author, May 30, 1990). *Cavalcade: The March of Southern Negro Youth*, the Southern Negro Youth Congress's short-lived monthly newspaper that was published in Birmingham, Alabama, from April to November 1941 and in May 1942, did not discuss the Waller case.

67. *The Daily Worker*, June 19, 1942, 4.

68. Ibid., June 26, 1942, 4.

69. *The Militant*, July 11, 1942, 1, 3.

70. Langhorne Jones to Darden, June 8, 1942, box 2, OWF. See also Hearing, 41. Jones was a law partner of Commonwealth Attorney Joseph Whitehead, Jr.

71. J. T. Clark to Darden, June 12, 1942, box 2, OWF.

72. Preston Moses to Darden, June 27, 1942, box 2, OWF.

73. John C. Roach to Darden, June 26, 1942, box 2, OWF.

74. James Cannon, Jr., to Darden, June 26, 1942, box 2, OWF.

75. *Pittsylvania Tribune*, June 19, 1942, 1.

Chapter 8

1. Finerty to Dabney, May 16, 1942, box 4, Dabney Papers.

2. Stuart I. Rochester and Jonathan J. Wolfe, "Colgate W. Darden, Jr.: The Noblest Roman of Them All," in Edward Younger and James Rice Moore, eds. *The Governors of Virginia, 1860–1978* (Charlottesville: Univ. Press of Va., 1982), 291–98; Virginia Waller Davis, "There's A Schoolboy Prophecy Darden Wants to Fulfill," *Richmond Times-Dispatch*, Feb. 2, 1941, sec. IV, 1, 5.

3. "Confidential exerpts [*sic*] from letter of Frank McCallister to M. Milgram, 6/10/42," box 188-21, WDLC.

4. See Hearing, 40–41, and Langhorne Jones to Darden, June 8, 1942, box 2, OWF.

5. Darden to Harry F. Byrd, June 17, 1942, box 2, OWF.

6. John Archer Carter to Darden, June 18, 1942, box 2, OWF.

7. Darden to Carter, June 25, 1942, box 2, OWF.

8. *Danville Register*, June 24, 1942, 5; *Pittsylvania Tribune*, June 26, 1942, 1; *New York Times*, June 25, 1942, 10.

9. *Pittsylvania Tribune*, June 26, 1942, 1.

10. Whitehead to Editor, *Richmond Times Dispatch*, June 28, 1942, sec. IV, 6. An editorial in the *Danville Register*, June 28, 1942, 6, entitled "Where the Press Failed," contained a similar criticism of several of the country's major newspapers for expressing views on the Waller case without having "any real understanding of the facts." It also portrayed Waller in hostile terms similar to those used by Whitehead. A few days earlier the *Richmond News Leader*, June 26, 1942, 1, 2, had published an article listing Waller's previous convictions.

11. "Memorandum of Mr. Justice Frankfurter," June 27, 1942, in "Legal File"—Memoranda, 1942, Container #218, reel 138, Felix Frankfurter Papers, Manuscript Division, Library of Congress; *New York Times*, June 28, 1942, 25; Hearing, 322–23.

In an account of his efforts with Chief Justice Stone, Finerty later wrote: "Stone told me that he believed the Court would have issued the Writ of Habeas Corpus had proof been made by Waller's trial counsel on the original

trial of the fact that non-payers of poll taxes were excluded from the jury. . . .
Stone having told me privately that this was the ground upon which the
Supreme Court denied the petition for certiorari, I then tried to file a petition
for Habeas Corpus . . . supported by affidavits showing that such exclusion of
non-payers of poll taxes was, in fact, made in connection with the jury trying
Waller. When the Supreme Court refused to issue Habeas Corpus, Stone told
me that the Court took the position that the failure to make this proof on trial
was fatal and that it could not be supplied collaterally on Habeas Corpus. I told
him that it was a barbarous doctrine that a man could be executed for the
procedural error of his counsel when there was no doubt as to the facts.
Nevertheless, I could not move him nor the other members of the Court."
Finerty to Thurgood Marshall, Sept. 26, 1952, Finerty Papers.

12. McCallister to Milgram, June 22, 1942, box 186-3, WDLC. Despite
McCallister's admonition not to use the petition publicly, in deference to the
wishes of some of the signers, a story about it went out on the AP wires and
appeared in several newspapers. See *New York Times,* June 28, 1942, 25; *Journal
and Guide* (Norfolk), July 4, 1942, 2; *Danville Register,* June 28, 1942, 5; *Richmond
Times-Dispatch,* June 28, 1942, sec. I, 2.

13. McCallister to Milgram, June 22, 1942, box 186-3, WDLC.

14. Dabney to Thomas Sancton, June 26, 1942, box 4, Dabney Papers.

15. "The Waller Hearing Today," *Richmond Times-Dispatch,* June 29, 1942, 6.

16. *Danville Register,* June 30, 1942, 1.

17. *Richmond Times-Dispatch,* June 30, 1942, 1, 4; *Richmond Afro-American,* July
4, 1942, 12; *The Christian Century* 59 (July 15, 1942): 892–93.

18. Hearing, 8.

19. Ibid., 2–3.

20. Ibid., 6. Darden repeated this promise later in the hearing. See Hearing,
247–48, 251–52.

21. Hearing, 27. The transcript of Annie Waller's testimony at the Hearing
filled some thirty pages (8–38), but that at the trial was only slightly over three
pages.

22. Hearing, 8–10, 11–22.

23. Ibid., 25–26, 28.

24. Record, 112.

25. Ibid., 113.

26. Hearing, 27.

27. See Record, 110.

28. Hearing, 35.

29. Ibid., 39–41.

30. Ibid., 65–66.

31. Ibid., 67.

32. Ibid., 124–25.

33. Ibid., 126–28.

34. Record, 95.

35. Hearing, 324. See also 103–4, 134.

36. Hearing, 324.

37. Ibid., 300–301; Record, 98.

38. Hearing, 326.

39. Ibid., 327.

40. Ibid., 152–55.

41. Ibid., 163, 165.

42. Ibid., 215, 219.

43. Ibid., 214–15.

44. Ibid., 307.

45. Ibid., 304–7.

46. Ibid., 228–29.

47. Ibid., 233.

48. Ibid., 243–46.

49. Ibid., 140.

50. Ibid., 140–42.

51. Ibid., 149.

52. Ibid., 206.

53. Ibid., 256.

54. Ibid., 257–58.

55. Ibid., 258–59.

56. Ibid., 265–70.

57. Ibid., 273.

58. Ibid., 300–301.

59. Ibid., 275–76.

60. Ibid., 309–11.

61. Ibid., 314.

62. Ibid., 315.

63. Ibid., 321.

64. Ibid., 324.

65. Ibid., 328. Earlier Finerty indicated that he believed there had been coaching in the testimony of John Curtis Williams at the trial. See Hearing, 177–79.

66. Hearing, 326.

67. Ibid., 336.

68. Ibid., 338.

69. Ibid., 331.

70. Ibid., 332.

71. Ibid., 332–33.

72. Ibid., 340–41.

Chapter 9

1. *Danville Register,* June 30, 1942, 4.

2. *New York Times,* June 30, 1942, 20.

3. Copy in box 15, OWF. The signers were: Elmer A. Carter, editor of *Opportunity*; Frank Crosswaith, director of Harlem Labor Center and a member of the New York Housing Authority; Layle Lane, vice-president of the American Federation of Teachers; George E. Haynes, secretary of the Race Relations Commission of the Federal Council of Churches; Carl Murphy, editor and publisher of the *Baltimore Afro-American*; A. Philip Randolph, president of the Brotherhood of Sleeping Car Porters; Channing H. Tobias, member of the National Council of the YMCA; and Walter White, secretary of the NAACP.

4. *Richmond Times-Dispatch,* June 1, 1942, 10.

5. Ibid. Milgram answered Darden's gratuitous comment a few days later by issuing a statement itemizing the WDL's expenditures in the Waller case and showing that they were going to end with a deficit. See *Richmond Afro-American,* July 11, 1942, 13. For a final summary of the WDL's income and expenditures in the Waller case see *Workers Defense Bulletin,* Summer 1942, 2, and the discussion later in this chapter.

6. *Richmond Times-Dispatch,* July 1, 1942, 10, 11.

7. *New York Herald Tribune,* July 1, 1942, 19.

8. McCallister to Eleanor Roosevelt, July 7, 1942, box 1653, Eleanor Roosevelt Papers. In the *Workers Defense Bulletin,* Summer 1942, 4, McCallister again stated that "we feel that his conduct was eminently fair and considerate, and can only differ with his conclusion." To Milgram he wrote that "my opinion of Darden wasn't lowered by his decision. It seems to me that he rose above political considerations in sticking to his guns." McCallister believed that, although Darden helped himself politically within Virginia, "he is ruined nationally" as a result of his decision. McCallister to Milgram, July 14, 1942, box 186-9, WDLC.

9. Murray, *Song,* 171.

10. "Odell Waller Must Die," *Richmond Times-Dispatch,* July 1, 1942, 14. A few days later, Dabney concluded that Darden's decision "was very popular in the State." Dabney to Thomas Sancton, July 6, 1942, box 4, Dabney Papers. An article by Parke Rouse in the *Richmond Times-Dispatch,* July 5, 1942, sec. 1, 14, claimed that Darden "grew in stature in the minds of Virginians" because of the way he handled the Odell Waller case.

11. *Richmond News Leader,* July 1, 1942, 10.

12. *Danville Register,* July 1, 1942, 6.

13. Sancton to Dabney, July 2, 1942, box 4, Dabney Papers.

14. Sancton to Dabney, July 9, 1942, box 4, Dabney Papers.

15. Sancton, "The Waller Case," *The New Republic* 107 (July 13, 1942): 45–47.

16. Murray, *Song*, 171–72; WDL, *Press Service*, July 6, 1942, 1; *New York Age*, July 11, 1942, 1; Layle Lane, "Land of the Noble Free," in *New York Age*, July 11, 1942, 6; *Richmond Afro-American*, July 4, 1942, 1, and July 11, 1942, 12; *Richmond Times-Dispatch*, July 1, 1942, 10, and July 2, 1942, 1; *New York Times*, July 1, 1942, 21.

17. Murray, *Song*, 172–73; Layle Lane, "Land of the Noble Free," *New York Age*, July 11, 1942, 6.

18. *Journal and Guide* (Norfolk), July 4, 1942, 2.

19. International Labor Defense, *News*, release of July 3, 1942, copy in file "Crime—Odell Waller, 1940–41," box 54, Group II, NAACP Papers; *The Daily Worker*, July 2, 1942, 1, and July 3, 1942, 3; *Richmond Times-Dispatch*, July 2, 1942, 1, 4.

20. *Evening Star*, July 1, 1942, A 19; Murray, *Song*, 172.

21. Lash, *Eleanor and Franklin*, 671. The WDL also wired Hopkins directly to plead for a presidential intervention similar to Wilson's in the Mooney case. See Eduard C. Linderman to Hopkins, [July 1, 1942], box 188-18, WDLC. Despite Mrs. Roosevelt's failure, the members of the delegation apparently felt that she "had done everything possible and had been a sympathetic friend to all of them." See Mary Pillsbury Lord to Eleanor Roosevelt, July 8, 1942, box 1651, Eleanor Roosevelt Papers. Mrs. Lord got her information from Anna Arnold Hedgeman, a member of the delegation and racial relations advisor to the New York Office of Civilian Defense.

22. Murray, *Song*, 172; Layle Lane, "Land of the Noble Free," *New York Age*, July 11, 1942, 6.

23. Finerty to Darden (telegram), [July 1, 1942], box 187-22, WDLC.

24. WDL, *Press Service*, July 6, 1942, 1, 4, 5; *Richmond Times-Dispatch*, July 2, 1942, 1; *New York Times*, July 2, 1942, 22.

25. *Daily Press* (Newport News), July 2, 1942, 1; *Journal and Guide* (Norfolk), July 4, 1942, 2.

26. *Richmond News Leader*, June 26, 1942, 1; *Richmond Times-Dispatch*, June 27, 1942, 4; *Pittsylvania Tribune*, July 3, 1942, 1; *Journal and Guide* (Norfolk), July 4, 1942, 2. McCallister concluded that Waller's behavior in prison had hurt his case and "was responsible for the Governor's characterization of him as 'fiery and somewhat lawless.'" He got his information from the Reverend Henry Lee Robinson, who was in charge of religious work in state institutions. Robinson said that Waller's bad behavior was not limited to the last two weeks and "that Odell was the most difficult prisoner that he had in the four years since Robinson had been connected with the institutions." See McCallister to Milgram, July 14, 1942, box 186-9, WDLC.

27. *Richmond Times-Dispatch*, July 2, 1942, 4.

28. Ibid., July 3, 1942, 6; *Richmond Afro-American*, July 4, 1942, 12.

29. *Richmond Times-Dispatch,* July 2, 1942, 4; *Richmond Afro-American,* July 4, 1942, 2; Preston to Milgram, Aug. 14, 1942, Finerty Papers.

30. *Danville Register,* July 2, 1942, 1; *The Commonweal* 36 (July 17, 1942): 301–2. Preston allowed the WDL to make photostatic copies of the document, but he insisted on retaining the original "as a memorial of a very remarkable though distressing three hours spent with Waller just before his execution." Preston to Milgram, Aug. 14, 1942, box 188-27, WDLC.

31. From photocopy of original, Finerty Papers. The version issued by the WDL made a few changes in spelling, capitalization, and punctuation. I have retained the original form.

32. *Richmond News Leader,* July 2, 1942, 1; *Richmond Times-Dispatch,* July 3, 1942, 6; *Danville Register,* July 3, 1942, 1–2; *Richmond Afro-American,* July 11, 1942, 12. The Price Funeral Home in Richmond handled the burial arrangements and shipment of Waller's body to Danville. The cost ($156.15) was paid by the WDL. See statement in box 183-10, WDLC.

33. Commonwealth of Virginia, *Annual Report of the Board of Directors of the Penitentiary With Accompanying Documents: For Fiscal Year Ending June 30, 1940* (Richmond: Division of Purchasing and Printing, 1940), 45, and *Annual Report of the Board of Directors of the Penitentiary With Accompanying Documents: For Fiscal Year Ending June 30, 1941* (Richmond, 1941), 56, and *Annual Report of the Board of Directors of the Penitentiary With Accompanying Documents: For Fiscal Year Ending June 30, 1942* (Richmond, 1942), 10; Commonwealth of Virginia, *Annual Report of the Department of Corrections, 1943* (Richmond: Division of Purchasing and Printing, 1943), 71; *Daily Press* (Newport News), July 2, 1942, 4; *Richmond News Leader,* July 2, 1942, 4; Paul W. Keve, *The History of Corrections in Virginia* (Charlottesville: Univ. Press of Va., 1986), 190–91. There had been five executions during the fiscal year ending June 30, 1940.

34. U.S. Dept. of Commerce, 16th Census of the United States, 1940, *Population,* 2d ser., Characteristics of the Population, *Virginia* (Washington, D.C.: GPO, 1941), 10.

35. WDL, *Press Release,* July 3, 1942; *New York Age,* July 11, 1942, 1. The signers were the Reverend Laurence T. Hosie, acting national chairman; Layle Lane, vice-chairman; Dr. George S. Counts, treasurer; and Morris Milgram, national secretary.

36. *Chicago Defender,* July 11, 1941, clipping in box 256, WDLC. For other editorials and articles, see notebooks of clippings in boxes 255–57, 259, 260, WDLC.

37. *New York Herald Tribune,* July 3, 1942, 30.

38. *New York Times,* July 3, 1942, 16.

39. *Richmond Times-Dispatch,* July 3, 1942, 4.

40. *Richmond Afro-American,* July 11, 1942, 1, 12, 13.

41. *New York Amsterdam News,* July [11] 1942, clipping in box 184-22, WDLC.

42. Layle Lane, "Land of the Noble Free," *New York Age*, July 18, 1942, 6, 8; Murray, *Song*, 174. Milgram wrote afterwards that Murray "couldn't bear to stand that sorrowful occasion," but that the service was a "tremendous tribute to Odell Waller." Milgram to Annie Waller, July 20, 1942, box 187-17, WDLC.

43. *Richmond Afro-American*, July 11, 1942, 12; Milgram, "The Last Mile," *Workers Defense Bulletin*, Summer 1942, 2; Milgram, "When it was my turn to speak. . . ," *Workers Defense League: A Journal to Mark the 35th Anniversary*, [5].

44. Layle Lane, "Land of the Noble Free," *New York Age*, July 18, 1942, 8.

45. *Richmond Afro-American*, July 11, 1942, 12.

46. *New York Age*, July 11, 1942, 3; *New York Amsterdam News*, July 11, 1942, clipping, box 155, WDLC; *The Voice* (New York), July 11, 1942, clipping, box 260, WDLC.

47. *The Daily Worker*, July 6, 1942, 1–2; flier, box 188-27, WDLC.

48. *The Daily Worker*, July 6, 1942, 6; *Richmond Afro-American*, July 11, 1942, 13; *New York Amsterdam News*, July 11, 1942, clipping, box 155, WDLC. Randolph also bitterly denounced the Communists in an editorial, "The Communists and the Negro," *Black Worker*, July 1942, 4. They "would sacrifice America, the Negro people and heaven and earth for Soviet Russia. . . . The Communists wanted and has [*sic*] brazenly attempted to horn in on, for unholy and selfish reasons, a struggle for the Negroes' democratic rights, made sacred by the blood of Odell Waller. Yes, the Communists have become the Number One Enemy of the Negro."

49. *New York Times*, July 17, 1942, 19; *New York Age*, July 18, 1942, 1, and July 25, 1942, 1; *Richmond Afro-American*, July 25, 1942, 1, 2; *The Crisis* 49 (Aug. 1942): 247. A total of six blacks were lynched in 1942. See Peter M. Bergman, *The Chronological History of the Negro in America* (New York: New American Library, 1969), 497.

50. *Richmond Afro-American*, July 25, 1942, 13; WDL, *Press Service*, July 20, 1942, 3; Murray, *Song*, 174–75. A typewritten copy of this letter, dated July 17, 1942, which varies slightly from the version that was published, is in folder "Odell Waller Case," box 57, Murray Papers. A few days earlier Murray had written another similar, equally bitter statement. In it she wrote that Waller's defenders "wanted to prove that the democratic process was workable, even in approaching the volcanic question of race relations." But they were rebuffed by "the legalistic refusal of the Virginia and Federal Courts to look beyond the technicalities." See "He Has Not Died In Vain," July 13, 1942, typed MS in box 183-6, WDLC. Some of this was published in *The Call*, July 17, 1942, copy in box 257, WDLC.

51. Murray to Roy Wilkins, July 15, 1942 and Robert Early, Jr., to Wilkins, July 17, 1942, in file "Crime—Odell Waller, 1940–41," box 54, Group II, NAACP Papers; press release of March on Washington movement, July 20, 1942, box 186-3, WDLC; *New York Age*, July 25, 1942, 1, 12; *The Daily Worker*, July

24, 1942, 4, and July 25, 1942, 3; WDL, *Press Service,* July 20, 1942; Murray, *Song,* 175–76; Garfinkel, *When Negroes March,* 99–102; Pfeffer, *A. Philip Randolph,* 78.

52. "ODELL WALLER CASE, Workers Defense League: SCHEDULE OF INCOME AND EXPENDITURE, November 1, 1940–July 28, 1942," box 183-10, WDLC.

53. "Remember Odell Waller!" *The Fighting Worker,* July 15, 1942, 1–3.

54. Ibid., 2–3.

55. Ibid., 4.

56. Stone to Editor, July 30, 1942, box 4, Dabney Papers. The letter was published in the *Richmond Afro-American,* Aug. 15, 1942, 20, but it did not appear in some of the other newspapers and journals to which he had sent it, such as the *Richmond News Leader,* the *Richmond Times-Dispatch,* and *The Nation.* It was noted, but not published, in *The New Republic* 107 (Aug. 24, 1942): 233.

57. Murray to *Richmond Afro-American,* Aug. 29, 1942, box 184-26, WDLC. The *Richmond Afro-American,* Sept. 5, 1942, 20, published an abridged version of this letter.

Epilogue

1. *Richmond Afro-American,* July 11, 1942, 13.

2. Annie Waller to Milgram, July 18, 1942, box 187-17, WDLC. This letter, and another written to Pauli Murray on August 30, 1942, was apparently dictated by Annie, but it was in the handwriting of Dollie Harris. Although newspaper stories stated that Mrs. Harris lived in Man, West Virginia, these letters gave Kistler, a neighboring community, as a postal address. Annie Waller wrote that she was planning to visit New York, but there is no indication that she ever made the trip. See Annie Waller to Murray, Aug. 30, 1942, and Murray to Annie Waller, Oct. 5, 1942, in file "Odell Waller Case," box 57, Murray Papers.

3. *Pittsylvania Tribune,* Nov. 24, 1944, 1, 4; *Danville Register,* Nov. 19, 1944, 1, 6.

4. *Proceedings of the Fifty-Sixth Annual Meeting of the Virginia State Bar Association, 1946* (Richmond, 1946), 153–56.

5. Murray to Darden, Aug. 24, 1942; Darden to Murray, Aug. 28, 1942, box 188-25, WDLC.

6. Keve, *Corrections in Virginia,* 181–83; Rochester and Wolfe, "Colgate W. Darden, Jr.," 300;

7. Rochester and Wolfe, "Colgate W. Darden, Jr.," 302–5; *Richmond Afro-American,* Aug. 28, 1943, 14, copy in file "Racial Problems," box 75, Colgate W. Darden, Jr., Executive Papers, VSL; Darden to Editor, *Richmond Afro-American,* Sept. 19, 1942, A 4; Robbins L. Gates, *The Making of Massive Resistance: Virginia's*

Politics of School Desegregation, 1954–1956 (Chapel Hill: Univ. of N.C. Press, 1964), 96 note #6, 163–65; *Richmond Times-Dispatch,* June 10, 1981, 1, 5.

8. Dabney, *Across the Years: Memories of A Virginian* (New York: Doubleday, 1979), 164; Dabney to Thomas Sancton, July 13, 1942, box 4, Dabney Papers; Dabney, "Nearer and Nearer the Precipice," *Atlantic Monthly* 171 (Jan. 1943): 94–100.

9. Virginius Dabney, *Virginia: The New Dominion* (Garden City, N.Y.: Doubleday, 1971), also fails to mention Waller. On Dabney's racial views see Morton Sosna, *In Search of the Silent South: Southern Liberals and the Race Issue* (New York: Columbia Univ. Press, 1977), 121–39. Sosna's assertion that Dabney "waged practically a one-man campaign in the state to save Odell Waller" (128) is misleading. See also Bruce Alan Brown, "Justice, Patience, Reason: The Writings of Virginius Dabney on Matters of Race" (M.A. thesis, College of William and Mary, 1987). Dabney, like Darden, believed (in 1956 at least) that the *Brown* decision was not truly legal. See Gates, *Making of Massive Resistance,* 96 note #6.

10. FBI, "Thomas H. Stone," file no. 100-6190 (5/29/43), 9.

11. *Richmond Afro-American,* Nov. 28, 1942, 13, and Dec. 5, 1942, 9; FBI, "The Labor Defense Congress," file no. 100-4891 (1/25/43).

12. FBI, "Thomas H. Stone," file no. 100-6190 (5/29/43) and no. 105-78 (Apr. 1945); "Revolutionary Workers League," file no. 100-6877 (Jan. 15, 1945).

13. *Danville Register,* July 7, 1942, 4. See also Dabney to Thomas Sancton, July 13, 1942, box 4, Dabney Papers.

14. *The Bulletin* (Martinsville, Va.), July 13, 1942, copy in box 259, WDLC.

15. Morris Milgram to John F. Finerty, Jan. 10, 1943, box 187-5, WDLC; *Workers Defense Bulletin,* Summer 1943, 2, 3.

16. *Richmond Times-Dispatch,* Mar. 22, 1945, 17; *Proceedings of the Fifty-sixth Annual Meeting of the Virginia State Bar Association, 1946* (Richmond, 1946), 245–47; Freeman, *The Style of a Law Firm,* 117–18.

17. U.S. Senate Committee on the Judiciary, *Poll Taxes: Hearings before a Subcommittee of the Committee on the Judiciary,* 77th Cong., 2d sess., Sept. 23, 1942, 394–99.

18. *Workers Defense Bulletin,* Fall 1942, 1; WDL, *Press Service,* Nov. 9, 1942; *New York Times,* Mar. 21, 1942, 28.

19. *Poll Tax: Hearings,* 394.

20. Finerty to Marshall, Sept. 26, 1952, Finerty Papers.

21. *New York Times,* June 6, 1967, 47.

22. Milgram, "When it was my turn to speak. . . ," *Workers Defense League: A Journal to Mark the 35th Anniversary,* [6]; Loeffel, history of the Workers Defense League, 11–12.

23. Milgram, "Introduction," in Pauli Murray, *Dark Testament and Other Poems* (Norwalk, Conn.: Silvermine Publishers, 1970); Morris Milgram, *Good Neighborhood: The Challenge of Open Housing* (New York: Norton, 1979), 11; Michael Capuzzo, "A Life Building Dream House to Unite Races," *The Philadelphia Inquirer*, Sept. 21, 1986; *Contemporary Authors* (Detroit: Gale Research Co., 1981), vol. 73–76: 433; Fund for an Open Society, *Open Forum* 10, no. 1 (Spring 1987); Jacob K. Javits, *Discrimination U.S.A.* (New York: Harcourt, Brace & World, 1960), 164.

24. "Interview with Pauli Murray, February 13, 1976," Southern Oral History Program, Univ. of N.C., Chapel Hill, 60–61; *Southern Exposure* 4 (Winter 1977): 4; Sandra G. Boodman, "The Poet as Lawyer and Priest," *Washington Post*, Feb. 14, 1977, B1, B4; Murray, *Song*, 160–62, 182–88, 206–8, 368, and passim.

25. Unpublished 1943 version in possession of Morris Milgram.

26. *South Today* 8 (Winter 1945): 35.

27. Murray, *Dark Testament and Other Poems*, 25.

28. *Washington Post*, July 4, 1985, C4.

29. See *Swain* v. *Alabama*, 380 U.S. 202 (1965); *Taylor* v. *Louisiana*, 419 U.S. 522 (1975); *Bateson* v. *Kentucky*, 476 U.S. 79 (1986); Edward S. Corwin, *The Constitution and What It Means Today*, rev. by Harold W. Chase and Craig R. Ducat, 14th ed. (Princeton, N.J.: Princeton Univ. Press, 1978), 410–11. In the case of *Holland* v. *Illinois*, 110 S. Ct. 803 (Jan. 22, 1990), Justice Antonin Scalia has recently held that "the Sixth Amendment requirement of a fair cross section on the venire is a means of assuring, not a *representative* jury (which the Constitution does not demand), but an *impartial* one (which it does)."

30. *Harper et al.* v. *Virginia State Board of Elections*, 383 U.S. 663.

31. Hearing, 89.

Bibliography

Note on Sources

Between 1940 and 1942 Waller's defenders, mainly the Workers Defense League, published a number of fliers and one significant pamphlet (Pauli Murray and Murray Kempton, *"All For Mr. Davis": The Story of Sharecropper Odell Waller*, New York: Workers Defense League, [1941]). Since then, the only substantial discussion of the case to appear in print has been the two chapters by Pauli Murray in her autobiography, *Song in a Weary Throat: An American Pilgrimage* (New York: Harper & Row, 1987), which has been reissued as *The Autobiography of a Black Activist, Feminist, Lawyer, Priest and Poet* (Knoxville: Univ. of Tenn. Press, 1989). The fact that historians have ignored the case, or forgotten it entirely, has been due in part at least to the elusive nature of the principal sources. However, there are substantial amounts of material available to the researcher. The two most important collections are in the Archives at the Virginia State Library in Richmond and in the Workers Defense League Collection at the Walter P. Reuther Library of Labor and Urban Affairs at Wayne State University in Detroit. Neither of these collections was listed in the National Union Catalog of Manuscript Collections. The Waller materials in the Archives at the Virginia State Library were also not even recorded in the Archives' registers and were, for all practical purposes, lost. Certain that Virginians would not have destroyed all the records of so important a case, I persuaded the archivists to keep looking in the nooks and crannies, and in the summer of 1987 they located fifteen manuscript boxes in the Executive Papers of the Secretary of the Commonwealth. These were all labeled "Odell Waller File—1942," but they were unnumbered and uncataloged. They had apparently not been opened since being deposited there in 1942. We arbitrarily numbered each box, but future processing of the material could result in changed box numbers. These boxes contain many of the important legal papers, including a printed copy of the transcript of the trial that was prepared for the appeal to the Supreme Court of Appeals of Virginia. Most of the boxes are filled with the thousands of letters, telegrams, and petitions sent to Governor Darden in the spring of 1942. There are also many interesting letters from citizens and officials of Pittsylvania County. In addition to this collection, the Archives of the Virginia State Library have documents pertaining to Waller's extradition and reprieves in the Executive Papers of the Secretary of the Commonwealth for 1940, 1941, and 1942 as well as other relevant items in the Executive Papers of Governors Price and Darden.

The Workers Defense League Collection in the Walter P. Reuther Library is a major depository of materials on labor issues since the mid 1930s. Those pertaining to the Waller case are in boxes 183 to 188 and 255 to 260 and are listed in the library's finding guide. The first six boxes contain letters, reports, financial statements, press releases, legal papers, and other documents. They include a copy of the printed transcript of the trial and a typescript of the transcript of the governor's commutation hearing. There are many letters by the key participants, including Pauli Murray, David Clendenin, Morris Milgram, Frank McCallister, Odell Waller, Annie Waller, and others. The other six boxes contain notebooks of newspaper clippings which were collected by a clipping service for the WDL. Most of these are from the spring of 1942, but they are valuable for showing the range of coverage across the United States and, in a few instances, beyond its borders.

In addition to these two major sources, documents on the Waller case can be found in a number of other manuscript collections. The papers of Pauli Murray in the Arthur and Elizabeth Schlesinger Library on the History of Women in America at Radcliffe College in Cambridge, Massachusetts, is one. This material, which was unprocessed and also not listed in the National Union Catalog of Manuscript Collections, has two folders relating to the Waller case containing fliers, clippings, legal materials, a photostat of Waller's "Dying Statement," and some Murray correspondence. The papers of Virginius Dabney in the Alderman Library of the University of Virginia in Charlottesville have many important letters and printed items and are essential for understanding his role in the case. The papers of John F. Finerty in the library of the University of Oregon in Eugene have a significant Waller file. This has many of the legal documents, including drafts of some of the briefs, a copy of the transcript of the governor's commutation hearing, and a photostat of Waller's "Dying Statement." The NAACP Papers in the Manuscript Division of the Library of Congress have some useful material. Series B, the Legal Files, contains three folders of correspondence and fliers on the case as well as a small but relevant folder on the Pittsylvania County schools. Another folder on Waller is located in the material on sharecroppers in Series A, the General Office Files. There are also a few scattered references to the Waller case in the Monthly Reports of NAACP Officers, which can be found in part I of the microfilm edition of the NAACP Papers. The papers of Eleanor Roosevelt at the Franklin D. Roosevelt Library, Hyde Park, New York, which contains a number of Pauli Murray letters, also have a few references to the case. Some manuscript collections that are apparently relevant to the subject were not helpful. Thus there are no files on the Waller case in the Claude Barnett Papers at the Chicago Historical Society, in the Moorland-Spingarn Research Center at Howard University, in the Southern Conference for Human Welfare Papers in the Hollis Burke Frissell Library at Tuskegee University, or in the Southern Tenant Farmers' Union Papers at the Wilson Library of the University of North Carolina, Chapel Hill. The Frissell Library at Tuskegee does have a clipping file that contains some newspaper references to the Waller case.

The numerous publications of the WDL, including the *Workers Defense Bulletin*, its regular *Press Service*, and other news releases, and its fliers and pamphlets, are essential in studying the Waller case. No one depository has all of these, although many are to be found in the Workers Defense League Collection at the Walter P. Reuther Library. There is a substantial (but incomplete) set of *Press Service* releases of the WDL in the Harvard University Library, Cambridge, Massachusetts, and a valuable collection of WDL pamphlets in the library of the University of California at Berkeley. Materials on the Revolutionary Workers League of the U.S. are not easily available. The Library of Congress has a copy of its constitution, and the State Historical Society of Wisconsin has a small collection of pamphlets of the RWL. A number of the fliers put out by the Richmond Waller Defense Committee are in the Dabney Papers. A small amount of material on the RWL's activities in the Waller case can also be found in the folder on the "Odell Waller Defense Committee" in the papers of Sidney Lens in the Chicago Historical Society. The RWL's newspaper, *The Fighting Worker*, is available on microfilm.

The involvement of the RWL attracted the attention of the FBI to the Waller case. As a result of a Freedom of Information Act request, I obtained copies of a number of files pertaining to Thomas H. Stone, the RWL, and Odell Waller. Although these were heavily censored, mainly to block out the names of agents and informers, they were useful, particularly on Stone.

The major Virginia newspapers, especially the *Richmond Times-Dispatch* and the *Richmond News Leader*, and the black press, especially the *Journal and Guide* (Norfolk) and the *Richmond Afro-American*, devoted a considerable amount of space to the Waller case. The local papers, the *Danville Register* and the *Pittsylvania Tribune*, are valuable for obtaining the perspective of whites, usually anti-Waller, in Pittsylvania County and vicinity. These, as well as the major national newspapers, are available on microfilm. Unfortunately, the microfilm edition of the *Pittsylvania Tribune* was filmed from an incomplete set and lacks the key issues for 1940. These can be read in the offices of the *Star-Tribune* in Chatham.

Nearly all of the people who were most closely involved in the defense of Odell Waller were deceased by the time I did my research. An important exception was Morris Milgram, who in numerous conversations was a helpful source of information. The late Samuel H. Friedman, who was WDL publicity director at the time, also shared his recollections with me. I have also benefited from conversations with Preston Moses, former editor and publisher of the *Pittsylvania-*

Tribune, Esther Cooper Jackson, former executive secretary of the Southern Negro Youth Congress; and with a number of people who live in the Gretna area, including Virginia Keatts, who helped me locate the house formerly owned by the Waller family, and Ruth and Cecil Motley, who live in the house that was occupied by Oscar Davis at the time of the shooting. Another person who had a considerable interest in the case is Virginius Dabney, who made some helpful observations on Thomas H. Stone and Edmund M. Preston.

The courthouse in Chatham has relevant material on the Davis and Waller families scattered among the Deed Books, birth records, marriage records, and voting registration records. There is also no substitute for on-site visits to Pittsylvania County. The house once owned by the Waller family was still standing in 1989, as was the house occupied by Oscar Davis, although it has been considerably modified since the time of the shooting. Oscar Davis's grave site is in Chatham Burial Park near the center of Chatham. Odell Waller's grave, overgrown by weeds, is in a small black cemetery at the junction of state routes 685 and 686 a few miles southeast of Gretna. Nearby is the small Fairview Baptist Church, the site of Waller's funeral. Because of renovations it is no longer the plain white structure it had been in 1942, but it remains an important institution in the lives of many black people in the area.

Primary Sources

Manuscript Collections

Congress of Racial Equality. Papers, 1941–67. Microfilm ed.

Dabney, Virginius. Papers (#7690). Manuscripts Division, Special Collections Dept., Univ. of Va. Library.

Finerty, John F. Papers. Manuscripts Dept., Univ. of Oregon.

Frankfurter, Felix. Papers. Manuscript Division, Library of Congress.

Frazier, E. Franklin. Papers. Moorland-Spingarn Research Center, Howard University.

Lens, Sidney. Papers. Chicago Historical Society.

Murray, Pauli. Papers. Arthur and Elizabeth Schlesinger Library on the History of Women in America, Radcliffe College.

National Association for the Advancement of Colored People. Papers. Library of Congress.

National Association for the Advancement of Colored People. Papers. Microfilm ed. Parts I and II.

Roosevelt, Eleanor. Papers. Franklin D. Roosevelt Library, Hyde Park, N.Y.

Swanson, Gregory H. Papers. Moorland-Spingarn Research Center, Howard Univ.

Workers Defense League Collection. Archives of Labor and Urban Affairs, Walter P. Reuther Library, Wayne State Univ.

Pittsylvania County Records

County Land Books, 1918–44. Archives and Records Division, Va. State Library.
Deed Books; Index to Marriage Register, vols. 4 to 6, 1901–39; Partial List of Birth Records, 1866–96; Voting Book, Pittsylvania County Court House, Chatham.

State Records

(In Archives and Records Division, Va. State Library)
Darden, Colgate W. Executive Papers.
Executive Warrants. Folder no. 1989.
Price, James H. Executive Papers.
Secretary of the Commonwealth. Executive Papers. July 1940–July 1942.
State Board of Education. Annual Reports of Division Superintendents, 1939–40.
Waller, Odell. File—1942. Secretary of the Commonwealth, Executive Papers.

Federal Bureau of Investigation Files

Committee for the Labor Defense Congress. 1942.
Harden, Thomas F. 1942–43.
Labor Defense Congress. 1942–43.
National Save Odell Waller Conference. 1942.
Revolutionary Workers League. 1945.
Stone, Thomas H. 1942–48.
Waller, Odell. 1940.

Workers Defense League Publications and Materials

Kempton, Murray. *Odell Waller's Mother.* New York, [1941].
Loeffel, Beatrice. Unpublished manuscript on the history of the Workers Defense League. Copy in office of executive director of the WDL.
Murray, Pauli, and Murray Kempton. *"All For Mr. Davis": The Story of Sharecropper Odell Waller.* New York, [1941].

Press Service. Feb. 3, 1941–Nov. 9, 1942.

"To Establish Justice. . .": Sharecroppers Under Planters Law. New York, 1940.

Workers Defense Bulletin. Oct. 1, 1940–Fall 1949.

Workers Defense League: A Journal to Mark the 35th Anniversary of the Workers Defense League. [1971].

Workers Defense League. Pamphlets. New York, 1936–45. Bound collection in library of the Univ. of Calif. at Berkeley.

Other Records

Alumni Records. Alderman Library, Univ. of Va.

Revolutionary Workers League, U.S. *Constitution of the Revolutionary Workers League, U.S. and its Position on Democratic Centralism.* New York, Demos Press, [1939].

Revolutionary Workers League, U.S. Miscellaneous Ephemeral Materials, State Historical Society of Wisconsin, microfilm edition.

Government Documents

U.S. Senate. Committee on the Judiciary. *Poll Taxes: Hearings Before a Subcommittee of the Committee on the Judiciary.* 77th Cong., 2d sess., Mar. 14 and Sept. 23, 1942.

———. *Congressional Record,* 77th Cong., 2d sess. (1942).

———. Dept. of Commerce. 16th Census of the United States. 1940. *Agriculture, Virginia.* 1st ser. Washington, D.C.: GPO, 1941.

———. Dept. of Commerce. 16th Census of the United States. 1940. *Agriculture: Crop-Sharing Contracts.* Washington, D.C.: GPO, 1943.

———. Dept. of Commerce. 16th Census of the United States. 1940. *Population.* 2d ser. Characteristics of the Population, *Virginia.* Washington, D.C., GPO, 1941.

———. Dept. of Labor. Bureau of Labor Statistics. *A Statistical Survey of the Danville Area, Virginia.* Industrial Area Statistical Summary no. 18 (Jan. 1943).

Virginia, Commonwealth of. *Annual Report of the Board of Directors of the Penitentiary With Accompanying Documents, 1940–1942.* Richmond: Division of Purchasing and Printing, 1940–42.

———. *Annual Report of the Department of Corrections, 1943.* Richmond: Division of Purchasing and Printing, 1943.

———. State Board of Education. *Annual Report of the Superintendent of Public*

Instruction, 1939–1940 and *1940–1941.* Richmond: Division of Purchasing and Printing, 1940–41.

———. Dept. of Agriculture and Immigration. *Virginia.* Comp. and ed. Charlotte Allen. Richmond, [1937].

———. State Library. *The General Assembly of Virginia, July 30, 1619–January 11, 1978: A Bicentennial Register of Members.* Cynthia Miller Leonard, comp. Richmond: Virginia State Library, 1978.

Waller Case Documents

"Brief on Behalf of the Commonwealth." Record no. 2442. *Odell Waller* v. *Commonwealth of Virginia.* Copy in Box 3, Odell Waller File—1942.

Commonwealth of Virginia v. *Odell Waller.* Circuit Court of Pittsylvania County. Sept. 19, 26, and 27, 1940. In Record no. 2442. *Odell Waller* v. *Commonwealth of Virginia,* submitted to the Supreme Court of Appeals of Virginia.

Ex parte Odell Waller, 316 U.S. 648 (June 1, 1942).

"Odell Waller, Petitioner, against Rice M. Youell, Superintendent of the State Penitentiary, Richmond, Virginia, Respondent, Petition For Writ of Habeas Corpus, December 3, 1941." Copy in Box 3, Odell Waller File—1942.

Odell Waller v. *Rice M. Youell, Superintendent.* "Argument on Petition For Writ of Habeas Corpus Before Hon. Robert N. Pollard, U.S. District Judge, Richmond, Virginia, June 10, 1942." Copy in Finerty Papers.

Odell Waller v. *Rice M. Youell, Superintendent.* "Motion in Support of a Petition for Writ of Habeas Corpus." June 10, 1942. Copy in Finerty Papers.

"Public Hearing Before Hon. Colgate W. Darden, Jr., Governor of Virginia, In re Odell Waller, Richmond, Virginia, June 29, 1942." Copy in Finerty Papers.

"Reply Brief for Plaintiff in Error." Record no. 2442. *Odell Waller* v. *Commonwealth of Virginia.* Copy in Box 3, Odell Waller File—1942.

U.S. Supreme Court. *Records and Briefs,* 316 U.S. 679, no. 1097, c.d., microfiche ed.

Waller v. *Commonwealth of Virginia,* 178 Va. 294 (Oct. 13, 1941). *Waller* v. *Youell,* 130 Fed. Reporter, 2d. ser. 486 (June 16, 1942).

Waller v. *Youell,* 46 F. Supp. 411 (June 11, 1942).

Waller v. *Youell, Superintendent,* 316 U.S. 679 (May 4, 1942).

Waller v. *Youell, Superintendent,* 316 U.S. 712 (June 1, 1942).

Other Court Cases

Bateson v. *Kentucky*, 476 U.S. 79 (1986).
Booth & al. v. *The Commonwealth*, 16 Gratt (57 Va.) 519 (1861).
Craft v. *The Commonwealth*, 65 Va. 602 (1873).
Harper et al. v. *Virginia Board of Elections et al.*, 383 U.S. 663 (1966).
Holland v. *Illinois*, 110 S. Ct. 803 (1990).
Joseph R. Mickins v. *Commonwealth of Virginia*, 178 Va. 273 (1941).
Pierre v. *State of Louisiana*, 306 U.S. 354 (1939).
Smith v. *State of Texas*, 311 U.S. 128 (1940).
Strauder v. *West Virginia*, 100 U.S. 303 (1880).
Swain v. *Alabama*, 380 U.S. 202 (1965).
Taylor v. *Louisiana*, 419 U.S. 522 (1975).

Interviews and Correspondence

Dabney, Virginius. Jan. 20, 1989. (Correspondence.)
Friedman, Samuel H. Jan. 20 and Feb. 23, 1990.
Hill, Oliver W. Aug. 28, 1990. (Correspondence.)
Jackson, Esther Cooper. May 30, 1990.
Keatts, Virginia. Aug. 8, 1988.
Milgram, Morris. Jan. 17, 1988 and numerous subsequent telephone conversations and letters.
Moses, Preston. Jan. 25, 1989.
Motley, Cecil and Ruth. Aug. 8, 1989.

Oral Histories

Alexander, Will W. Oral History Research Office, Columbia Univ., 1972.
Baldwin, Roger Nash. Oral History Research Office, Columbia Univ., 1972.
Mitchell, Harry Leland. Oral History Research Office, Columbia Univ., 1957.
Murray, Pauli. "Interview with Pauli Murray." Feb. 13, 1976. Southern Oral History Program, Univ. of N.C., Chapel Hill.

Newspapers and Journals

The Black Worker. 1940–42.
The Catholic Worker. 1940–42.
Cavalcade: The March of Southern Negro Youth (Birmingham, Ala.). 1941–42.

Civil Liberties Quarterly. 1940–42.

The Commonweal. 1940–42.

The Communist. 1940–42.

The Crisis. 1940–42.

The Daily Press (Newport News). 1940–42.

The Daily Worker. 1940–42.

The Danville Register. 1940–42.

The Evening Star (Washington, D.C.). 1942.

The Fighting Worker. 1935–47.

International News. 1939–42.

The Journal and Guide (Norfolk). 1940–42.

The Militant. 1941–42 (successor to the *Socialist Appeal*).

The Nation. 1940–42.

The New Republic. 1940–42.

The New York Age. 1940–42.

The New York Herald Tribune. 1942.

The New York Times. 1940–42.

The News (Lynchburg). 1940–42.

Newsweek. 1940–42.

Ohio State Journal (Columbus). 1940.

Opportunity: Journal of Negro Life. 1940–42.

The Pittsylvania Tribune (Chatham, Va.). 1940–42.

PM (New York). 1942.

The Richmond Afro-American. 1940–42.

The Richmond News Leader. 1940–42.

The Richmond Times-Dispatch. 1940–42.

Socialist Appeal. 1940–Jan. 25, 1941.

The S.T.F.U. News (Southern Tenant Farmers' Union News). 1938–41.

South Atlantic Quarterly. 1940–42.

The Southern Frontier. 1940–45.

Tenant Farmer (successor to *S.T.F.U. News*). 1941–42.

Time. 1940–42.

Virginian-Pilot (Norfolk). 1940–42.

Books and Articles

Brewer, William M. "The Poll Tax and the Poll Taxers." *Journal of Negro History* 29 (July 1944): 290–99.

Broady, T. Rupert. "Poll Tax: Symbol of Oppression." *Crisis* 48 (June 1941): 192, 204–5.

Dabney, Virginius. *Below the Potomac: A Book about the New South.* New York: Appleton-Century, 1942.

———. "Civil Liberties in the South." *Virginia Quarterly Review* 16 (Winter 1940): 81–91.

———. "Nearer and Nearer the Precipice." *Atlantic Monthly* 171 (Jan. 1943): 94–100.

———. "Reflections." *Virginia Magazine of History and Biography* 93 (July 1985): 279–90.

Daniels, Jonathan. "A Native at Large." *The Nation* 151 (Dec. 21, 1940): 635.

Davis, Ben, Jr. "The Communists, the Negro People and the War." *The Communist* 21 (Aug. 1942): 633–35.

Ford, James W. "The Negro People and the New World Situation." *The Comminist* 20 (Aug. 1941): 696–704.

Gooch, Robert K. "The Poll Tax in Virginia Suffrage History: A Premature Proposal for Reform." Mimeographed report. Charlottesville: Institute of Government, Univ. of Va., 1969.

Hall, Rob Fowler. "New Forces for Peace and Democracy in the South." *The Communist* 19 (Aug. 1940): 690–706.

Jackson, Luther P. *The Voting Status of Negroes in Virginia: 1942.* Petersburg: Va. Voters League, 1943.

Murray, Pauli. *Dark Testament and Other Poems.* Norwalk, Conn.: Silvermine Publishers, 1970.

———. *Song in a Weary Throat: An American Pilgrimage.* New York: Harper & Row, 1987.

Plunkett, Moss A. *The Skeleton in Democracy's Closet.* Richmond: Southern Electoral Reform League, n.d. [1940].

Richmond Waller Defense Committee. "A Story of Social Injustice." [Richmond, 1941].

———. *They Call It Murder.* Richmond, [1941].

Roosevelt, Eleanor. "Some of My Best Friends Are Negro." *Ebony* 9 (Feb. 1953): 16–20, 22, 24–26.

Sancton, Thomas. "Segregation: The Pattern of a Failure." *Survey Graphic* 36 (Jan. 1947): 7–11.

———. "The South and the North: A Southern View." *American Scholar* 12 Winter 1942–43): 105–15.

———. "The Waller Case." *The New Republic* 107 (July 13, 1942): 45–47.

Thompson, Charles H. "Mr. Dabney and the 'Precipice'." *Journal of Negro Education* 12 (Spring 1943): 141–43.

Secondary Sources

Anderson, Jervis. *A. Philip Randolph: A Biographical Portrait.* New York, Harcourt, Brace, Jovanovich, 1972.

Ashby, Warren. *Frank Porter Graham: A Southern Liberal.* Winston-Salem, N.C.: John F. Blair, 1980.

Bardolph, Richard, ed. *The Civil Rights Record: Black Americans and the Law, 1849–1970.* New York: Crowell, 1970.

Bell, Daniel. *Marxian Socialism in the United States.* Princeton, N.J.: Princeton Univ. Press, 1967.

Bergman, Peter M. *The Chronological History of the Negro in America.* New York: New American Library, 1969.

Biographical Directory of the Governors of the United States, 1789–1978. Ed. Robert Sobel and John Raimo. Westport, Conn.: Meckler, 1978.

Brown, Bruce Alan. "Justice, Patience, Reason: The Writings of Virginius Dabney on Matters of Race." M.A. thesis, College of William and Mary, 1987.

Bruce, Philip Alexander, et al. *History of Virginia.* Vol. 6. *Virginia Biography.* Chicago: American Historical Society, 1924.

Bryson, W. Hamilton. "The History of Legal Education in Virginia." *University of Richmond Law Review* 14 (Fall 1979): 155–210.

Buni, Andrew. *The Negro in Virginia Politics, 1902–1965.* Charlottesville: Univ. Press of Va., 1967.

Carter, Dan T. *Scottsboro: A Tragedy of the American South.* Baton Rouge: La. State Univ. Press, 1969.

Clement, Maude Carter. *The History of Pittsylvania County.* Lynchburg, Va.: J. P. Bell Co., 1929.

Colgate Darden: Conversations With Guy Friddell. Charlottesville: Univ. Press of Va., 1978.

Commission on Interracial Cooperation. *The South's Landless Farmers.* Atlanta: Commission on Interracial Cooperation, 1937.

The Constitutional Law Dictionary. Volume 1: Individual Rights. Ed. Ralph C. Chandler, Richard A. Enslen, and Peter G. Renstrom. Santa Barbara, Calif., 1985.

Contemporary Authors. Detroit: Gale Research Co., 1981.

Corwin, Edward S. *The Constitution and What It Means Today.* Rev. by Harold W. Chase and Craig R. Ducat. 14th ed. Princeton, N.J.: Princeton Univ. Press, 1978.

Dabney, Virginius. *Across the Years: Memories of a Virginian.* New York: Doubleday, 1978.

——. *Richmond: The Story of A City.* New York: Doubleday, 1976.

——. *Virginia: The New Dominion.* Garden City, N.Y.: Doubleday, 1971.

Dictionary of America Negro Biography. Ed. Rayford Logan and Michael R. Winston. New York: Norton, 1983.

DiPerna, Apula. *Juries on Trial: Faces of American Justice.* New York: Dembner Books, 1984.

Directory of Afro-American Resources. Ed. Walter Schatz. New York: Bowker, 1970.

Dodson, E. Griffith. *The General Assembly of the Commonwealth of Virginia, 1940– 1960.* Richmond, 1961.

Draper, Theodore. *American Communism and Soviet Russia.* New York: Viking, 1960.

Dunbar, Anthony P. *Against the Grain: Southern Radicals and Prophets, 1929–1959.* Charlottesville: Univ. Press of Va., 1981.

Dykeman, Wilma, and James Stokely. *Seeds of Southern Change: The Life of Will Alexander.* Chicago: Univ. of Chicago Press, 1962.

Dyson, Lowell K. "Radical Farm Organizations and Periodicals in America, 1920–1960." *Agricultural History* 45 (Apr. 1971): 111–20.

Eagles, Charles W. *Jonathan Daniels and Race Relations: The Evolution of a Southern Liberal.* Knoxville: Univ. of Tenn. Press, 1982.

Encyclopedia of Southern Culture. Ed. Charles Reagan Wilson and William Ferris. Chapel Hill: Univ. of N.C. Press, 1988.

Encyclopedia of Southern History. Ed. David C. Roller and Robert W. Twyman. Baton Rouge: La. State Univ. Press, 1979.

Encyclopedia of the American Left. Ed. Mari Jo Buhle, Paul Buhle, and Dan Georgakas. New York: Garland, 1990.

Fleischman, Harry. *Norman Thomas: A Biography, 1884–1968.* New York: Norton, 1969.

Franklin, John Hope. *From Slavery To Freedom: A History of American Negroes.* 3d ed. New York: Knopf, 1967.

Freeman, Anne Hobson. *The Style of a Law Firm: Eight Gentlemen from Virginia.* Chapel Hill, N.C.: Algonquin Books, 1989.

Frost, Richard H. *The Mooney Case.* Stanford, Calif.: Stanford Univ. Press, 1968.

Fuller, Mabel C., Viola W. Shorter, and Landon E. Fuller. *Pittsylvania County Geography Supplement.* Pressittsylvania County School Board and Univ. of Va., 1925.

Gaines, William H. Jr. "Courthouses of Halifax and Pittsylvania Counties." *Virginia Cavalcade* 20 (Spring 1971): 5–11.

Garfinkel, Herbert. *When Negroes March: The March on Washington Movement in the Orgnizational Politics for FEPC.* Glencoe, Ill.: Free Press, 1959.

Gates, Robbins L. *The Making of Massive Resistance: Virginia's Politics of School Desegregation, 1954–1956.* Chapel Hill: Univ. of N.C. Press, 1964.

Gavins, Raymond. "Hancock, Jackson, and Young: Virginia's Black Triumvirate, 1930–1945." *Virginia Magazine of History and Biography* 85 (Oct. 1977): 470– 86.

————. *The Perils and Prospects of Southern Black Leadership: Gordon Blaine Hancock, 1884–1970*. Durham, N.C.: Duke Univ. Press, 1977.

Gentry, Curt. *Frame-Up: The Incredible Case of Tom Mooney and Warren Billings*. New York: Norton, 1967.

Ginger, Ann Fagan, and Eugene M. Tobin, eds. *The National Lawyers Guild: From Roosevelt through Reagan*. Philadelphia: Temple Univ. Press, 1988.

Goldwater, Walter. *Radical Periodicals in America, 1890–1950: A Bibliography With Brief Notes*. New Haven: Yale Univ. Press, 1966.

Grubbs, Donald H. *Cry from the Cotton: The Southern Tenant Farmers' Union and the New Deal*. Chapel Hill: Univ. of N.C. Press, 1971.

Guild, June Purcell. *Black Laws of Virginia*. Richmond: Whittlet & Shepperson, 1936.

Hall, Alvin LeRoy. "James H. Price and Virginia Politics, 1878–1943." Ph.D. diss., Univ. of Va., 1970.

Hall, Jacquelyn Dowd. *Revolt Against Chivalry: Jessie Daniel Ames and the Women's Campaign Against Lynching*. New York: Columbia Univ. Press, 1979.

Harris, William H. *Keeping the Faith: A. Philip Randolph, Milton P. Webster, and the Brotherhood of Sleeping Car Porters, 1925–37*. Urbana, Chicago, London: Univ. of Ill. Press, 1977.

Heinemann, Ronald L. *Depression and the New Deal in Virginia: The Enduring Dominion*. Charlottesville: Univ. Press of Va., 1983.

Hershan, Stella K. *A Woman of Quality*. New York: Crown, 1970.

Hill's Richmond Virginia City Directory: 1941: Richmond: Hill Directory Co., 1941.

A History of the National Lawyers Guild, 1937–1987. New York: National Lawyers Guild Foundation, 1987.

Hopkins, Ernest J. *What Happened In The Mooney Case*. New York: Brewer, Warren & Putnam, 1932.

Howe, Irving, and Lewis Coser. *The American Communist Party: A Critical History (1919–1957)*. Boston: Beacon, 1957.

Jackson, Luther P. *Race and Suffrage in the South Since 1940*. Atlanta: Southern Regional Council, 1948.

Javits, Jacob K. *Discrimination U.S.A.* New York: Harcourt, Brace & World, 1960.

Kempton, Murray. *Part of Our Time: Some Ruins and Monuments of the Thirties*. New York: Simon and Schuster, 1955.

Keve, Paul W. *The History of Corrections in Virginia*. Charlottesville: Univ. Press of Va., 1986.

Klehr, Harvey. *The Heyday of American Communism: The Depression Decade*. New York: Basic Books, 1984.

Kluger, Richard. *Simple Justice: The History of Brown v. Board of Education and Black America's Struggle for Equality*. New York: Knopf, 1976.

Kneebone, John T. *Southern Liberal Journalists and the Issue of Race, 1920–1944*. Chapel Hill: Univ. of N.C. Press, 1985.

Konvitz, Milton R. "A Nation Within A Nation: The Negro and the Supreme Court." *The American Scholar* 11 (Winter 1941–42): 69–78.

Krueger, Thomas A. *And Promises to Keep: The Southern Conference for Human Welfare, 1938–1948.* Nashville, Tenn.: Vanderbilt Univ. Press, 1967.

Lash, Joseph P. *Eleanor and Franklin.* New York: Norton, 1971.

Lens, Sidney. *Radicalism in America.* Updated ed. New York: Crowell, 1969.

————. *Unrepentant Radical: An American Activist's Account of Five Turbulent Decades.* Boston: Beacon Press, 1980.

Mangum, Charles S., Jr. *The Legal Status of the Negro.* Chapell Hill: Univ. of N.C. Press, 1940.

Marks, Thomas C., and J. Tim Reilly. *Constitutional Criminal Procedure.* North Scituate, Mass., Duxbury Press, 1979.

Martin, Charles H. *The Angelo Herndon Case and Southern Justice.* Baton Rouge: La. State Univ. Press, 1976.

Martindale's American Law Directory: 1929. New York, Martindale, 1929.

The Martindale-Hubbell Law Directory: 1940. 72d ed. New York: Martindale-Hubbell, 1940.

Martindale-Hubbell Law Directory: 1955. Summit, N.J.: Martindale-Hubbell, 1955.

Mason, Alpheus Thomas. *Thomas Fiske Stone: Pillar of the Law.* New York: Viking, 1956.

Mason, Robert. "V. Dabney: The Quintessential Virginian." *Virginia Quarterly Review* 55 (Winter 1979): 160–63.

Meier, August, and Elliott Rudwick. *From Plantation to Ghetto.* 3d ed. New York: Hill and Wang, 1976.

Milgram, Morris. *Good Neighborhood: The Challenge of Open Housing.* New York: Norton, 1979.

Miller, Francis Pickens. *Man From the Valley: Memoirs of a 20th Century Virginian.* Chapel Hill: Univ. of N.C. Press, 1971.

Myrdal, Gunnar. *An American Dilemma: The Negro Problem and Modern Democracy.* New York: Harper & Row, 1942.

Naison, Mark. *Communists in Harlem during the Depression.* Urbana: Univ. of Ill. Press, 1983.

The Negro Handbook: 1942. Comp. and ed. Florence Murray, New York: Wendell Malliet, 1942.

The Negro Handbook: 1944. Comp. and ed. Florence Murray. New York: Current Reference Publications, 1944.

The Negro in Virginia. Comp. Workers of the Writers' Program of the Works Projects Administration. New York: Hasting House, 1940.

Ogden, Frederic D. *The Poll Tax in the South.* University: Univ. of Ala. Press, 1958.

Outside the Magic Circle: the Autobiography of Virginia Foster Durr. Ed. Hollinger F. Barnard. University: Univ. of Ala. Press, 1985.

Pfeffer, Paula F. *A. Philip Randolph, Pioneer of the Civil Rights Movement.* Baton Rouge: La. State Univ. Press, 1990.

Price, Margaret. *The Negro and the Ballot in the South.* Atlanta: Southern Regional Council, 1959.

Proceedings of the Fifty-sixth Annual Meeting of the Virginia State Bar Association, 1946. Richmond, 1946.

Raper, Arthur F., and Ira De A. Reid. *Sharecroppers All.* Chapel Hill: Univ. of N.C. Press, 1941.

Record, Wilson. *The Negro and the Communist Party.* Chapel Hill: Univ. of N.C. Press, 1951.

Reed, Linda. "The Southern Conference for Human Welfare and the Southern Conference Educational Fund." Ph.D. diss., Ind. Univ. , 1986.

Scales, Junius Irving, and Richard Nickson. *Cause at Heart: A Former Communist Remembers.* Athens: Univ. of GA Press, 1987.

Seidler, Murray B. *Norman Thomas: Respectable Rebel.* 2d ed. Syracuse, N.Y.: Syracuse Univ. Press, 1967.

Seidman, Joel, comp. and ed. *Communism in the United States: A Bibliography.* Ithaca and London: Cornell Univ. Press, 1969.

Simon, Rita J. *The Jury: Its Role in American Society.* Lexington, Mass.: Heath, 1980.

Sitkoff, Harvard. *A New Deal for Blacks: The Emergence of Civil Rights as a National Issue.* Vol 1. *The Depression Decade.* New York: Oxford Univ. Press, 1978.

Smith, Gibbs M. *Joe Hill.* Salt Lake City: Univ. of Utah Press, 1969.

Sosna, Morton. *In Search of the Silent South: Southern Liberals and the Race Issue.* New York: Columbia Univ. Press, 1977.

Suggs, Henry Lewis. *P. B. Young, Newspaperman: Race, Politics, and Journalism in the New South, 1910–1962.* Charlottesville: Univ. Press of Va., 1988.

———. "Black Strategy and Ideology in the Segregation Era: P. B. Young and the Norfolk *Journal and Guide,* 1910–1954." *Virginia Magazine of History and Biography* 91 (Apr. 1983): 161–90.

Swanberg, W. A. *Norman Thomas: The Last Idealist.* New York: Scribner's, 1976.

Tindall, George B. *The Emergence of the New South, 1913–1945.* Baton Rouge: La. State Univ. Press, 1968.

Trotsky, Leon. *Writings of Leon Trotsky.* Ed. Naomi Allen and George Breitman. 2d ed. Vols. 9, 10, 11. New York: Pathfinder Press, 1974, 1976, 1978.

Virginia State Bar Association. *Proceedings of the Fifty-sixth Annual Meeting of the Virginia State Bar Association, 1946.* Richmond, 1946.

Wald, Alan M. *The New York Intellectuals: The Rise and Decline of the Anti-Stalinist Left from the 1930s to the 1980s.* Chapel Hill: Univ. of N.C. Press, 1987.

Warren, Frank A. *An Alternative Vision: The Socialist Party in the 1930s.* Bloomington: Ind. Univ. Press, 1974.

Williamson, Joel. *The Crucible of Race: Black/White Relations in the American South*

Since Emancipation. New York: Oxford Univ. Press, 1984.

Weiss, Nancy J. *Farewell to the Party of Lincoln: Black Politics in the Age of FDR.* Princeton, N.J.: Princeton Univ. Press, 1983.

Wilson, Woodrow. *Papers.* Ed. Arthur S. Link et al. Vol. 46. Princeton, N.J.: Princeton Univ. Press, 1948.

Wolfe, Jonathan James. "Virginia in World War II." Ph.D. diss., Univ. of Va., 1971.

Wymar, Lubomyr, comp. *American Political Parties: A Selective guide to Parties and Movements of the 20th Century.* Littleton, Colo.: Libraries Unlimited, 1969.

Virginia: A Guide to the Old Dominion. Compiled by Workers of the Writers' Program of the Works Projects Administration, New York: Oxford Univ. Press, 1946.

Younger, Edward, and James Tice Moore, eds. *The Governors of Virginia, 1860–1978.* Charlottesville: Univ. Press of Va., 1982.

Index